Coaching the
Female Athlete

Coaching the Female Athlete

DONNA MAE MILLER

Professor and Director
Department of Physical Education for Women
University of Arizona, Tucson, Arizona

Lea & Febiger 1974 Philadelphia

253497

Health Education,
Physical Education, and
Recreation Series

Ruth Abernathy, Ph.D., Editorial Adviser,
Professor Emeritus, School of Physical and Health Education,
University of Washington, Seattle, Washington 98105

Library of Congress Cataloging in Publication Data

Miller, Donna Mae.
    Coaching the female athlete.

    1. Sports for women.   2. Coaching (Athletics)
I. Title.
GV709.M49   796'.019'4   73-11156
ISBN 0-8121-0448-X

Published in Great Britain by Henry Kimpton Publishers, London

Library of Congress Catalog Card Number 73-11156

PRINTED IN THE UNITED STATES OF AMERICA

To my own great mentors and coaches—
Mom, Dave, and Minnie.

Preface

From the enormous developments in and applications of technology in sports in recent years have come volumes of literature on every aspect of this growing field. Despite the consuming interest in and the surge of knowledge and talent in sports, the coaching of girls and women appears to be still in its infancy. For that matter, coaching in general is regarded by some as being somewhere in the Bronze Age in light of the spasmodic connections between knowledge and practice.

But, why the gaps? Certainly the quality of research done in recent years not only in physical education, but in many related areas as well, is vastly improved and of considerable significance to all teachers and coaches of sports activities. Unfortunately, there is a tendency for research to be dismissed as holding no promise of practical application. Indeed, much data from research concentrated on Olympic performers may seem quite irrelevant to the teacher or coach grappling with large classes or groups of athletes with various abilities (ranging, for the most part, from low to average) whose first and most urgent task is to cater to the many students fully capable of a life of sport but who for one reason or another do not get it. Another gap apparently occurs because much research is widely scattered throughout various technical sources. For those with limited scientific backgrounds, making sense out of all the data may offer little enticement for keeping abreast. Moreover, serious writings on coaching, outside research journals, have tended to center on the analyses of sports skills and instant how-to-do-it techniques. Perhaps the widest gap is the time-lag between knowledge and practice. Good research is longitudinal; it requires replication under a variety of conditions and this takes time. In the past some research information was misleading and erroneous because such procedures were not employed. During this time-gap teaching and coaching continue, and in many instances practices are handed down from one coach to another, despite the fact that what may work for one coach may not work for another, or even repeatedly work for the same coach.

I do not propose that this book will solve the dilemma, although I hope that by providing a compendium of research, example, and practical wisdom, heretofore not available in one source, some gaps may be closed.

I have drawn upon my experiences as a participant and a coach, as well as my study in relevant disciplines, to answer the increasingly apparent need for literature in the teaching and coaching of girls and women. Although my intent is to cover the field exhaustively, no one book or author could present a complete treatise on the present comprehensive state of coaching theory and practice and the diverse subject matter of sports. A sustained attempt is made, however, to bring together information, inferences, and hypotheses from diverse fields such as physical education, psychology, physiology, sociology, physics, philosophy, and the world of the sports superstar.

This volume may confirm familiar ways of doing things or may expose the readers to propositions and possibilities outside their preferred theoretical position or experience. The book makes no pretense of analyzing specifics of each sport. Aspiring performers may turn to numerous books for help, and most coaches have in their personal library handy paperback primers and pamphlets that detail the specifics of strategy and offer diagrams and concise analyses of techniques. In addition, the very nature of sports in today's multimedia world exposes both coach and athlete to new techniques within an instant. Soon after exposure, what is new is analyzed, imitated, and, in many instances, mastered.

This book does address itself to the numerous inhabitants of the sports world—physical educators, coaches, athletes, interested laymen, and members of the various subdivisions or related specialties in sports—who are concerned not only with the theory and practice of coaching, but also with the total operation of sports programs for girls and women. The format is intended to be suitable for self-study by the athlete as well as by the discriminating teacher/coach who may incorporate suggestions from different portions that apply to a particular concern. The material may be applied according to the specific needs of the beginner as well as of the outstanding athlete. Or the book can be used as a "polishing" device by seasoned coaches who seek the opportunity of catching up with some material and data that may have escaped them. More importantly, the format is unified by the theme of education's commitment to the individual athlete and is written with the hope that all readers will derive a sense of relevance of his or her role in that commitment.

The subject matter is presented in eleven chapters. In Chapter 1 the scope and significance of contemporary sports programs for girls and women are discussed, and the perspectives of such programs are presented in dimensions of historical roots as well as the roots of modern dilemmas. Problems to ponder and questions are posed to entice philosophic inquiry. Chapter 2 considers the physiologic and psychologic dimensions of the athlete. Questions explored include: Who is the female athlete? What is her personality structure? Do sports influence personality? What are the marks of a champion? Are strenuous training and competition harmful? Chapter 3 is addressed to the preparation and behaviors of the coach and attempts to expose some of the soft-spots in the teaching/coaching relationship. The scope and potentials of coaching are set out in Chapters 4, 5, 6, 7, and 8 in such headings as Facilitating Skill Acquisition, Multiplying Motivation, Exploring Mechanical Principles, Harnessing Technologic Assistance, Analyzing and Assessing Athletic Potential.

In Chapters 9 and 10 are topics focused on preparing the athlete through conditioning and training programs and taking care of the athlete through injury prevention, control, and recognition. Chapter 11 anticipates some new priorities or focal problems in coaching, such as spectator behavior and crowd control, legal liability, and coach-player relationships. Information relative to the various organizations that guide and conduct programs for girls and women is provided.

A book is always the product of the interest and help of a large number of people. Among the many friends who offered valuable suggestions for this book I thank in particular Anne E. Atwater, Fred B. Roby, and Kathryn R. E. Russell. I am grateful to Lee Schwager, who handled the bulk of the stenographic work, and to Judy Spray, Kathy Mounier, Diane Rothe, and Darry Ware for their efficient and cheerful assistance.

I am, of course, indebted to the publishing companies that granted permissions to use quoted and paraphrased materials from their books, and to the authors who wrote these materials.

Tucson, Arizona   DONNA MAE MILLER

Contents

5. Actualizing Potential by Multiplying Motivation

6. Exploring Mechanical Principles

7. Harnessing Technologic Assistance for Analyzing Performance

8. Analyzing and Assessing Athletic Potential

1. Dimensions of
Athletic Programs
for Girls and Women

The future is certain. We must make some specific
designs for participation in women's sport in America.

Leona Holbrook

SOME HISTORICAL ROOTS

When reviewing the early history of sports, it is sometimes
difficult to realize that half the human race is female. In ancient
Greece, religious and social mores precluded the participation of
women in such events as the Olympic games, which were not sporting events as we know them, but religious festivals dedicated to the
glory of the gods. Thus, the priestesses of Demeter, who were con-
secrated to the goddess, were the only women permitted to attend
the games. (In Sparta, women regularly took part in athletic events,
and Sparta was notorious for allowing young women to go naked
in public.) The behavior of the female members of the Greek pan-
theon, however, did not reflect the subordinate, indeed almost invis
ible, role to which women were relegated.

In early America, the history of women in sports was not too
different from that of ancient times. Prior to the 1900s, there were
few accounts of women in sports. Until recently, they rarely intruded on the sports page. The emergence of the female in sports
is largely a twentieth-century phenomenon, and rather closely interwoven with her appearance in the Olympic Games. In 1896, when
the Olympics were reestablished by Baron Pierre de Coubertin,
women could watch but could not compete. Four years later, at the
Olympics in France, staged more or less as a sideshow for an international exposition in Paris, women competed in tennis and golf
(sports no longer in the Olympics). Women's swimming events
were added to the Olympics in 1912, women's fencing in 1924, and
women's gymnastics and track in the 1928 Olympic Games.

Although sports fans may remember Mildred ("Babe") Didrikson best as a professional golfer, she was perhaps the first woman Olympic performer to receive headlines equal to those of the men. In 1932, then just 18 years old, the "Babe" was America's number one track star. At the Olympic Games at Long Beach, California, she won gold medals in the javelin throw and the 80-meter hurdles, setting world records in both. In the high jump, because she was disqualified for diving over the bar, she had to settle for the silver medal, although she had previously cleared the bar at a height of 5 feet 5¼ inches (also a world record).[28] The Olympic Games of 1960, in which America's favored men runners and jumpers did not even advance to the finals, will be remembered because the long-legged Wilma Rudolf of Clarksville, Tennessee, dominated the contests, winning three gold medals.

Although sports programs for women were not at first sponsored by colleges and universities, no narrative of early beginnings would be complete without a mention of Catherine E. Beecher and Delphine Hanna. In 1828 at Hartford Female Seminary, Catherine E. Beecher planned a physical education program consisting primarily of calisthenics performed to music, and in 1904 Delphine Hanna of Oberlin College started the first organized Women's Gymnasium and Field Association. These associations, the forerunners of the present athletic associations, began the conducting of intramural programs of competition.

One of the activities in these intramural program beginnings, and the first team sport played by American women, was the game of basketball, invented by James Naismith in 1891. The rapid rise in popularity of basketball is credited with providing an impetus to the first stirrings of women's intercollegiate sports programs.[10]

For the most part, the creation of the sportswoman in the twentieth century closely parallels the changing role of women in this century. Margaret A. Coffey capsuled the then and now sportswoman in these words:

> The progress of civilization in the twentieth century has drastically altered the image of the sportswoman. Fifty or sixty years ago, she was a rare creature, encumbered by rigid social mores as well as by yards of gabardine. Today, she ventures into virtually every area of physical endeavor, performing with grace and skill. Benefitting from the past six decades of both economic and social growth, her opportunities are unlimited.[5]

THE CONTEMPORARY SCENE

Today, despite the notion that in terms of sport "women sit in the back of the bus,"[13] as Marie Hart put it, there are many evidences of departure from tradition.

Biologically the old arguments about the weaker sex are becoming passé, although the mystique surrounding the female's physical prowess is deeply embedded in society. The myths and old wives' tales about sports being unfeminine have been explored in depth and are beginning to be exploded as well. The emphasis upon women as attractive objects rather than as skilled performers has begun to give way. For example, for the first time in its history, for the 19th Glen Campbell–Los Angeles Open Golf Tournament, a real, honest-to-goodness golfer was chosen to be queen—the U.S. Women's Amateur Champion, 16-year-old Laura Baugh. There is a golf course in Georgia designed expressly for women only, "something golf hasn't seen since Mary, Queen of Scots, was batting a leather bag of feathers over gorse-grown dunes the Firth of Forth."[29]

In Rome in 1960, 537 of the 5396 competitors in the Olympics were women. By 1964, 732 women, as contrasted to 5588 men, had managed to become participants in 13 of the 21 events. And, in 1972, of 10,000 participants in the games, at least 3000 were women. Women today have their own separate competitions in track, swimming, gymnastics, fencing, and volleyball (added in 1964). And, in the Winter Olympics, women compete in everything but ski jumping and ice hockey. There is no doubt that in the Winter Olympics of 1970 in Sapporo, Japan, women added not only to the color. The theme song of that occasion, "Thank Heaven for Little Girls," was evidently justified by the victories of the three women who received gold medals, two in speed skating and one in skiing. The American men's ice hockey team won the silver medal. Another highlighted first for women came when Enriqueta Basilio was designated to complete the dramatic relay of carrying the Olympic flame to the ceremonial urn at the 19th Olympiad at Mexico City in 1968. (The Olympic flame, generated on Mt. Olympus in Greece, from the heat of the sun, is relayed by thousands to the place of the official Olympic urn.)

The range of activities acceptable for women also has greatly increased, and women have now breached almost all the long-recognized all-male preserves. Some undaunted women now engage in hazardous sports. Rhonda Martin, who goaltended for an intramural league at the University of Minnesota, apparently was not too worried about stopping pucks that can reach a speed of more than 100 miles per hour. There are lady umpires, girl jockeys, women professional football teams, and those who aspire to becoming football coaches. Kerry Kleid, who has made history already by becoming America's first professional woman motorcycle racer, simply said, "I just never bought all that about what ladies should not do."[1] Not only do women today participate in almost every sport that men do, they are even competing with their male counterparts in some sports. Although the U.S. Polo Association does not recognize girls in polo, Debbie Lee made history in 1972 at Yale University as the first woman in Yale athletics to compete against men. She scored one goal and assisted in three others in a 14–6 victory over Harvard.[11] More than 100 New York high schools, in a 16-month experiment, tested girls as competitors on all-male squads in noncontact sports such as tennis, golf, bowling, riflery, swimming, and track. In 1971 the New York State Board of Regents approved the recommendation of integration, although not in football or other contact sports. The only dissenting vote of the 15-member board was that of a woman. The physicians who acted as advisors were unanimous in declaring that there were no medical reasons to prohibit girls from competing on boys' teams in the non-contact sports listed above. What do the students themselves think of coed teams? In a poll conducted by *Scholastic Magazine,* only 7 per cent of the high school seniors opposed coed teams in any sport.[30]

Obviously, today's sportswoman is witnessing the ushering in of a new era of interscholastic sports, and there are current trends with far-reaching implications. Women today not only are seeking more sport opportunities but also are pointing out discriminatory practices and debating with renewed vigor their right to support in budget, facilities, coaching staff, and competitive events equal to that afforded athletic programs for men. The 1970s mark the beginnings of reorganization of the governance and conduct of interschool competition sports programs for girls and women. In 1971 this development culminated in the establishment of a new organization, the Association for Intercollegiate Athletics for Women (AIAW), which, among other purposes, sponsored national championships in women's intercollegiate athletics. In 1973, the Association (AIAW), experiencing its first lawsuit in a challenge of the scholarship policy of the Division of Girls and Women's Sports (DGWS), called for a vote of its member institutions on whether the existing statement on scholarships for women students should be changed. Of those institutions responding to a mail vote, more than 80 per cent agreed that a change should be made. A special committee met in Washington, D.C., on March 25–27, 1973, to re-write the DGWS philosophic statement and to formulate interim regulations for the awarding of financial aid to women athletes and for recruitment of athletes.

The trend toward a greatly increased emphasis on sports for girls and women will continue and will be matched by women expanding their authority in athletic programs in the schools. But there is still a long way to go. Some old problems do remain and some new ones intrude upon the scene.

PROBLEMS TO PONDER

Interscholastic and intercollegiate and professional sports for girls and women undoubtedly have arrived. Yet, in the literature are found both a total critique of competitive sports programs for girls and women and compelling proposals for the reorientation of thought and practices. Enough athletic history has been written (although women rarely intruded on the course of events) that women are, or should be, well aware of the problems to be reckoned with and the importance of understanding their responsibility in the so-called new era of sports competition for women.

The Feminine Problem?

As noted in the previous section, apparently many persons prior to the twentieth century gave obeisance to one version or another of the old dictum: girls are made of sugar and spice and everything nice. And, in keeping with that metaphor, a feminine picture of women was conjured up, which seemed to militate against females doing anything more physical than stamping their feet and screaming. The image persists in some quarters even today. Margaret Clark and Margaret Lantis may have summarized the attitudes that persist and the problems that face the woman who pursues an interest in sport: "A vigorous and 'athletic' woman may be respected and admired but seldom emulated."[4] And, in an article written in 1971, Marie Hart decried the fact that the roles of being a woman and of being a successful female athlete are almost incompatible in the United States because "women in sport do not fit our particular concept of femininity and those who persist in sport suffer from it."[13]

At least such may be the case with *some sports*. In 1955, Naomi Leyhe found that woman members of the American Association of Health, Physical Education and Recreation (AAHPER) were much less favorable in their attitudes toward competition in the team sports than they were in the individual sports.[18] In 1968 an attitude inventory by Bea Harres showed that students' attitudes toward the desirability of athletic competition were influenced positively by their participation.[12] Again, an interesting finding was that the individual sports, swimming and tennis, were considered most desirable, followed by volleyball, track and field, softball, and basketball. Ulrich, in her book *The Social Matrix of Physical Education* written in 1968, declared that women in the individual sports tend to acquire status whereas women in the team sports, which "still have masculine overtones in terms of cultural identification," tend to lose status.[31]

Theresa Malumphy's study of the factors affecting the personality of women athletes in intercollegiate competition indicated that the effect of competition on the feminine image was dependent upon the personal feelings of the participant herself.[21] Girls who participated in archery, golf, gymnastics, fencing, tennis, and swimming saw their participation as enhancing their feminine image, but those who played badminton, basketball, field hockey, softball, and volleyball were not as sure that participation enhanced their feminine image. Of significance to the physical educator and coach, Malumphy's findings showed that participants in the team sports and team-individual sports reported that their first participation was in the school setting under the leadership of physical educators, whereas those in the individual sports started participating earlier and in a club or recreational setting.

In 1972, Ken Foreman, Chairman of the Women's Long Distance Running Sub-Committee of the Amateur Athletic Union of the United States, reported a survey in which respondents were asked to rate 75 different sports activities according to a masculinity-femininity scale. The whole group (men and women) classified two activities as essentially feminine—field hockey and ballet. The whole group classified 15 activities as exclusively masculine—boxing, roller skating, soccer, motorboat racing, handball, motorcycle racing, weight training, wrestling, ice hockey, pole vault, crew racing, riflery, bait casting, bullfighting, and cross-country skiing. Of the remaining 55 activities, the great majority were ranked as primarily masculine; only running, softball, volleyball, ice skating, diving, tennis, bowling, and water skiing were classified as being suited to the female performer. As Foreman pointed out, although these findings are shocking enough, it was even more revealing to consider that "the men who responded to the opinionaire virtually relegated women to the home, where house work, child bearing and sewing were said to be her primary modes of bio-physical expression."[8] Foreman suggested that the real clue to the status of the female is not something implicit in the nature of the female, but rather a manifestation of the male ego. "Males simply cannot tolerate a serious challenge from a woman."[8]

The problem of femininity and sport is one that will not easily be resolved, despite the fact that even the American Medical Association Committee on the Medical Aspects of Sports expressed the belief that participation in sports is now accepted as contributing to rather than detracting from the feminine image. As Foreman stated, "only now are we beginning to see that masculinity and femininity are tentative things, that humanness is the certainty with which we deal."[8]

As long as there is a question of femininity perhaps it will continue to need no other refutation than that provided by the individual. Certainly the concept of the unsightly, bulging muscle has been changed by the appearance of a number of women in the Olympic competitions. The criticism that sports tend to masculinize the behavior of girls and women can only be changed in the same way, by the behavior of the individual athlete and coach. Such behaviors do not imply the necessity for dressing women in satin or scanty outfits. Women should above all be themselves. If a woman likes feminine finery, she need not smother it, nor should she indulge in ruffles in order to prove her womanhood. As Phoebe Scott pointed out, "of central importance is good taste and attendance to the task at hand."[27]

And, perhaps beyond being themselves, women in sport need to take the hazing they are bound to receive, good naturedly and in stride. Embittered defensive attitudes may be indicative of uncertainty and do little to convince the critic. After all, is not the maintenance of balance, an ability to roll with the punch, a large part of the makeup of the real champion?

Students First, Athletes Second?

In all instances it is expected that athletic programs in schools will be educative. That sports have been shown to educate man personally, socially, and culturally in the world at large and, in a sense, without benefit of a cent of the taxpayer's education dollar is the thesis of my book *Sport: A Contemporary View.*[22] That physical educators—teachers and coaches—have a special responsibility to educate through sport seems to be an accepted fact, although institutional guardians of education are somewhat vague, divided, and ambivalent about the place, value, and conduct of that particular treasure called "interscholastic athletics."

Certainly, a crippling disjunction in the troubled history of athletics for boys and men has been whether players are students or athletes first. A great deal has been said and written within recent years to suggest that the era of the Knute Rockne image in athletics is gone, at least in athletic programs for men. Many books portraying the anti-hero seem to confirm the notion that even in sports, the most traditional stronghold of such educational values as sportsmanship, the at one time safe statement that sports build character calls for some reflection on the problems encountered in reality. The athlete himself decries the system that creates what he calls the "hero-worshippers" and "phoney stereotypes." He considers himself to be the victim of the big athletic machine, abused by students and faculty who see him only as a number, position, and defender of the glory of good old alma mater.

Not unlike their predecessors of the 1920s, women physical educators of today appear to approve of programs of intercollegiate athletics for women if they are conducted not as men's intercollegiate athletics are conducted, but as Mabel Lee, well known for her articles on competition for women, expressed in 1923, ". . . free of all taint of professionalism and commercialism . . . informal, entirely sane, and absolutely wholesome."[17] Although competitive sports programs for girls and women have not been plagued by some of the problems attendant in programs for men—undesirable recruitment practices, stringent schedules, costly operations, the entourage of athletic personnel, publicity, boosters clubs, and the like—this is not to suggest that such problems could not exist. Some persons have contended that only more money, gate receipts, and scholarships are needed to upgrade women's programs. Probably typical of many sports page assessments is this one: "There is no drive for competition between men and women by women athletic directors who shudder at the thought of upgrading their programs to include admission fees, scholarships and recruiting—the backbone of men's programs."[15] And, as if to put frosting on the cake, an athletic director sized up the women's problem as: "The women's program is hampered by the fact that they won't charge admission or look at the competitive angle."[14] Recently the policies related to the awarding of financial aid to women athletes were changed (see previous section, The Contemporary Scene), and there is concern that the provision for athletic scholarships for women may create a potential for many abuses, including pressure recruiting and performer exploitation. And it is responsible men in athletic programs, out of their own troubled history, who have repeatedly advised women to avoid any practice that would lead to recruitment of athletes and all the attendant problems. Some suggest that, even in men's programs, recruitment should be where Bob Cousy, the great basketball player, would like to have it return. It would "consist of pinning a notice on the gym door that anyone who wants to come out for basketball is welcome—provided he's paid his tuition, passed his subjects, and gotten his own girlfriend."[23]

Of course, the notion that one school is better than another because it can buy its talent is a fraud foisted not only on the student but also on the various persons who support such programs. Coaches themselves may come to believe that buying talent is the same as developing it. The basic hypocrisy underlying scholarships and consequent recruitment, however, may be the pretense that it is for the good of the disadvantaged student who otherwise might not be able to attend a university. The figures on the disadvantaged athletes who go to colleges on athletic scholarships appear impressive, at first glance. According to other figures, however, three out of four black athletes on college athletic scholarships get virtually no education and emerge from college semiliterate. And, perhaps it is equally unfortunate that many teachers and coaches, women and men, have come to believe that all human activity in highly competitive sports programs can be governed by them as well as improved by them once the door is opened to a paying public.

Nonetheless, obtaining *financial support* for athletic programs is a perennial problem. The tendency is to believe that women's athletic programs are less important than are men's athletic programs, which in turn implies that women who work in women's programs perform a less valuable function than do men who work in men's programs. As a result, women are seeking equal opportunity, including financial support for their programs and more time for their work load in these programs.

The basic philosophy of the governing bodies of women's sports is that the program of interscholastic athletics for girls and women should be funded by the institution and not be dependent on variable sources. What is actually happening? Schools surveyed in one region offer a picture perhaps indicative of most other regions.[3] There is wide diversity from school to school in the amount of funds and in funding procedures. Money may be allocated from such various sources as: the associated student organizations, special administrative budgets, the physical education department, the athletic department, student-earned money from various projects, students and faculty pay their own expenses. Frequently the faculty coach or sponsor absorbs the additional responsibility with neither financial reimbursement nor load credit.

Because the objectives of athletic programs are considered to be an integral part of the physical education program, it is most desirable that proper funding be made through educational channels, not through gate receipts, donations, special projects, booster clubs, alumni sponsorship, scholarships, or capricious committee allocations. "Unless this fact is recognized," as Breeding pointed out, competitive sports programs risk sporadic development and, if they become dependent upon gate receipts the emphasis very likely would change from an educational objective to " 'play for pay.' "[3]

Thus, a glimpse of today's sport scene reveals some paradoxes. There is a resolute determination to raise the consciousness of women as to their rights and privileges, and at the same time some ponderables suggest cautious application of these new freedoms. What will be the plight of women in the pressurized chamber of the highly competitive sports arena? Will she be a damsel in distress, caught hopelessly in the same machine that is said to have ground up her male counterpart? How can girls and women be induced to take on desirable kinds of behavior within the framework of a highly competitive sports program? How can the undesirable effects of such programs—the exploitation of the players and intensification of individual emotional conflicts and resentments—be avoided? Do women want equal pressure to win, equal problems associated with entertainment and public athletics? Are there possibly unwanted consequences of financial equality? It is possible for women to direct the course of overly zealous competition?

Edith Betts, a past Chairman of the Division of Girls and Women's Sports, in the 1971 Conference on Sports Programs for Secondary Schools, expressed the sentiments of those who have the highest hopes for the future:

> The greatest thing we have is an intangible thing . . . the desire to do what is best for our girls; a self-imposed restraint to follow guidelines without having a policing body over our heads; a belief that is strong enough to deter those who would impose less educational goals upon our programs.[32]

Sports for All or Spectacles for Spectators?

It may be of historical interest, as well as helpful in mapping the future of competitive athletics for girls and women, to know what some of the leaders of former days had to say about the difficulties confronting athletics in education.

Mabel Lee, a leader in organizing the Women's Division of the National Amateur Athletic Federation and the National Section on Women's Athletics, is well known for her views on competition for women. In 1923 she was asked to present a study of the situation of intercollegiate athletics for women, including the cases both "for" and "against" such activities. Some of the disadvantages cited in that study are among those that are apparently of great concern even today: neglect of school work, idea of winning at all cost, undesirable newspaper notoriety, distortion of values, many girls who need "training for their physical welfare" the most would be neglected.[17]

In 1928 Ethel Perrin, then Chairman of the Executive Committee of the Women's Division of the National Amateur Athletics Federation, wrote about the crises in girls' athletics. She warned:

> Further when you hear that interest in athletics for women will be increased you may care to ask what kind of interest. Will it be the interest that has the welfare and happiness of the girls at heart? Or will it have the success of the Olympiad at heart? How much will it be concerned with the individual girls? How much will it consider what the ultimate effect on them will be? Very little. And for the rest, the great mass, it will not care at all. It will already have disposed of them— "dead wood." But they are not "dead wood." They are normal, adolescent American school girls, who have a right to the opportunity for athletics and many of them will be told that the training of Olympic teams takes nothing away from the girls who are not on the teams, that their program goes on just the same. Perhaps it does, but they know and you know that it is comparatively speaking an inferior program. They are, so to speak, getting an athletic diet of left-overs. Another fallacious argument which I, at least, have heard, maintains "Girls want it. God bless them—they shall have it." We might as well approve of giving matches to a child or of giving ice cream to one child while all the others watch him eat it.[26]

Men, too, offered early cautions about the conduct of athletics in education. Jay B. Nash stated in 1928:

> The earmarks of bad athletics, whether they involve boys or girls, will always center around *intensive coaching of a few, neglect of the many, spectators, gate receipts, State and National Championships.*[24]

Nash warned that such activities are not educational:

> They exist to give publicity to the coach, the principal of the school, the president of the university, the alumni, some local newspaper, the town boosters' club, and the players.[24]

In the 1900s, R. Tait McKenzie saw some of the difficulties confronting amateurism in his day as being:

> 1. The standard of performance is raised so high that the ordinary student, realizing he is hopelessly outclassed, gives up playing the game he would otherwise enjoy and that should be kept within his reach.
>
> 2. The competitor is elevated and separated into a special class apart from his fellows, requiring separate quarters, special diet, and consequent privileges to make the drudgery less irksome.
>
> 3. The publicity that accompanies the contest puts them into the class of public entertainers for which the spectator pays to see and so acquires certain rights over the players, who become mere performers. Pressure is thus brought to bear on athletic authorities and rules committees to consider the spectator rather than the man for whom the game should be designed.
>
> 4. The winning of the game becomes more important than the observance of the spirit of the law and the practice of fair play. It is the professional motive which is the thrill of the contest.[19]

Sound strangely familiar, even today? Today is not different from yesteryear in the concern expressed for preserving the values and eliminating the evils in sports programs for all girls and women. Certainly the need for increasing the motivation of the general female population for regular physical exertion and sports activities is repeatedly underscored in the more recent writings, such as those of Evalyn S. Gendel, physician, who points out that continuing sequential energetic programs from primary grades through college not only would produce women available to Olympic superwoman criteria but also would benefit the "common woman," athlete or not.[9]

Closely related to the matter of sports for the common woman is the question: Do those who participate in interschool competitive sports continue to play their game after high school or college, or has the fun been wrung out? Real enjoyment of the game, the kind that extends beyond school walls, may be endangered by the growth of spectator spectaculars in women's sports. If players begin to seek something beyond mere participation, if they are led astray by those seductive goddesses, victory and prestige, the urge to participate for its own sake may indeed be inhibited.

Hubbard, describing the "Merriwell Obsession" (the idea that if you cannot do something well you should not do it), reiterated the dangers that J. B. Nash saw in the 1930s with the growth of "spectatoritis" and the decline of amateur participation.

> We are in no danger as long as a sufficient proportion of the population remains sufficiently uninhibited to go on making spectacles of themselves for their own profit rather than watching spectacles promoted for the profit of others.[16]

That sports should remain playful, joyful, spontaneous,[25] rather than being a job, is a thesis about which there is rather general agreement, although it may very well be that this is the major problem women will have to ponder as they devise sports programs for the future.

Many persons who place great value on the interscholastic sports experience and who believe that girls and women are being cheated by not having this experience are at the same time apprehensive about expanding the programs because the fun has been wrung out of the experience. Perhaps too typical of many programs is this experience described by one teacher.

> Recently, I attended two basketball tournaments which left me with the impression that the players were not competing against the opponent, but were at war with an enemy! We've actually had some of our players followed and attacked after an athletic event by athletes from one of our opponent schools. I have also been faced with the disturbing fact that my girls' locker room, which was used by the visiting team, was pretty well torn up—clothing pulled from baskets and taken (a nice word for stolen), baskets bent up and just plain abused. To me, a demonstration that was the straw that broke the camel's back—were the players, whose team lost the championship game, and then refusing to accept their

awards. Is being second that bad? Maybe this is just a woman's view. But whatever happened to taking pride in doing something well? Even when defeated by someone better, the player usually had the courtesy, and pride in a job well done, to congratulate the winner.[6]

Women's Athletic Liberation and Leadership?

With the emancipation of women in the world at large, it also appears that the attitudes and rules that limit sports choices for women are being challenged and the barriers to women competing on men's teams are being eliminated. Numerous articles justifying a woman's right to compete with men have been written. Policy-making bodies have revised discriminatory clauses that existed in the regulations for varsity sports. Cases of litigation are pending in several states, and courts either have determined or will determine discrimination in sport on the same basis that it is determined in employment. It is even no longer unacceptable for a girl to defeat a boy, although some persons contend it is hard to do if he is more than 10 years old.

And yet, problems remain unsolved. The Association of Intercollegiate Athletics for Women and the Division of Girls and Women's Sports took the position that, although positive experiences for the exceptional girl or woman may occur through participation in boys or men's competitive groups, such instances are rare and should be judged acceptable only on an interim basis until women's programs could be initiated. Officers of AIAW, however, have been troubled by contradictory expectations held for this organization and many physical educators have expressed concern for the direction in which the equality movement is heading. Some persons are concerned about whether or not women's programs will remain as such if women can be absorbed into men's teams. Others are concerned about women coaches being replaced by men. Men athletic directors are even worried that the added emphasis on women's programs will cut into their own programs.

There appears to be at least one point on which women are agreed. They want the equal right to determine their own destiny in interscholastic athletics. Moreover, emancipating women, a theme harking back to earlier attempts to liberalize girls and women's programs and take them out of the bondage of incompetent leadership, should be the responsibility and privilege of women. Men should not be the arbitrators for women's programs. But as one male author put it: "If women do not accept leadership roles, they will be criticized for any program, however bad, which arises under other leaders."[2]

Obviously, the acquisition of positive outcomes from the sports experience will not be automatic. Even though the governing organizations of sports declare a philosophy rooted in the primacy of the individual, the key to values will continue to rest in the hands and thoughts of those who engage in and conduct competitive sports programs—responsible leaders. Every responsible leader will attempt to find answers for the following questions.

1. Purposes

Do interscholastic athletic programs for which players are recruited and subsidized have a place in higher education? If so, what is the place and what are the purposes of such programs? If not, why not?

Are the objectives, purposes, and methods associated with interscholastic athletics sufficiently in harmony with those of physical education to justify interpreting the former as a phase of the latter?

In what terms should interscholastic athletics programs be evaluated? in gate receipts? in games won and lost? in, public and alumni opinion and/or support? in effect on participants? in effect on nonparticipants? in cost per participant?

What is the relationship (if any) between successful athletics teams and (1) alumni gifts for educational purposes and/or (2) appropriations for education from state legislatures?

2. Faculty and Leadership

Who should control interscholastic athletics? university presidents? school principals? faculty? athletic directors? physical educators? outside committee? students? legislators?

Should the general requirements for initial employment, professional rank, tenure, promotion, and salary be the same for athletics coaches as for all members of the faculty?

Should athletics coaches be required to meet specific minimum requirements in professional training in physical education?

3. Participants and Program

How can the unwholesome aspects of interscholastic athletics be effectively eliminated (or controlled)?

How can interscholastic athletics be administered and controlled so that the experiences offered the participants are truly *educational*?

Should interscholastic programs be enlarged to serve more students than the programs currently serve?

What minimum standards of scholarship and morality should be required of participants in interscholastic athletics?

Should interscholastic athletics programs be widened to include most or all the sports included in the Olympic program?

What limitations should be imposed on schedules? on number of games? on length of playing season? on distance traveled? on class time lost? on number of years for which schedules are made in advance?

On what basis should opponents be selected? on philosophy of interscholastic athletics? on recruiting practices? on natural rivalry? on admission standards? on scholarship standards? on potential gate receipts? on enrollment?

How can overemphasis of a few sports to the exclusion of others be avoided?

How can reliable and valid data concerning the effect of participation in interscholastic athletics on the participants be obtained?

4. Facilities and Finances

Should new facilities be designed primarily for intramural and classroom use or for spectator capacity?

Should receipts from intercollegiate athletics go into the general university fund and the interscholastic athletics program be financed by budget allocation in the same manner as are the other departments in the university?

Should sports for which players are subsidized and that are utilized chiefly for student and public entertainment be self-supporting? Should student fees be used to support such sports?

Can the financial support of interscholastic teams in sports in which few students participate (golf, tennis, fencing, and the like) be justified when thousands of students are to be served by the school?

In view of rising costs and increased enrollments, how can interscholastic athletics programs and facilities be adequately financed? How can facilities be provided for "low income" sports?

5. Public Relations

What should be emphasized in the publicity given to interscholastic athletics?

Do interscholastic athletics suffer from *too much* publicity?

How can the interpretation of interscholastic athletics to the public, to the faculty, to the administration, to the legislature, and to the press and radio be improved?

How can the dichotomy—physical education versus athletics—in publicity be changed? Should it be changed?

How can publicity related to interscholastic athletics be effectively directed and controlled?

In summary, women have had no sports history in the annals of their own kind. They have been shrouded in myth. Their history now will be written perhaps in the way they engage the opportunities and the well-known problems. And it seems that new priorities are rooted in old problems. Elwood Craig Davis, examining professional efforts, proferred: "If man has been trying for quality since the days of antiquity, what possibly could now be suggested which has not been tried a thousand times? Yet, perhaps some idea might pop into your head as we try to ferret out some tempting touch or tool that will help bring our quarry to bay." Davis suggested that there are at least five kinds of attempts to pursue to find and gain at least a passing brush with quality: (1) following our expectations, (2) relying on our estimates, (3) persevering, (4) pursuing topmost values, and (5) adapting to situations.[7]

Perhaps the response to such a challenge is best summed up in the words of Theresa Malumphy:

> Competition does not need to be destructive of femininity, budgets, administrative relationships, physiology, or the psyche. Our role as model is an exciting one. Our realization of the soundness of a bit of Aristotelian philosophy, "nothing in excess," is demanded.[20]

REFERENCES

1. Barth, I. Girl on a hot seat. *Parade Magazine*, January 16, 1972, p. 12.
2. Bowen, R. T. A man looks at girls' sports. *Journal of Health, Physical Education and Recreation*, November-December 1967, pp. 42-44.
3. Breeding, B. Funding intercollegiate sports programs in the intermountain area. *The Physical Educator 28*(3), 1971, pp. 133-134.
4. Clark, M., and Lantis, M. Sports in a changing culture. *Journal of Health, Physical Education and Recreation*, May-June 1958.
5. Coffey, M. A. Then and now the sportswoman. *Journal of Health, Physical Education and Recreation*, February 1965, pp. 38-50.
6. Dalsheimer, B. Physical education: Involvement in education? *The Foil*, Fall 1972, pp. 16-20.
7. Davis, E. C. Quest toward quality. Speech presented at the AAHPER Southwest District Convention, Las Vegas, Nevada, April 21, 1972.
8. Foreman, K. What research says about the female athlete. Report presented at the Pacific Northwest Sports Medicine Seminar, Seattle, Wash., March 19, 1972.
9. Gendel, E. S. Fitness and fatigue in the female. *Journal of Health, Physical Education and Recreation*, October 1971, pp. 53-58.
10. Gerber, E. W. The changing female image: A brief commentary on sport competition for women. *Journal of Health, Physical Education and Recreation*, October 1971, pp. 59-61.
11. Girls on the team. *Parade Magazine*, May 14, 1972.
12. Harres, B. Attitudes of students toward women's athletic competition. *Research Quarterly, 39*(2), 1968, pp. 278-284.

13. Hart, M. Sport: Women sit in the back of the bus. *Psychology Today*, October 1971, pp. 64-66.

14. Henry, J. Lack of funds limits women's athletics. *The Arizona Daily Star*, June 23, 1972, p. 1-D.

15. Henry, J. Women's collegiate athletics growing slowly. *The Arizona Daily Star*, June 22, 1972, p. 1-E.

16. Hubbard, A. W. Some thoughts on motivation in sport. *Quest*, X, 1968, pp. 40-46.

17. Lee, M. The case for and against intercollegiate athletics for women and the situation since 1923. *Research Quarterly*, *2*, 1931, pp. 93-127.

18. Leyhe, N. L. Attitudes of the women members of AAHPER toward competition in sports for girls and women. (Doctoral dissertation, Indiana University) Bloomington, Indiana, 1955.

19. Leys, J. F. The power and the glory of physical education with some illustrations from the works of R. Tait McKenzie. In *Proceedings of the Big Ten Symposium on History of Physcial Education and Sport*, Ohio State University, March 1-3, 1971. Bruce L. Bennett (Ed.). Chicago: The Athletic Institute, 1972.

20. Malumphy, T. M. Athletics and competition for girls and women. In *DGWS Research Reports: Women in Sports*. Dorothy V. Harris (Ed.). Washington, D.C.: American Association for Health, Physical Education and Recreation, 1971, pp. 15-19.

21. Malumphy, T. M. Personality of women athletes in intercollegiate competition. *Research Quarterly*, *39*(3), 1968, pp. 610-620.

22. Miller, D. M., and Russell, K. R. E. *Sport: A Contemporary View*. Philadelphia: Lea & Febiger, 1971.

23. Murray, J. Genius non-transferable. Source unknown.

24. Nash, J. B. Athletics for girls. *The North American Review*, January 1928, pp. 99-104. (*Chronicle of American Physical Education, 1855–1930*, compiled by Aileene S. Lockhart and Betty Spears.) Dubuque, Iowa: Wm. C. Brown, 1972.

25. Park, R. J. The human element in sport: Play. *The Physical Educator*, *28*(3), 1971, pp. 122-124.

26. Perrin, E. A crises in girls' athletics. *Sportsmanship*, *1*(3), 1928, pp. 10-12. (*Chronicle of American Physical Education, 1855–1930*, compiled by Aileene S. Lockhart and Betty Spears.) Dubuque, Iowa: Wm. C. Brown, 1972.

27. Scott, P. M. Food for thought for the future. *Proceedings: Fourth National Institute on Girls' Sports*. Washington, D. C.: American Association for Health, Physical Education and Recreation, 1968.

28. Smith, L. The girls in the Olympics. *Today's Health*, October 1964, pp. 28-31, 72, 75.

29. Smith, R. Golf course for women only. *The Arizona Daily Star* (© 1972 *New York Times News Service*), April 30, 1972.

30. Swift, P. Keeping up with youth. *Parade Magazine*, September 19, 1971.

31. Ulrich, C. *The Social Matrix of Physical Education*. Englewood Cliffs, N.J.: Prentice-Hall Inc., 1968.

32. *Update*. Washington, D.C.: American Association for Health, Physical Education and Recreation, November 1971.

2. Dimensions of the Athlete

Genius, in truth, means little more than the faculty of
perceiving in an unhabitual way.

William James

PSYCHOSOCIOLOGIC EXPLORATIONS

An inquiry into female athletes leads to such questions as:
Who are they? What makes them act as they do? Why do they
choose certain sports? Are there any common denominators among
sport participants? Does sport participation have any effect upon
personality development? What are the marks of a champion?

The psychosociologic dimensions of sport related to the why of
challenge, the makeup of personality, and more specifically the
psyche of an athlete are not easily generalized. Nor should they be.
No doubt all generalizations about people get stuck in the dilemma
that mankind is not uniform but compounded of individuals whose
psychic structures spread them over a wide span of differences.
Even the identification of an athlete cannot be made with any degree of certainty. "If one compares personality measures of a large
group of athletes from many different sports, it is likely that the
average scores will approximate those found within a normal population of young men and women of a similar age and living in a
similar culture."[60] Nonetheless, by stretching the limited data, some
possible insights into the nature of the competitor in sport may be
provided.

Who Is the Female Athlete?

A great many persons play at sports. They may be doing it for
personal therapy, to overcome an opponent or the odds of nature,
to deal with self-doubt and fear, just for the fun of it, or for any
number of personal reasons.

Why people compete in sports is a profound question that is
explored in the vast literature of the sport world. It is a question to
which I devoted a book.[37] There are as many reasons for involvement in the competitive world of sports as there are competitors.
Sports are, after all, an individual matter.

Frequently mentioned reasons for competing, as revealed in the limited research on girls and women engaged in sports competitions, include the opportunity to meet people and develop friendships, love of sport, and the challenge of testing their skills.[32] And there may be a certain truth in the notion that sports are among the most romantic, captivating engagements that women may encounter. Sportscaster Howard Cosell stated that "Sports is maybe the primary reason in the United States for sustaining illusion and delusion."[5] Today, sports figures are among those most glamorized by television, clothing designers, and beauty contests.

Despite certain romantic views of the sport competitor, however, she is not usually a member of the jet set, or a "social athlete." She may be on the economic fringes with small monetary rewards. She may be rather functionless in the typical sense of preparing herself for a vocation. The limited research indicates that female individual sports participants come from medium-sized cities, from middle-class and high economic and high educational levels, and that they develop their skills in locations other than public school facilities under the direction of specialists (e.g., country club professionals) in the sport.[33] Apparently the female athlete grows up in a family and among friends who warmly approve of and encourage her involvement in sport. Women golfers seem to be reared in families in which there is a history of parents' participation in sports. It is suggested that the mother, who is a model of womanly activity, by her active involvement in sport perhaps influences her daughter's positive self-concept as an athlete and a woman.[34]

In short, at least the competitive golf and tennis players appear to come from backgrounds in which they had the opportunity and resources for participation, they received professional coaching at an early age, and they feel secure about their femininity and popularity.

What Is Her Personality Structure?

Perhaps the most extensively investigated topic in the field of sports psychology is that of the personality of the athlete. Some questions studied have included: Do athletes differ from non-athletes? What personality traits characterize participants in the various sports subgroups (e.g., individual versus team)? Are there differences between the personality characteristics of male and female sports competitors? What about the personality characteristics of those who continue and those who drop out of sports? Other questions at least raised if not researched have included:

Does the participant in more than one sport differ from the athlete who participates only in one sport? Does the athlete who is a substitute, that is, the one who "rides the bench" most of the time, differ from the regular or "starter" who might be considered the more successful member of the team? In reviewing research studies concerned with the relationship between athletics and various personality factors, Cooper stated, "more questions are raised than answered."[9]

Morgan and other investigators commented on the many methodological problems and shortcomings that have plagued the study of personality dynamics of the athlete, some of which are the operational definitions employed, the variety of instruments used to make comparisons, questionable sampling methods, and failure of investigators to pursue the study of personality and sports within a theoretical framework.[38] Morgan proposed that a gravitational model be adopted to explain personality differences in sports, that is, *athletes are different at the outset and gravitate toward a sport because of inherent constitutional differences*. This suggestion was made on the basis of theoretical views and experimental findings from Eysenckian theory. Eysenck emphasized the biologic basis of personality, that is, personality is largely fixed by heredity.[15] Heredity accounts for 75 to 80 per cent of variance. Eysenck and his adherents demonstrated relationships between extraversion and variables such as pain tolerance, conditioning, level of aspiration, somatotype, degree of excitation and inhibition prevalent in the central nervous system (CNS), and this research has provided convincing evidence to suggest that these functions are largely inherited. Therefore, Morgan has speculated that the differences between athletes are due to gravitation of certain types rather than the result of sport participation.

Investigators interested in Eysenckian theory in sports psychology or in employing this theoretical model in an attempt to understand the psychodynamics of sports will want to read more comprehensive discussions than can be presented here.[16,17,25]

Research on the personality characteristics of the female sport competitor is very limited, except for that done on the Olympic-caliber athlete whose psyche has been rather thoroughly plumbed. And, as those done on the male athlete, such personality investigations, appear to be contradictory, misleading, and unproductive. Researchers more recently have urged critical examination of the controversial problems and relevance of personality testing such as the traditional comparisons between athletes and nonathletes, highly skilled and low skilled, individual and team sports, males and females, and so forth. Despite the limited data, the dubious connections and inconsistencies, and the lack of definitive answers, some findings are presented to illustrate the research that has been done, some of which may be enlightening.

There are some observations about the personality characteristics of *women athletes in general.* Neal found that United States women athletes in the 1959 Pan-American Games scored higher on the Edwards Personality Preference Schedule in variables such as achievement, autonomy, affiliation, and nurturance than did non-athletes.[40] Peterson and colleagues, using the Sixteen Factor Personality Questionnaire (16 FPQ), found that women athletes in general tend to be a little more serious than are average women, and may have a tendency to express themselves less freely.[44] Women competitors also are intellectually brighter, more conscientious, aggressive, and persevering than the norms for other women of equivalent age and education.

Malumphy found that the intercollegiate competitors in tennis and golf appear to be more intelligent, tough-minded, assertive, stable, and happy-go-lucky than are their college peers. They also may be more reserved, suspicious, casual, and placid.[34] They may be more intelligent, more self-sufficient, and more open to change.[32] These women may display such differences because of sports competition, and they do not seem to suffer anxiety over the possible lack of societal acceptance of the woman athlete. In fact, they feel that their participation in sports enhances their feminine image, makes them more datable, more interesting to be with.

Musier, investigating the differences in personality factors on the High School Personality Questionnaire (HSPQ) and 16 FPQ of girls and women in competitive lacrosse at the junior high school, senior high school, college, adult, and national levels, found significant differences between each group and its norm on one or more factors. Although these findings indicate a competitive girls and women's personality type, personality development appears to be independent of sports competition.[39] These findings suggest, as does the work referred to previously, the validity of the gravitational theory—the individual who already possesses certain characteristics is attracted to competitive sports.

In contrast to other findings, Berkey reported no significant differences between the athletic (in this case, intercollegiate basketball players) and nonathletic groups in aggression, deference, dominance, nurturance, and succorance needs as measured by the Edwards Personal Preference Schedule.[2]

Perhaps these contradictory findings can be explained by possible differences in personality traits of *participants in different types of sports* activities. In fact, Cratty, declaring that "present studies of the personalities of groups of athletes are of relatively little help to the coach," suggested that significant differences in personality traits are uncovered only within specific sports and subdivisions of a sport, for example, sprinters on a track team.[10] The problems of determining the relationship between personality and participation in specific sports, however, are as difficult as those posed in other areas of investigation. The limited research on women athletes does point to some distinguishing characteristics.

The study of Peterson and co-workers showed that women athletes in individual sports rate higher on personality factors of dominance, adventurousness, sensitivity, introversion, and self-sufficiency than do women in team sports.[44] They are also more radical and independent in their thinking, more self-assured, and less inhibited than are the team sports athletes. On the other hand, team sports athletes are self-reliant, steady, practical, dependable, emotionally disciplined, and higher in sophistication than individual sports athletes. No differences are found in such factors as sociability, intelligence, stability, and conscientiousness.

Malumphy found college women participants in team sports to be more group-dependent, more anxious, and lower in leadership interest than are their peers in individual sports.[33] She indicated that women in team sports are more like their nonathletic peers, and they express their feelings of unsureness about the contribution that athletics make in their femininity and social acceptability.[32] A study of the personality traits of female champion fencers showed a definite fencer's personality closely related to that of the competitive race car driver, male and female. The female fencer can be described as ambitious with a strong desire to succeed. She enjoys accomplishing difficult tasks requiring abundant skill and knowledge. She is well informed, imaginative, and independent.[63]

What about differences between males and females? Wyrick, describing how sex differences affect research in physical education, confirmed the idea that there are many variables in which men and women have been found to be statistically different, and she suggested that it is important to determine whether the environment is actually creating differences that do not exist biologically. Throughout research studies, motivation is a confounding factor. Apparently there is a need to determine how sex differences might evoke special problems when women are subjects in research investigations.[65]

Ogilvie contended that the trends for female competitors seem to be highly consistent with those for males, except that females appear less extroverted but possibly more stable, tough-minded, lower in neuroticism, higher in independence, and much less creative. They are "as well equipped to handle stress situations as Olympic males."[42]

Perhaps the significance of these reports is simply that, for whatever reasons, cultural or otherwise, women are different from men, and the same generalizations regarding the psychology of coaching cannot be applied to both.

Do Sports Influence Personality?

The evidence in favor of the theory that sport competition tends to develop certain personality traits is very scanty, controversial, and of questionable significance. One matter of seeming importance for women is that concerning *femininity*. It often has been assumed that girls and women committed to sports differ in the trait of femininity from those who are not in sports. Research indicates that the effect of participation on the feminine image primarily depends upon the participant herself.[33]

Furthermore, the findings, being limited and inconclusive, suggest cautious application. They also suggest, as Malumphy reminded coaches, the need to accept the woman athlete "primarily as a young woman and secondarily as one who is interested in activity and competition." She is just another young woman in school who has a sport skill and a desire to test it.[32]

To the question, can sport have a positive effect on personality, some writers contend that "harmonious development of the person comes through sport participation."[60] In the *stability-neuroticism* aspects of personality, a consistent observation is that athletes tend to be more stable, extroverted, and social than are nonathletes. After reviewing the literature pertaining to personality and physical ability, Kane concluded that a positive relationship exists between "athletic ability and (1) stability as opposed to anxiety, and (2) extroversion as opposed to introversion."[28]

A different interpretation, however, may be drawn from the work of other researchers. Pitts and McClure suggested that physical activity may actually evoke undesirable changes. They reported that infusion of lactate produces symptoms and attacks of anxiety in anxiety neurotics.[47]

Some writers declare that sports expose personality flaws. Ogilvie and Tutko, suggesting that if you want to build character try something other than sport, wrote: "When an athlete's ego is deeply invested in sport achievement, very few of the neurotic protective mechanisms provide adequate or sustaining cover."[41]

Ogilvie attempted to cover both horns of another dilemma: does competition increase emotional stability or are the less emotionally stable driven out of competition? Based upon limited data, he offered the following observations:

1. There seems to be a tendency for competitive girl swimmers to become less reserved as they move up the competitive ladder; or, there is a tendency for the less outgoing girls to be gradually eliminated from competition.

2. There is some evidence that competition increases emotional stability; or, perhaps the less emotionally stable are driven out of competition.

3. Highly assertive youngsters become slightly less so under the discipline of coaching; or, the more self-assertive girls are weeded out of competitive swimming.

4. There seems to be a dramatic change in conscience development as the young ladies move up the competitive ladder; or, a process of elimination occurs under the direction of the coach.

5. There is a significant shift of personality toward becoming much more tough-minded and to be less willing to accept nonsense; or, the child must get tough or drop out.

6. There seems to be no established theory to account for the degree to which the 10-year-olds have become shrewd, calculating, and worldly wise. Unfortunately, we do not have this measurement for 14-year-olds. Is it possible that "survival" depends upon the development of such characteristics?

7. There is a most dramatic shift from extreme apprehension and a tendency to worry, to self-assurance and self-confidence. Is this a result of the weeding process, or are we building character?

8. There is a shift toward self-control and self-discipline from the age of 10 to 14, but our data does not support the assumption that it will remain that high by college age.

9. There is a systematic reduction of tension and anxiety with increased age; or, children of a highly anxious type cannot stand the pressure.[42]

A report on high level Japanese sports showed that male athletes who dropped out of their athletic clubs were not as stable as those who stayed.[66]

These reports and similar research findings seem to confirm the theory of gravitational relationships and selective mortality in sport.[38] Morgan, reporting on several studies, pointed out that actual increases and decreases in psychologic *states* have been associated with acute, but generally not chronic, athletic participation. *States* are transitory and situational features of personality; *traits* are enduring and stable features of personality. Psychologic *traits* fixed by heredity do not change following participation in athletics.

In short, sports do not appear to cause stable mental health. Rather, those with stable profiles gravitate toward sports, and stability may be considered as a prerequisite to continued high level performance.

Of further interest in the stability-neuroticism aspect of personality is Morgan's observation that, although athletes display fewer neurotic symptoms than do nonathletes, once the athlete is referred to a psychiatric service, his prognosis is less favorable than that of the nonathlete. The implication for those concerned with athletic programs, as Morgan pointed out, is that "psychological first aid is just as important as physical treatment for the injured athlete."[38]

A further aspect of personality dynamics in sports concerns the matter of *aggression*. Sports have been generally recognized as a catharsis—an acceptable channel for the expression of aggressive tendencies, of reasonable benefit in sublimating antisocial tendencies, and a means for compensating for inferiority feelings or imagined incompetencies. Lorenz proposed that sport, being a "specifically human form of non-hostile combat," may educate man to "a conscious and responsible control of his own fighting behavior."[31] Schafer pointed out that competitive sports serve a "social control" function—inhibiting abnormal interest, harnessing adolescent energies, encouraging yet controlling physical force, providing opportunities to struggle against an enemy, and exerting a deterring influence on delinquency.[53] Lawther declared that sports seem to make athletes a little less "thin skinned" when it comes to criticism and a little more realistic about public acclaim, a little more inclined to enjoy social contact: "the sports expression of aggression renders him more sociable and friendly away from the contest."[30]

Certainly it is a well-known fact that coaches practice numerous techniques and place great faith in their effectiveness to arouse or to calm athletes prior to, during, and following competition, although there is little scientific verification for these techniques.

Some psychologists point out that the cathartic effect occurs only when anger is present,[8] and other researchers report that aggression is reduced if the athlete wins the contest but not if he loses.[35] And quite in contrast to the *cathartic* theory is the *circular* theory—that aggressive tendencies are heightened following an aggressive act; thus, the expression of aggression becomes a habit and leads to increased aggression.[3]

The only firm conclusion that can be drawn from the literature related to the effect of sport participation on personality is that more research is needed, particularly on female athletes. Perhaps this further conclusion may be warranted: because all experiences tend to shape personality, sport too may be said to shape personality. The more intense the experience, the more effect it may have on forming personality characteristics, both good and bad.

Are There Marks of a Champion?

What makes a champion? It may be easier to answer the question: what does not? Perhaps championship performance cannot be generalized or predicted. Nonetheless, to speculate about the vital virtues of a champion performer is most inviting, and I shall not ignore the temptation to proffer some observations.

The matter of *psychologic championship,* or what makes the champion tick differently from, say, the near-champion, is of considerable interest to the world of sports in general. An ABC sports special devoted to the theme of "What Makes a Champion?" highlighted the notion that they are much like anyone else except for this difference: they act upon their dreams. They have an urge to excel, an iron determination, a total singlemindedness that can overcome almost anything. They have no regrets that they missed out on something else.

Payton Jordan and Bud Spencer, in their excellent book *Champions in the Making,* admonish not only coaches but also athletes to keep in mind one basic principle: "There is no single formula for success in track and field unless it might be the idea of staying in balance. . . ."[27] The *balance* they were referring to applies not only to methods of work schedule and training rules, but to attitude patterns as well.

The concept of *balance* or its synonyms is found in many writings aimed at distilling the qualities that make a champion. Fred Russell, sports reporter, acknowledged a "special kind of skill polished by practice and fully harnessed by understanding," as well as the common denominators of determination and pride. But above all Russell considered emotional *balance* a vital component, because it enables the competitor to operate at his optimum level regardless of the situation, success or failure. The time comes when an athlete gains confidence.

> . . . emotional maturity of being at his best when the going is roughest, when he experiences that tremendous satisfaction of keeping his presence of mind in the deepest difficulty, that genuine joy of being able to function in disaster—and finish in style. That's a true champion.[50]

Apparently, being in balance includes *being able to fail* in good spirits. Norman Vincent Peale attributed this quality of having a "balance wheel" to the right disposition to do one's best, to stand the wear and tear. How a person performs when he is getting beaten offers a good clue to the right disposition.[43] Peale, contending that faith makes champions, pointed to some characteristics that make a champion's ability and capacity meet: never being a quitter; believing in oneself; a desire to win, to be great; mastering the little skills that go with excellence and that make the difference between the ordinary and the exceptional. Russell, explaining that the real champion "is the person whose heart can be educated," pointed to the prime factor as being "the experience of having failed." In distilling the essence of this championship quality of having failed, Russell used such descriptions as: he has developed a feel for pressure; he is "clutch-worthy"; he has conquered the fear of making a mistake; he keeps presence of mind in the deepest difficulty; he is able to function in disaster and finish in style; he has a funny bone as well as a backbone. This is why "in defeat, one can rest on his character and keep a stout heart."[49]

The difficult art of losing, according to a *Time Magazine* essay concerning the great losers of this century, is that ". . . the loser controls his attitudes, he can always change that attitude and regard defeat as unimportant."[12] The art of losing is focusing on what can be, not on what might have been. Defeat, which is both a humbling and corrective process, is in many ways a better teacher than is success. In a sense, then, champions are good losers because they use defeat to examine why they lost.

The limited research on this topic reveals that, at least in the sports investigated, the female competitor's reactions to winning and losing depend primarily upon her feelings about how well she played and the opponent's skill. The groups investigated, participants in tennis and golf, appear to be typified by a wholesome discontent related to losing rather than being characterized by prima donna and poor-sport behaviors.[32]

In addition to being able to tolerate and learn from defeats, apparently the champion is able to withstand whatever *discomfort or pain* is demanded by pushing to extremes in hard, grueling practices and contests. Sport literature has an abundance of references to the aspects of pain and discomfort related to performance. Seemingly typical of the champion's attitude is that of Don Schollander, whose reflections on top competition in swimming were that, if you push yourself through the pain barrier into real agony, you are a champion.

> You can back off, or you can force yourself to drive to the finish, knowing that the pain will become excruciating. Right there, the great competitors separate from the rest, for it's those last few meters that count.[54]

Schollander's female counterpart and Canada's swimming champion, Elaine Tanner, also seemed to sum up the attitudes of the champion who puts mind over matter: "If I felt pain I almost enjoyed it because that meant I was working hard and it spurred me to work even harder."[55]

And now there is evidence in research to support the belief that athletes are able to withstand high levels of pain. Insofar as females are concerned, the athletes in college basketball show a decidedly higher pain tolerance than do nonathletes, although there are no differences between these groups in pain threshold (the minimum stimulus that can produce pain).[61] Apparently an explanation of the athlete's ability to tolerate pain might be that she is so engrossed in the activity or distracted by it that pain goes unnoticed.

The work of Petrie, who has investigated pain in many subjects although not in athletes, and the work of Ryan and colleagues, who investigated characteristics of pain tolerance common to certain male athletic groups, should be of further interest to coaches.[45,52] Petrie identified three kinds of persons: the reducer, the augmenter, and the moderator; the differences between these types involve numerous aspects of personality that contribute to the sensation of suffering. The reducer has the greatest tolerance for pain. Because he tends to reduce all sensation received, he suffers from a "sensory lack," thus he has a greater desire for physical activity and for sensation of almost any type as a source of stimulation. Essentially the reducer is extroverted and suffers from isolation, thus he has a greater number of friends than does the augmenter. The augmenter does not suffer from sensory deprivation, does not tolerate pain well, does not need the stimulation of exercise, and has fewer friends than does the reducer, although the relationships are deep.

Ryan and Kovacic and Ryan and Foster reported that, in keeping with the work of Petrie, male athletes have higher pain tolerance than do nonathletes, the characteristics of the reducer being even more common to the contact sports group than the noncontact sports group.[51,52]

Walker, summarizing the literature on pain and athletics, suggested that more information is needed regarding concerns such as whether athletes possess pain tolerance or develop it during participation, the effect of pain on performance, and pain tolerance according to sport and position played.[62]

In summary, the studies of personality characteristics of athletes, however nebulous, have been intended to help to answer such questions as: Can personality be improved or modified by participation in sport? Will high level competition have special effects upon the structure of the athlete's personality? What personality characteristics distinguish the outstanding athlete?

Perhaps too much emphasis has been placed on attempting to

distinguish certain personality types in sports. Perhaps traits found in highly skilled athletes are not significant to their performance. High achievers in any field of endeavor may be characterized by similar traits. One common trait that high achievers in any field appear to have is the willingness to work hard and to work long hours. Absorption, commitment, concentration, vigor, boldness, courage, resourcefulness, self-actualization, flexibility, acceptance of conflict and tension, and many synonyms are used to describe the creative person. If creativity is a way of life, then the characteristics of a creative person also would be those that describe an outstanding sport performer who has immersed herself in the activity and who has a rich background of knowledge and experience in it to be a winner.

Insofar as research in general gives clues to what makes a champion, there are, it seems, personality traits that characterize the exceptional athlete and there are numerous exceptions. If there is a championship personality, perhaps the explanation confirms the theory that athletes are different at the outset and gravitate toward sport according to their personality differences.[38] In any case, an abundance of literature deals with the male athlete, but very scanty information regards the female, except at the highly skilled level. More studies of personality are needed, especially longitudinal studies and those related to women. Moreover, there appears to be a real need for improving the research designs and for asking more pertinent questions.

One large question remains: How can these various findings and observations regarding the personality of female sport participants be related to teaching and coaching? Would it not be convenient if findings could be used to help prescribe some magic, all-purpose formula for recognizing the potential athlete? Using this formula, the coach or teacher could assign people to the area they match on their personality test. Perhaps fortunately for the future of sports, this will never become reality. There is no guarantee involved, no assurance that these generalized characteristics molded into an individual would make a complete performer. Some athletes who do not possess any of these so-called sport-type personalities will succeed in competition. And there may be some with all the characteristics mentioned who will never pass within the realm of sports. Thus the freedom to choose any area of participation and to excel will always belong to the individual. Chapter 8 provides further information regarding the assessment of personality as a factor in athletic achievement.

PHYSIOLOGIC EXPLORATIONS

In addition to assessments of the personality and motives of the female athlete, there is need for understanding her physiologic makeup and her physiologic response to vigorous programs of training and competition.

Although much remains to be learned about the effects of competitive sports on girls and women, research to date tends not only to dispel the notion of biologic inferiority of females but to provide evidence in support of rigorous training and competitive sports programs for them. In fact, such programs, properly conducted, enhance the health of young women. Some of the physiologic parameters are discussed in the following pages.

The Weaker Sex?

A framework for generalizing about physiologic superiority resists easy description and resolution just as does the concept of psychologic championship.

Bernauer, suggesting that the physical performance of the female shows an apparent superiority over that of the male, raised a question of just what superior means. "If you function in such a way as to live longer, be more resistant, survive more efficiently, then by measure of this definition of superiority you are superior to others."[4]

Bernauer argued that, using physiologic tests of capacity and the physiologic parameters favoring the males' greater response level, it is not surprising to find a bias in favor of male superiority. However, he made a compelling case for the biologic superiority of the female while urging continuing study of the problems attending the female engaged in physical competition.

It is a matter of fact that women perform physically on a much more comparable basis with men and in many cases are superior to men than was previously thought. Foreman reported that records concerned with four of the most highly trained athletes in the world reveal a startling similarity in various physiologic parameters between male and female distance runners.[21] Other studies of the net efficiencies of men and women in prolonged work (on a treadmill) under thermal stress show men and women to be strikingly similar—in some instances the data favor the men and in others the women. In general the female manifests a large measure of regulation (balance or homeostasis) under prolonged work.[4] Women are considered to be biologically superior to men in their resistance to illness and death, which may indicate that they could cope with a more consistent and prolonged participation in sports.[24]

However, in noting anatomic and physiologic differences between males and females, with special reference to athletic competition, deVries made a plea for establishing sensible programs for girls and women not merely those based upon modification of men's sports.[11] Some sex differences that do exist may have bearing on sport performances and participation in competitive athletics, although more research is needed to establish the significance of these differences. Perhaps the most obvious structural difference is that the female has a "poorer" strength-weight ratio than does the male due to the smaller proportion of muscle in relation to larger amount of adipose tissue. This fact, coupled with the fact that the ratio of heart weight to body weight in the female is only 85 to 90 per cent of the value for the male, makes it obvious that the performances of males and females are not comparable. Females adjust to heavy training, however, much the same as do males (see Chapter 9 for further discussion).

Sex differences in fat storage and center of gravity (slightly higher in males than in females) or differences between the height of males and females are not significant as isolated facts. Actually there may be greater differences among individuals of the same sex than between the sexes. Moreover, the importance of these differences may be relative. For example, the larger stores of fatty tissue in women may be regarded as an advantage in some activities; they provide greater buoyancy in swimming and lesser heat loss in cold water.

A finding of some significance appears to be the difference in the incidence of athletic injury between males and females. The overall incidence of athletic injuries is much greater for women than for men. The fact that the highest percentage of injuries for women is found in sports that require explosive efforts may indicate that the musculoskeletal system of the female is not suited to some activities such as short runs and the long jump (see Chapter 9 for further discussion on injuries).

There are physiologic differences between the sexes that may imply the need for programs designed specifically for females. Basal metabolic rate (BMR) is higher for males than for females although this difference is significant only in regard to resting heat dissipation, not efficiency of muscular activity. Limited data have shown that the female may be less able to deal with hot environments than can the male because her threshold for sweating is higher, thus the physiologic cost of maintaining heat balance is greater. Microcirculation (or the resistance of the capillary wall to break down from mechanical manipulation) is greater in males than in females, which may account for the females' greater susceptibility to bruises.

The implication of such studies and facts is not that women are superior or inferior to men, but rather that females can and should participate in vigorous programs of sports activities selected and designed for them. Clayton L. Thomas, Vice President, Medical Affairs, Tampax, Incorporated, summarized the emancipated view of the female sports participant: "Apart from menstruation, parturition, and lactation, there are no essential differences in physiology of male and female, and the special anatomical characteristics of the female offer no bar to athletic sports."[57]

That the female athlete is clearly superior to the sedentary female in general health and physiologic functioning appears to be an acknowledged fact. The need for increasing the motivation of the general female population for regular physical exertion is underscored by Evalyn S. Gendel in her studies of the fitness and fatigue in the common woman not just the Olympic or national sport superwoman.[23] General results of her study showed that those young women who are physically active or who score highest on work capacity have fewer complaints of fatigue, menstrual difficulty, backaches, and related problems, and were rated physiologically fit.[23] Gendel suggested that attention to fitness for increasing numbers of girls and women would mean removing competitive sports programs from the realm of outside activity to the area of regular school environment.[23]

Are Strenuous Training and Competition Harmful?

Considerations concerning the menstrual cycle, pregnancy, and fear of physiologic damage have long been the basis for withholding from girls and women the encouragement and permission to participate in sports to the same extent as boys and men. Research has revealed generally that intense training and competitive programs do not have a deleterious effect on girls and women. Data and opinions from numerous medical and sport sources are briefly summarized in the following section.

Menstruation and Childbearing. Erdelyi stated that active, competitive sport does not disturb the *onset of menarche* and noted that research findings in other countries support her own experience, that the menstrual cycles of athletes are generally the same as for nonathletes.[18]

In discussing the *effects of menstruation on performance,* Erdelyi reported poor performance in tennis and rowing, but improved performance in ball games, swimming, gymnastics, and track and field during menstruation.[19] Erdelyi referred also to the work of Bausenwein and Ingmann, who reported that female participants in the Helsinki Olympics were not affected by their menstrual period. Ray Goddard, U.S. Olympic team physician, noted that four world records were set by girls who were menstruating during the Olympics in Tokyo.[19]

Ken Foreman, Chairman of the Women's Long Distance Running Sub-Committee of the Amateur Athletic Union of the United States, reported on a study he conducted involving two groups of nationally ranked athletes.[21] It revealed that 25 per cent of the track and field performers thought they performed better during menstruation, 25 per cent thought they performed less well, and the remaining 50 per cent stated that there was no difference in their performance. When the nationally ranked softball and basketball players responded to the same questions, 18 per cent stated that they performed better while menstruating, 48 per cent said that they performed less well, and 24 per cent indicated that their performance was about the same. One of the athletes in this study reported adverse effects from strenuous training, or performance, during menstruation, although 29 per cent of this group stated emphatically that they had less menstrual pain when they were training regularly.

To the question of whether girls should *train during menstruation,* studies show that work loads may change during menstruation. Erdelyi referred to studies by Duentzer, Hellendall, Kiss, and Haraszthy, who found that from 42 to 48 per cent of female athletes achieved above their average during their menstrual period.[19] Fifteen per cent showed improved performances, with the remaining athletes doing less well. Inferior performances were most common in the premenstruum. A study by Phillips revealed that, during menstruation, fluctuations occurring in pulse rate and blood pressure before and after exercise cannot be attributed to menstruation.[46] Garlick and Bernauer reported that blood hemoglobin and hematocrit are related to the menstrual cycle at rest, but apparently are not influenced by moderate exercise.[22]

Some authorities do point out, however, that overtraining and excessive stress may cause *menstrual disorders.* Girls who start intensive training programs before menarche have a higher percentage of menstrual disorders than those who start training later, and these disorders tend to disappear when the work load is reduced.[48] Although greater incidence of menstrual cycle abnormality has been noted among girls who started heavy training before menarche, Erdelyi found no cause-and-effect relationship.[18] Some research indicates that gynecologic problems occur more frequently among competitive girl swimmers and skiers than among those in other sports.[18] According to Duentzer, however, the alleged harm stemming from participation in aquatic activity during menses is is largely myth.[14] Simple rules should be followed to avoid ill effects —being fit, moderation of activity, avoidance of extreme cold or heat.

As to whether strenuous training and competition adversely affect *reproduction,* there is evidence to the contrary. There are documented instances in which pregnant women not only have competed but have won championships. Although deVries maintained that strenuous activity should be avoided because of the extra pressure already put on the body by fetal circulation, he quoted Noach who cited the case histories of 15 German women champions who have borne children: five of the women gave up sport, two showed comparable performance records after retraining, and eight of the women markedly improved their performance.[11] The latter group reported that they "felt tougher." Noach concluded that pregnancy is a "special kind of nine month conditioning program because of increased demand on metabolism and the cardiovascular system."

Clayton Thomas cited studies by Astrand, Anderson, Erdelyi, and Gendel in which the obstetric and gynecologic histories of athletes were revealed.[58] He noted that the athletes proved to be normal in every respect, except that in those athletes who bore children the "length of labor was shorter, and the necessity for cesarean section was 50% less than for the control group."

Physiologic Adaptation to Stress. The physiologic implications of intense overloading also have been important concerns within recent years because of the increasing number of female competitors and the greater intensity of the training programs. Maximum oxygen uptake, which is indicative of *aerobic capacity* or the capacity to pay as you go, has become a fruitful area of study. A few pertinent highlights of such investigations on girls and women are presented here.

According to a report by Ken Foreman, Donald Knowlton of Southern Illinois University, who is conducting a long-term study involving members of the Ozark Track Club, reported findings representing several months of over-distance training by 10- to 16-year-old girls with oxygen uptake records ranging from 51.0 to 69.6 ml/kg/min as compared to maximum scores for the control group of 42.7 ml/kg/min.[21] Brown, reporting on the effects of cross-country running on preadolescent girls, noted that six weeks of intense training resulted in a 20 per cent increase in aerobic capacity with maximum uptake scores ranging from 47 to 78 ml/kg/min.[6] Brown emphasized that "the development of aerobic capacity is directly related to the duration of each training bout as well as to its intensity."

With regard to *loss of fluids* and *increased body temperature,* the physiologic cost of maintaining heat balance in hot weather is greater for women because the threshold for sweating in women is approximately 2 to 3 degrees centigrade above that in men and the temperature gradient from core to skin is smaller in women than in men.[11] C. H. Brown, Chief of Medical Services at the Veterans Administration Hospital in Livermore, accrued data from 11 female distance runners ranging in age from 9 years 10 months to 29 years.[21] Following a 13-mile run he found that weight loss among the participants varied from 2.06 to 3.28 per cent, with the average loss being 2.68 per cent. Although only four of the participants would permit the taking of rectal temperature, the four showed an average increase of 2.6 degrees F, with the highest recorded temperature being 103.6 degrees F. When compared to the critical levels stated above, it is obvious that these runners were nearing the limits of their adaptative potential. The fact that females perspire at a higher temperature threshold than do males may mean that they would be adversely affected by heat earlier than would their male counterparts, and thus they would require markedly different rules pertaining to their participation in long-distance races.

It has been reported that persistent stress may cause hypertrophy of the *adrenal gland,* and some medical persons wonder if persistent stress can interfere with the normal interplay of the *endocrine glands.* Nonetheless, thus far reports indicate that adrenal hypertrophy is reversible after the stress is stopped.

Another physiologic parameter of concern is that of *blood changes.* Studies concerned with women, which have included the analysis of blood samples, have shown little if any change in hematocrit from stress of intense overload. However, there have been small but significant changes in hemoglobin with a tendency for blood counts to decline following intense exercise.[21] It has been suggested that the decline in hemoglobin is temporary and probably represents a high rate of destruction of red blood cells as a consequence of stress of heavy overload.[7]

Perhaps the question of whether or not females can adapt to the stress of intense overload is best summed up in the words of Eric Banister, of the Preventive Medical Center in Vancouver, British Columbia: "I see no dramatic difference between male and female response to the stress of exercise or in the tenor of the subsequent adaptation to the repeated stress which constitutes training."[21]

How About Muscles?

Probably the most common concern relative to sport competition for girls and women pertains to the fear of building muscles and thus masculinization. Ken Foreman, citing numerous studies, concluded that "there is growing evidence that highly skilled female athletes possess great natural strength and an essentially ecto-mesomorphic body structure, but the supposition that girls will become heavily muscled, male-like creatures as a consequence of intense training is a tragic distortion of reality."[21]

Harmon Brown, endocrinologist and field event coach for the Milbrae Lions Track Club, has conducted extensive research on girls and women and concluded that women are capable of performing heavy exercises and achieving considerable strength without showing muscle hypertrophy, probably due to these factors: hypertrophy is marked by loss of adipose tissue, and hypertrophy is revealed much less in women than in men because women produce only about 10 per cent as much androgen (male hormone) as do males.[7]

A study reported by Wilmore and Brown, involving 80 women who had been using heavy-resistance exercises for a period of 10 weeks or more, showed that there were substantial increases in strength but slight muscle hypertrophy.[64] They concluded, however, that the extent of increases was small relative to the men due to the fact that the secretion of testosterone is considerably higher in men than in women.

It should be noted that muscular strength is considered to be the most important factor in successful sport performance. Marie-Therese Eyquem, although citing studies undertaken at the Center for Gynecological Consultation in Prague which concluded that the masculinizing influence of sport was nonexistent, declared that "there is no doubt that some women whose morphology or functional characteristics are closer to men's are first in great competitions . . . since certain handicaps are thus overcome."[20]

Frances McGill, in personal communication with Foreman,[21] cited research conducted at Loveless Foundation, Albuquerque, New Mexico, showing that partly because of increasing deposition of fat in the female, the physical performances of girls fall behind those of boys. McGill's study showed that the physical performances of men and women are quite similar when they related to fat-free weight.[36] Unpublished data provided Ken Foreman by Dr. Furchner of the Los Alamos Medical Center strongly support McGill's notation. Dr. Furchner revealed that 17 of the 24 members of the U.S. Women's Olympic team showed higher lean body scores (relationship of muscle to fat) than does the average male in the normal population.

What About Injuries?

Research bearing upon the incidence of injuries to girls and women in sports appears to be scanty, and largely centered on track and field events. The research seems to indicate that the female does have certain proclivities toward injury, although such evidence could be considered as underscoring the general neglect of the female as a viable participant in sport who needs careful training and preparation.

Klaus reported that the incidence of athletic injuries sustained by women is almost double that of men.[29] Strain-type injuries such as inflammation of tendons, tendon sheaths, and periosteum, and bursitis are sustained four times more often by women than by men. The highest incidence of injury occurs in ballistic or explosive events such as sprints (54 per cent), or long jump (31 per cent).

Ken Foreman, reporting on data derived from a variety of sources including medical records and accident reports, stated that accidents and injuries in specific track and field events follow a rather predictable pattern.[21] Distance runners have foot problems, including blisters, corns, and plantar warts. Girls having exceptionally long toes suffer fatigue fractures of the second metatarsal bone. Medial displacement of the navicular bone, associated with long arch strain, is a common problem for distance runners who are forced to train on streets or other hard surfaces. Javelin throwers suffer from severe inflammation of the flexor attachments at the medial epicondyle of the humerus. This becomes a particularly serious problem for girls who use a three-quarter or sidearm delivery. Tendonitis of the wrist flexors is a common problem for shot-putters, but it can often be eliminated or corrected by a protracted period of squeezing a firm sponge ball. Because the brass shot is relatively small, frequent traumatic abduction, hyperextension of the index finger, occurs when the shot slips off the hand during the ballistic flip at the instant of delivery.

Foreman reported further that the female athlete seems to be highly susceptible to soft tissue injuries. Hurdlers frequently bruise their shins, knees, and gluteal muscles while jumping over the hurdle. The hamstring pull is a common consequence of early season sprinting. Perhaps the underlying causative factor is a marked imbalance between the agonistic and antagonistic muscles due to minimal long-term training by a majority of girls and women. In recent years inflammation of Achilles tendon with the classic edema and squeaky tendon has become a major problem. Although the causative factors are not clear, Foreman strongly recommended that early season stair running be eliminated and that athletes train on soft surfaces in running flats or tennis shoes.

Perhaps Celeste Ulrich best summed up the matter of injuries in these words: "Women can be injured, as can males. But they will not collapse because they are females."[59]

Which Sports Do What?

Interest in the strenuousness of sports for young women has raised such questions as what the various sports relatively contribute to fitness and what comparative energy demands are made by various sports and training programs. With few exceptions, most of the studies concerned with assessment of energy cost of sport participation have used male subjects and have been conducted in a laboratory. In a study supported in part by the Division of Girls and Women's Sports, Vera Skubic and Jean Hodgkins tested women participants in archery, badminton, basketball, bowling, golf, hockey, softball, tennis, and volleyball in order to determine the relative strenuousness of these sports.[56] Comparisons of energy expenditure for each sport were made by calculating mean heart rate, oxygen uptake, and ventilation. The subject's heart beats were telemetered during her actual participation in each sport. The center halfback position in hockey and the roving player position in basketball were found to be heavy activities, requiring a significantly greater oxygen uptake than did positions in all other sports. Rated as moderate activities were the nonroving forward and guard positions in basketball, badminton, tennis, softball pitching, and volleyball. Golf, archery, and bowling were classified as light activities in energy expenditure.

These findings are similar to what might be expected of these various sports, but further implications are of more interest. Although the exceptionally high heart rates of the roving player in basketball and center halfback in hockey were not maintained continuously for long periods of time, an interesting finding is that players average approximately 180 beats/min for games lasting 50 to 60 minutes. Physiologists have indicated that pulse rates from 180 to 200 beats/min are exhausting and can be maintained only for short periods. One possible explanation for the findings is that the "women in general are physiologically capable of meeting far greater energy requirements than is generally believed."[56]

Drinkwater and Horvath studied 15 female track athletes, ages 12 to 18 years, in order to determine the effects of treadmill simulation of a standard track and field workout.[13] The results showed that "the two most strenuous events during practice were the 220 yard maximum speed runs and the 880 yard moderate speed endurance run." Mean maximum oxygen uptake values derived from this study ranged from 42.5 to 51.1 ml/kg/min. Of course, these findings do not refer to those girls and women in the highly competitive sport programs; however, there is no experimental evidence to suggest that women are as fragile as they are commonly believed to be.

Because women are not blessed with as great a muscle mass as men and tend to be fatter, they have a distinct disadvantage in performing sports with a high priority for strength. This generalization, however, refers more to the average female. Without doubt, the Olympic champion discus thrower Olga Connally could hardly be regarded as lacking in strength or, for that matter, in femininity.

On the other hand, although feminine women may be wrestlers and boxers and may not be harmed in any way even by intense contact sports, the aggressive, body-contact sports do not typify the American girl, and other sports may be better adapted to girls and women.[1,26]

Perhaps the matter of which sports girls should participate in and which demand the greatest energy expenditure cannot be resolved by any generalization. It is apparent that, at the highly skilled level, endurance and physical strain are as involved in the so-called womanly sports of skating and gymnastics as they are in any other. A person who intensively trains and competes in vigorous sports is in effect fit—she has a slower pulse rate, has deep respiration and lower respiration rate, has normal blood pressure, has strong heart stroke and large heart, recovers rapidly from exercise, and tolerates lack of oxygen for long periods.[1] Actually, few injuries occur in individuals who are fit. And for many persons, the relative strenuousness of various sports, or the fact that the body responds to intensive activity by becoming fit, is of secondary importance, if considered at all, to the fact that they want to participate in the sport of their choice.

REFERENCES

1. Albright, T. E. Which sports for girls? In *DGWS Research Reports: Women in Sports.* Dorothy V. Harris (Ed.). Washington, D.C.: American Association for Health, Physical Education and Recreation, 1971, pp. 53-57.
2. Berkey, R. Psychology of women who compete. *California Association for Health, Physical Education and Recreation Journal,* January/February 1972, pp. 6, 18.

3. Berkowitz, L. *Aggression: A Social-Psychological Analysis.* New York: McGraw-Hill Book Co., 1962.

4. Bernauer, E. Physical performance by the female: An apparent superiority. Proceedings of the 43rd Annual Conference of the Western Society for Physical Education of College Women, Asilomar, Calif., November 9-11, 1967, pp. 41-45.

5. Braun, S. The voice you love to hate. *TV Guide,* August 28, 1971, pp. 22-27.

6. Brown, C. H., et al. Girl power: The effects of cross-country running on preadolescent girls. Presented at the Annual Meeting of the American College of Sports Medicine, Atlanta, Ga., May 1, 1969.

7. Brown, H. New dimensions in physical activity and fitness for girls and women. *American Corrective Therapy Journal, 25*(3), 1971.

8. Buss, A. *The Psychology of Aggression.* New York: John Wiley & Sons, Inc., 1961.

9. Cooper, L. Athletics, activity and personality: A review of the literature. *Research Quarterly, 40,* 1969, pp. 17-20.

10. Cratty, B. J. Coaching decisions and research in sports psychology. *Quest, XII,* 1970, pp. 46-53.

11. deVries, H. A. *Physiology of Exercise.* Dubuque, Iowa: Wm. C. Brown, 1966.

12. The difficult art of losing. *Time Magazine,* November 15, 1968, pp. 47-48.

13. Drinkwater, B. L., and Horvath, S. M. Response of young female track athletes to exercise. *Medicine and Science in Sports, 3,* 1971, pp. 56-62.

14. Duentzer, E. Le sport et la femme. XI International Congress Sport Medicine, 1956, p. 378.

15. Eysenck, H. J. *The Biological Basis of Personality.* Springfield, Ill.: Charles C Thomas, 1967.

16. Eysenck, S. B. G., and Eysenck, H. J. A factor-analytic study of the lie scale of the junior Eysenck personality inventory. *Personality, 1,* 1970, pp. 3-10.

17. Eysenck, H. J., Easting, G., and Eysenck, S. B. G. Personality measurement in children: A dimensional approach. *Journal of Special Education, 4,* 1971, pp. 231-268.

18. Erdelyi, G. J. Women in athletics. *Proceedings of the Second National Conference on the Medical Aspects of Sports,* November 27, 1960. Chicago: American Medical Association, 1961.

19. Erdelyi, G. J. Gynecological survey of female athletes. *Journal of Sports Medicine and Physical Fitness, 2,* 1962, pp. 174-179.

20. Eyquem, M. T. Women and the Olympic games. 4th International Congress on Physical Education and Sports for Girls and Women, Washington, D.C., August 6-12, 1961.

21. Foreman, K. What research says about the female athlete. Report made at Pacific Northwest Sports Medicine Seminar, Seattle, Wash., March 19, 1972.

22. Garlick, M. A., and Bernauer, E. M. Exercise during the menstrual cycle: Variations in physiological baselines. *Research Quarterly, 39,* 1968, pp. 533-542.

23. Gendel, E. S. Fitness and fatigue in the female. *Journal of Health, Physical Education and Recreation,* October 1971, pp. 53-58.

24. Gendel, E. S. Physicians, females, physical exertion and sports. *Proceedings: Fourth National Institute of Girls' Sports.* Washington, D.C.: American Association for Health, Physical Education and Recreation, 1968.

25. Gray, J. A. The psychophysiological basis of introversion-extroversion. *Behavior Research and Therapy, 8,* 1970, pp. 249-266.

26. Huelster, L. J. The role of sports in the culture of girls. *Proceedings: Second National Institute on Girls' Sports.* Washington, D.C.: American Association for Health, Physical Education and Recreation, 1966.

27. Jordon, P., and Spencer, B. *Champions in the Making.* Englewood Cliffs, N.J.: Prentice-Hall, Inc., 1968.

28. Kane, J. E. Psychological correlates of physique and physical abilities. In *International Research in Sport and Physical Education.* E. Jokl and E. Simon (Eds.). Springfield, Ill.: Charles C Thomas, 1964, pp. 85-94.

29. Klaus, E. J. The athletic status of women. In *International Research in Sport and Physical Education.* E. Jokl and E. Simon (Eds.). Springfield, Ill.: Charles C Thomas, 1964.

30. Lawther, J. D. *Sport Psychology.* Englewood Cliffs, N.J.: Prentice-Hall, Inc., 1972.

31. Lorenz, K. *On Aggression.* Translated by Marjorie Kerr Wilson. New York: Harcourt, Brace & World, 1966.

32. Malumphy, T. M. Athletics and competition for girls and women. In *DGWS Research Reports: Women in Sports.* Dorothy V. Harris (Ed.). Washington, D.C.: American Association for Health, Physical Education and Recreation, 1971, pp. 15-19.

33. Malumphy, T. M. Personality of women athletes in intercollegiate competition. *Research Quarterly, 39,* 1968, pp. 610-620.

34. Malumphy, T. M. The college woman athlete—questions and tentative answers. *Quest, XIV,* 1970, pp. 18-27.

35. Martin, L. A. The effects of competition upon the aggressive patterns of wrestlers and basketball players. (Doctoral dissertation, Springfield College), Springfield, Mass., 1969.

36. McGill, F., and Luft, U. C. Physical performance in relation to fat free weight in women compared to men. *Physiological Aspects of Sports and Physical Fitness.* (A selection of papers presented at Scientific Meetings of the American College of Sports Medicine.) Chicago: The Athletic Institute, 1968, p. 82.

37. Miller, D. M., and Russell, K. R. E. *Sport: A Contemporary View.* Philadelphia: Lea & Febiger, 1971.

38. Morgan, W. P. Reprint of Chapter 15, Sport psychology. In *Psychomotor Domain: Movement Behaviors.* Robert N. Singer (Ed.). Philadelphia: Lea & Febiger, 1971.

39. Musier, C. L. Personality and selected women athletes. *International Journal of Sport Psychology, 3,* 1972, pp. 25-31.

40. Neal, P. Personality traits of United States women athletes who participated in the 1959 Pan-American games, as measured by the Edwards personal preference schedule. (Master's thesis, University of Utah), Salt Lake City, Utah, 1963.

41. Ogilvie, B., and Tutko, T. Sport: If you want to build character, try something else. *Psychology Today, 5,* 1971, pp. 61-63.

42. Ogilvie, B. What is an athlete? *Journal of Health, Physical Education and Recreation,* June 1967, p. 48.

43. Peale, N. V. *Faith Made Them Champions.* New York: Guideposts Associates, 1954.

44. Peterson, S., Trousdale, W. W., and Weber, J. C. Personality traits of women in team sports vs women in individual sports. *Research Quarterly, 38,* 1967, pp. 686-689.

45. Petrie, A. *Individuality in Pain and Suffering.* Chicago: University of Chicago Press, 1967.

46. Phillips, M. Effects of the menstrual cycle on pulse rate and blood pressure before and after exercise. *Research Quarterly, 39,* 1968, pp. 327-333.

47. Pitts, F. D., Jr., and McClure, J. N., Jr. Lactate metabolism in anxiety neurosis. *New England Journal of Medicine, 277,* 1967, pp. 1329-1336.

48. Rarick, G. L. Competitive sports for girls: Effects on growth, development and general health. In *DGWS Research Reports: Women in Sports.* Dorothy V. Harris (Ed.). Washington, D.C.: American Association for Health, Physical Education and Recreation, 1971, pp. 48-52.

49. Russell, F. What makes a champion? *California Association for Health, Physical Education and Recreation Journal, 8,* 1968, p. 26.

50. Russell, F. What makes a champion? *Sportlight, 4,* 1969, pp. 5-8.

51. Ryan, E. D., and Foster, R. Athletic participation and perceptual augmentation and reduction. *Journal of Personality and Social Psychology, 6,* 1967, pp. 472-476.

52. Ryan, E. D., and Kovacic, C. R. Pain tolerance and athletic participation. *Perceptual and Motor Skills, 22,* 1966, pp. 383-390.

53. Schafer, W. E. Some social sources and consequences of interscholastic athletics: The case of participation and delinquency. In *Aspects of Contemporary Sport Sociology.* Gerald S. Kenyon (Ed.). Proceedings of C.I.C. Symposium on the Sociology of Sport, University of Wisconsin, Madison, Wis., 1968, pp. 29-44.

54. Schollander, D., and Savage, D. Not the triumph but the struggle. *Reader's Digest,* June 1971, pp. 222-257.

55. Scott, M. Elaine Tanner's "secret" success story. *Sports and Fitness Instructor, 1,* 1972, p. 4.

56. Skubic, V., and Hodgkins, J. Relative strenuousness of selected sports as performed by women. *Research Quarterly, 38,* 1967, pp. 305-313.

57. Thomas, C. L. The female sports participant: Some physiological questions. In *DGWS Research Reports: Women in Sports.* Dorothy V. Harris (Ed.). Washington, D.C.: American Association for Health, Physical Education and Recreation, 1971, pp. 37-44.

58. Thomas, C. L. Effect of vigorous athletic activity on women. *American Academy of Orthopedic Surgeons Symposium on Sports Medicine.* St. Louis: C. V. Mosby Co., 1969.

59. Ulrich, C. Women aren't so fragile. *Science Digest,* December 1969, pp. 53-54.

60. Vanek, M., and Cratty, B. *Psychology of the Superior Athlete.* New York: Macmillan, 1970.

61. Walker, J. Pain parameters of athletes and non-athletes. (Doctoral dissertation, University of Texas), Austin, Texas, 1970.

62. Walker, J. Pain and athletics. In *DGWS Research Reports: Women in Sports*. Dorothy V. Harris (Ed.). Washington, D.C.: American Association for Health, Physical Education and Recreation, 1971.

63. Williams, J. M., Hoepner, B. J., Moody, D. L., and Ogilvie, B. C. Personality traits of champion level female fencers. *Research Quarterly, 41,* 1970, pp. 446-453.

64. Wilmore, J. H., and Brown, C. H. The effects of maximal resistance training on strength and body composition of women athletes. Presented at American College of Sports Medicine, Albuquerque, N.M., May 9, 1970.

65. Wyrick, W. How sex differences affect research in physical education. In *DGWS Research Reports: Women in Sports*. Dorothy V. Harris (Ed.). Washington, D.C.: American Association for Health, Physical Education and Recreation, 1971, pp. 21-30.

66. Yanada, H., and Hirata, H. Personality traits of students who dropped out of their athletic clubs. Proceedings of the College of Physical Education, University of Tokyo, Tokyo, Japan, 1970, p. 5.

3. Dimensions of the Coach

In hewing the wood for an axe-handle, how do you proceed? Without another axe, it cannot be done.

Confucianist Scriptures

Highly competitive interscholastic programs for girls and women, being somewhat in their infancy, have not placed heavy demands on experienced women coaches. It often has been assumed that there are few if any qualified women coaches and that men are not qualified to coach women. Both assumptions warrant further examination. It is even possible to detect C. P. Snow's "two cultures" battle pattern between physical educators and coaches, wherein each rejects the theories and importance of the other. In some instances, students have been harassed into competition for allegiance to one group or the other.

There is no doubt that the growth of competitive sports programs for women has expanded horizons for women coaches until presently there is a shortage of experienced women coaches and qualified women officials. And there is no doubt that women as well as men who coach girls and women need to be mobilized properly to address the problems and situations that now exist. They need to reassess the role of the coach in today's society and the responsibilities of coaching, whether practiced in collaboration with physical education, sport agencies outside the schools, or on the broad scale of Olympic development programs.

TEACHER AND COACH: TWO PART HARMONY

It has been traditionally accepted that not only are coaches men, but that coaches differ from teachers. In a way, both of these notions are true, but only in a way. The assumption that teaching and coaching differ has largely been based upon the distinction that physical education teachers are those who teach classes whereas coaches are those who handle the after-school varsity athletic programs. Accompanying these somewhat fragile distinctions

45

have been such commonly held beliefs that coaches should be paid more than are teachers and that their preparation should be largely in terms of their own performance skills, i.e., an all-American quarterback makes the best coach. The argument that few women physical educators are highly skilled enough as performers may have some validity. But here again it cannot be assumed that competitive experience is a measure of anything other than being eligible to compete in terms of grades, time, and similar circumstances.

Miss Sue Clark, a physical education teacher at Tucson High School, who became the girls' tennis coach somewhat by chance (she agreed to take over girls' tennis until a permanent coach could be found), put together a rather incredible record of coaching achievement. With no previous coaching experience and admittedly no great player herself, her varsity teams compiled a fantastic record of 213–0, which is believed to be a national scholastic record. Her junior varsity team had a win-loss record of 159–3, and the freshmen 90–4. Her teams won 14 straight divisional championships and failed only three times to win the state championship. What is the secret of her success? Surely not having experienced and skilled players or being highly skilled herself. Only 14 of the girls she coached had ever played tennis before. The secret to her success seemed to be devotion to the players and to the game, and to do that "you have to be a teacher first and a coach second . . . there's no other way."[2]

A look at the functions of teacher and coach reveals that there are certain common roles both must fulfill in order to produce winners. First, for real learning to take place, sound *principles of instruction* must form the basis of either effective teaching or effective coaching. Actually, "teacher" and "coach" are synonomous terms in the sense that they mean to instruct, to lead, to guide the actions of students. Both teaching and coaching are a process of giving some pattern, order, and meaning to learning.

Coaching may be viewed as that phase of instruction within a class period in which the players are engaged in the game and meaningful coaching clues to improve play are offered by the teacher. The distinction, therefore, that a class situation involves little coaching is inaccurate. Viewed in a similar perspective, but outside the classroom, coaching and teaching complement each other. Coaches at times become instructors in the after-school athletic program, because the performer is a learner at one time or another. Even the highly skilled performer must learn new skills in her own sport specialty; thus, facilitating the learning process is a function of coaches as well as of teachers.

Second, both teacher and coach must remain *constant students of their game,* willing to study, work, and think. In addition to teaching knowledges and skill, a teacher and coach must recognize the power of knowledge in general and be dedicated to the pursuit of knowledge throughout a lifetime. The need for and importance of a knowledge of psychologic, physiologic, kinesiology concepts and their application are just as basic to skill acquisition as to improving the performance of the highly skilled athlete.

A third common role is that both the teacher and the coach are *educators,* not only in the sense of possessing highly qualified technical skills, but also in the sense of being a professional. A profile of the professional teacher or coach includes the same broadly recognized criteria of participation in affairs of the profession; development of a distinctive competence; contribution to knowledge; assumption of responsibility for the preparation of younger members of the profession; commitment to the discovery and development of human potential, without concern for the remunerative rewards.

Finally, both teacher and coach are *concerned with various public*—students, parents, faculty, alumni, even the so-called "Monday morning quarterback."

In short, the differences between teacher and coach are somewhat fragile in that they both must live certain roles in order to touch the core of learning and both have similar designs as professionals. Perhaps the problem of nomenclature can be resolved by considering coaching as an extension of teaching and adopting the semantic use of the term "coaching" as a descriptive adjective —a teacher who coaches.

SOME FACILE DISTINCTIONS

Although the differences between coaching and teaching may not be the commonly held position that the teacher instructs the beginner and novice in the fundamentals whereas the coach uses the skills already developed in working with the highly skilled, it is true that the coach is usually involved with players who are already highly skilled, who are highly motivated, and who are voluntarily engaged in the sport of their choice. The coach must manage extensive organizational and procedural details, such as tournament planning, scheduling, publicity, eligibility, and the like. The coach is concerned with intensive training and competitive situations in which stress on both player and coach and emphasis on winning are part and parcel of the game. In coaching, some unique problems are faced—the language, the attitudes, the spectators, even the goals, and a host of uncontrolled variables—all of which may be difficult. Audiences may expect entertainment above educational outcomes, and therefore may consider booing, exploitation, and all other acknowledged evils of competitive athletics to be among their fundamental rights as supporters of the institution.

Although the differences between coaching and teaching are primarily differences in situational environment rather than differences in knowledges, technical skills, and professional commitment, these distinctions are such that the person needs to decide whether she wants to be a coach and whether she has the disposition and the talent demanded by the coaching situation.

THE CARE AND PREPARATION OF COACHES

A prevailing notion is that professional preparation programs for women do not emphasize preparation for coaching as contrasted to men's programs which are said to be geared to coaching. Can it be, however, that women will become better coaches if more coaching courses are added, "structured like those for men," as some persons assert? Responsible educators, pointing out the need to upgrade girls' athletic programs, raise further questions such as: "Should coaching of girls' sports remain exclusively in the hands of the profession instead of making use of teachers from other subject matter areas as the men do? Or perhaps making use of talented and available parents?"[9]

Without a doubt, a new conceptual model of the coaching profession seems urgently needed. One might even venture to say that if a clear picture of the basis of professionalism had been the first order of business in men's athletics, it would not be facing many of the problems it is now. Without a clear picture of coaching as a profession for women, there may be much nibbling away at bits and pieces to patch up the old model, or curricular decisions may be made simply to meet the exigencies at the time.

In response to the need for women coaches, there may be no pretense of producing professionals capable of overall design but merely a sporadic attempt to train technicians who may assist, say, in the development of Olympic athletes. Thus, some larger questions seem to be: Will the overall curriculum design for preparing coaches be compromised by the objective of preparing skilled technicians? Or, will interest and pride be expressed in educating both those who would be called teachers and those who would be called coaches? Furthermore, is it not reasonable to suggest, despite the fact that at present there may be a shortage of qualified women coaches, that mass production of coaches would be a great disservice to all concerned? When obviously the job market for teachers has been steadily diminishing, should less emphasis be placed on numbers alone?

In general, coaching as a profession should have as its goal the production of the professional person, a mixture of technician and scholar, who is recognized by peers and colleagues in the practice of the profession at large. Each coach recognized as a member of the profession should maintain currency, giving evidence of suitable education and periodic updating.

Various studies have been conducted concerning the professional preparation of male coaches. Maetozo, from a study of 200 coaches representative of 50 states, concluded that there are almost twice as many majors in physical education coaching as majors in any other subject; that only a few of those coaching who have majors in other subjects have a minor in physical education; that regardless of their major, coaches are assigned to teach a variety of subjects; and, that few written statements of qualifications for coaches are in use.[5] This conclusion, supported by various other studies, reveals that there is no consistent pattern of professional preparation for men coaches, although considerable unanimity exists concerning the kinds of experiences that should be included in the preparation of coaches. According to Perry, Maetozo tended to tie together the thinking and conclusions of most of the writers in the field when he stated:

> In general, most of those involved with athletics agree that professional preparation programs should provide for the development of the following competencies over and above those required for standard teacher certification.
>
> 1. An understanding of the relationship of the interscholastic athletic program and the particular sport they are coaching to the total educational program.
>
> 2. A knowledge of first aid and the safety practices and techniques pertinent to the sport they are coaching.
>
> 3. An understanding of the possibilities of legal liability as well as sound practices and preventative measures.
>
> 4. A thorough knowledge and understanding of the biological, social, moral, emotional, and spiritual values which may accrue from the activity and the best methods of bringing about these desirable outcomes.
>
> 5. A knowledge of the most accepted principles of growth and development and their implications for sports.
>
> 6. An understanding of the best methods of developing and conditioning members of athletic squads.
>
> 7. A knowledge of the basic principles in the care and prevention of injuries together with an understanding of the proper relationship of the coach to the school or team physician.
>
> 8. The ability to speak in public so as to bring credit to the profession and the school and so as to more effectively inform the public of the educational possibilities of the sport.

9. An understanding of the basic physiologic principles of motivation, stress, play, emotion, and group interaction.

10. A thorough knowledge of the fundamental offenses, defenses, strategies, and teaching methods involved in the particular sport. Included will be squad organizations, coaching techniques, and sound motivational procedures.

11. A knowledge of and a sense of responsibility for local, state, and national rules and regulations.[5]

Although women have not set forth specific statements for the preparation of women coaches, writings to date would appear to be in keeping with the statements outlined by Maetozo. Acknowledged *technical preparation skills and knowledges* demanded of coaching may be summarized as follows:

1. A thorough knowledge of the sport, including understanding of advanced skills and strategies, effective practice procedures, rules and their interpretation, officiating techniques and practices.

2. Knowledge of kinesiology, mechanics of movement, and exercise physiology in order to effectively evaluate competencies, to elicit skill improvement and proper physical conditioning, to impart such information to players as will make their practice sessions and training programs meaningful. The technical work of scholars, which has made possible numerous advances in the understanding and improvement of human motor performance, requires of the coach at least a basic acquaintance with the fields of kinesiology (or biomechanics) and exercise physiology. Anatomy should also be a requisite, in order to understand the lever system of bones and muscles. A kinesiology course will help in the understanding of pertinent anatomic data such as centers of gravity and basic laws of momentum, friction, ball restitution, and the like, and will aid in understanding the language of the kinesiologist and interpreting the data of relevant research studies.

3. Knowledge of psychology and sociology in order to understand oneself as well as other people—individual differences; personality structure and motivation; the nature of group behavior and interaction, including interpersonal relations between players, between coach and player, and between coach and various public, such as fellow teachers, administrators, the press, and other community groups.

4. Knowledge of organization and administration of competitive sports that will enable the coach to be thoroughly conversant with various governing organizations and be

able to plan and stage successful events, including procedural matters such as budgets, schedules, travel, and the like.

It also has been suggested that not only does the importance of athletic training warrant its inclusion in all physical education programs, but also there is a great need for *women athletic trainers*. Trainers of women's competitive teams are men for the most part, and they are often placed in difficult situations when attempting to handle adequately the physical, psychologic, and emotional problems of female athletes.[3] Some women express a desire also to inaugurate the *coaching minor* program for nonphysical education majors, such as men have done as a result of the evidence concerning the need for at least a minimum of professional preparation in physical education.

At least one state has established some standards for certifying those who coach girls' interscholastic programs.[4] In 1971 the Minnesota State Board of Education approved a certification for any man or woman who coaches a girls' interscholastic team. In order to attain approval, programs leading to a certificate as a Public School Coach, Girls' Interscholastic Sports must provide for:

1. Eighteen quarter hours (or the equivalent) of experiences designed to develop competencies in all the following areas:
   The Foundation of Girls and Women's Sports
   Theory and Techniques of Coaching
   Organization and Management of Girls' Interscholastic Sports
   Growth and Development and Psychology of Adolescent Behavior
   Medical Aspects of Coaching Girls' Sports (Prevention and Care of Girls' Athletic Injuries)
   Scientific Basis of Conditioning and Skills Performance
   Sports Officiating
2. A Practicum, Inservice Coaching for Women
3. Means for Assessment of the Competencies to be Developed.

The Practicum was designed to provide the prospective coach with practical experience with girls for one full season in a sport sponsored by the Minnesota State High School League. Because there is no grandfather clause, physical education teachers who do not wish to be coaches are not forced to enter that sphere, but persons who do enter the field must meet the requirements originally and continue to meet them every five years when certificates are renewed.

It must be remembered, however, that much of the impetus and direction in the professional preparation for the coaching minor program for men was largely due to the fact that too many coaches had little if any physical education preparation. It has been contended, therefore, that the coaching minor is "at least one vehicle to help bridge the gap between theory and practice in professional preparation."[5]

Until such time as women are fully prepared to assume roles as coaches and as teachers of coaches, or when women are not available to train coaches, it has been suggested that women seek help from qualified men coaches. Some ways in which men could assist women in specific coaching situations are that the woman could be a "trainee" either by observing the training of a men's team or by a cooperative venture in which the male coach works with her as a trainee in coaching the women's team, or that women might enroll in coaching courses taught by men.[7]

The most appropriate coaching preparation for women, however, appears to be the existing programs of professional physical education curricula. Existing courses (e.g., kinesiology, exercise physiology, motor learning) can be adapted or amplified to include the specialized needs of coaches and athletic trainers. Offering high level skill courses and proficiency testing programs provides an avenue for physical education majors to develop into more highly skilled performers. It is also important to seek opportunities to improve communication skills and to seek situations in which to obtain coaching experience—test your wings—in order to discover one's suitability for a coaching career.

As suggested previously, *other personal and professional qualities* demand some homework and perhaps soul-searching by those who aspire to a coaching career in athletics for girls and women.

Coaching, insofar as boys and men's athletics are concerned, seems to have worked itself into an almost untenable situation in its quasi-professional image. The reasons are not difficult to uncover: disenchantment with the athletic establishment and considerable suspicion about *values* being taught and learned. Students no longer have a naive belief that competitive sports represent an absolute good. They are asking questions. They are greatly concerned about the direction in which interscholastic athletics are heading. They have, to borrow a term used by Reich in *The Greening of America,* developed a new "head."

Although responsible coaching may not mean providing a code of ready-made orthodox beliefs, participants in sports are concerned with matters other than purely technical skill performance. Coaches must respond to this fact to be effective. Practical guides to the ethics, principles, and organization of a coaching career are available.[6] Several questions related to a philosophy of athletic programs are presented in Chapter 1. Similar questions, which were obtained from various college and university women teachers (Western Society for Physical Education of College Women) involved in the coaching of the highly skilled college women, warrant further analysis.

1. How does the coach go about developing a philosophy of coaching?

2. Upon what criteria should the coach develop her value system?

3. Is a question of ethics involved when a coach tries to adjust her players to her standards by psychologic motivations, and physiologic stimulants in order to ensure their best playing performance?

4. How can a coach best teach moral values in a highly competitive contest?

5. In higher education what is the coach's commitment to discover and develop human potential in sports?

   a. Upon what criteria or standards should a coach assign highly competitive activities?

   b. What are the criteria for evaluating the level of skill performance that need to be developed in many of the sport areas to ensure a good competitive experience in extramurals?

   c. Does a coach have the right to impose rigid standards regarding these competitive experiences (for example, grades and participation during off season)?

   d. Is there a need for a top level control group to enforce standards?

   e. Are extramurals valuable enough to have an adequate subsidy?

   f. Are the values of extramurals inherent within the activity and/or should the values extend into the lives and vocations of students?

   g. Should the program in higher education be based upon the needs and interests of students or should it be provided regardless of their needs and interests?

   h. Should higher education reflect the culture of which it is a part, and how does this affect a woman's role in sports and the development of her potentialities as a human being?

6. Is there a difference between sportsmanship and ethics?

In addition to these questions of values posed by today's competitive sports programs, the matter of the coaching personality and all the complex concerns surrounding the relationships between athlete and coach are of importance in personally sizing up those who coach girls and women.

A key to successful coaching is the coach's own desire and need to achieve. At the same time, there seems to be great concern about the *coaching behaviors* that contribute to real achievement. Numerous writings, which bear directly or indirectly on this matter, emphasize the special problem of authority involved in the coaching situation and the importance of effective communication between coach and athlete. Relationships between coach and athlete are discussed more fully in the chapter dealing with motivation. Attention is drawn to the matter here in order to highlight coaching behavior as a professional concern.

The view of James Counsilman, noted swimming coach, is that psychology takes precedence over physiology in coaching know-how. If a person is just good at stroke mechanics and physiology but has no ability to use psychology, he cannot coach. The best type of coaching psychologists, Counsilman contends, are actual coaches, and because the key to coaching success is the "psychology of confidence" many coaches have the ability to inspire confidence just through their reputation.[1]

According to the studies of Ogilvie and Tutko, perhaps the most vital character trait of a coach, on a long-term basis, is his "psychological endurance," his willingness to apply himself and stay with the task to completion. They also found that this trait is related to the coach's high threshold for stress. The good coach, at least at the top level, is able to operate on a low level of anxiety.[7]

Thomas Tutko, Director of the Institute for the Study of Athletic Motivation at San Jose State University, called the coaching personality the ultimate limitation. Asking the question of how the coach can spend so much time in something that may have minimal rewards, Tutko explored the motivational, interpersonal, and communication aspects of the coach's repertoire. He presented several styles or models of coaching personalities, although some researchers take issue with such pure categorization of coaching behavior. Tutko described the pure authoritarian coach who is without empathy or sympathy or understanding as one who leaves only cruelty, lack of cohesion, and resentment, and when he is not present the athletes do not produce. Other styles of coaching include the easygoing coach (the team may have difficulty facing stress), the intense, temperamental type (great for motivating except for the youth who is nervous), the business type (here are the facts), the democratic type (the athletes are part of the decision-making process). Regardless of whether or not coaches can be strictly categorized in terms of these models, there is little doubt that the coach has to look at what his functions really are, and what his reactions are: to motivate, to communicate, to be a father-figure, to depress people, to push people.[7]

With some care, those engaged in competitive sports programs for girls and women can be well prepared to meet the challenges and commitment of coaching. Like the human organism, on the one hand they must be specialized enough to occupy an important niche that no other can contest, and on the other they must be versatile enough to adapt to various conditions. They will know that their preparation is right when it tends to preserve the integrity, stability, and beauty of sport and the people in it, and wrong when it tends to do otherwise.

REFERENCES

1. Counsilman, J. Psychology and coaching. *Swimming World,* April 1972, pp. 11, 48.

2. Foust, T. The Sue Clark story. *The Arizona Daily Star,* April 23, 1972, pp. 1-B, 7-B.

3. Hutton, L. I., and Silken, J. Needed: Women athletic trainers. *Journal of American Association for Health, Physical Education and Recreation,* January 1972, pp. 77-78.

4. McIntyre, D. A coaching certificate for girls' interscholastic sports. *The Foil,* Fall 1972, pp. 13-15.

5. Perry, R. H. Coaching minor: Research and implementation. A talk presented at a joint convention of the Southwest District of the American Association for Health, Physical Education and Recreation and the California Association for Health, Physical Education and Recreation, Sacramento, Calif., March 1969.

6. Sabock, R. J. *The Coach.* Philadelphia: W. B. Saunders Co., 1973.

7. Spasoff, T. C. Needed: More women coaches. *Journal of Health, Physical Education and Recreation,* June 1971, p. 55.

8. Tutko, T. The coaching personality—The ultimate limitation. *Proceedings of the First International Symposium on the Art and Science of Coaching,* October 1-5, 1971. Willowdale, Ontario, Canada: F. I. Productions, 1971.

9. The writing is on the wall. *Update.* Washington, D.C.: American Association for Health, Physical Education and Recreation, December 1972, pp. 6-7.

4. Facilitating Skill Acquisition

"Can you teach me to fly like that?"
Jonathan Seagull tumbled to
  conquer another unknown.
"Of course, if you wish to learn."

Richard Bach
(Jonathan Livingston Seagull)

"Life," a cynical philosopher once shrewdly observed, "is a supremely illogical business. One can become dark from excess of light." This statement is so directly applicable to the study of learning theory that it ought to preface any such study. There are innumerable theories of learning, but what combinations of characteristics make teachers teach better are still much in the dark. For that matter, as Ernest Hilgard pointed out, the typical theory of learning may have little relation to what goes on inside a human being when he learns.

Despite the fact that there is considerable turmoil within learning theory, and despite the fact that knowledge of learning theory may provide an incomplete basis for dealing with problems of teaching, teachers and coaches, whether aware of it or not, do have theories about how learning takes place. Therefore, they should understand some of the assumptions upon which their own methods of teaching are founded. Each theory of learning is connected to *philosophic* assumptions concerning the moral and psychologic nature of man, e.g., is he good or evil or neutral, active or passive or reactive. Bigge provided a good discussion of these distinctions among 10 representative theories.[2] Furthermore, each theory of learning represents a *psychologic* system and its unique approach to learning or emphasis upon different sources of learning, i.e., connectionism, behaviorism, reinforcement, feedback, insight, cognition, or a combination of factors. Different theories provide diverse approaches to readiness, perception, motivation, transfer of learning, retention, role of practice, and so forth.

Even though some terms prominent in early learning theory may be passé, the old knowledge has not necessarily disappeared. Although no longer indexed under the same terminology, the ideas crop up in new forms. For example, perhaps beneath such contemporary terms as "display," "feedback," and "structure" are hidden the basic notion and once-fruitful ideas associated with the earlier Gestalt term "insight."[10] Whether or not a system or theory of learning remains identifiable or is transformed, some fertile notions have been developed from each.

It is not my purpose here to describe complex learning theories or to analyze the research underlying the development of theories more directly related to motor learning and skill acquisition. Numerous books present extensive analyses of various learning theories and their implications for teaching.[8,10,11,16] Reasonably sound guidelines for the teaching and improvement of skill performance have been formulated by authors of several excellent texts in motor learning and skill acquisition.[4–7,12,14,15,19,22–26,29]

A vast, sophisticated literature deals with the study of skill learning, although the special jargon and obscurity in some readings make difficult problems more difficult, or, worse, may confuse comparatively simple problems. Researchers themselves contend that the approach to the study of skills has resulted in "disconnected pockets of data."[1] Gentile observed that most motor learning textbooks have a "supermarket quality" in which topics such as massed/distributed practice, feedback, mental rehearsal, and so forth are "piled about in disarray."[9] Some persons may even acknowledge that theoretical structures and research designs cannot be reduced to simple explanations and often make necessary the use of special words, however obscure, because of the limitations of the language. Yet, at the same time these persons may argue that such investigations have little if any practical value to the teacher or coach.

Obviously the research literature on skill learning and performance needs to be integrated into some kind of unifying package that would serve as a practical guide for the teacher of skills. The problem is how to package such material without substituting new jargon for old and without presenting another disjunctive collection of overelaborated theories. Despite the hazards involved, my intent is to present some guidelines gleaned from experience and some theoretical viewpoints within which the teacher/coach may wish to operate. Many of these guidelines may be obvious to the seasoned coach. Many things a coach does simply make sense and probably need no supporting research evidence to be proved valuable. On the other hand, some persons operate on passé principles and old wives' tales because they have not bothered to keep abreast of the latest findings. The following material may offer one source of guidelines for the teacher/coach to which each may add the more complex understandings included in the research literature and his or her own empiric sources.

SHAPING SKILLS

The process of skill learning may be likened to the process of biologic development, that is, skill progresses from the general to the specific, from gross to refined movements by a process of individuation of parts within wholes. Actually, the critical concern for the teacher frequently revolves around the classic part-whole problem with a somewhat different emphasis than that given to the problem in the past. In a sense, the contemporary approach to skill learning is analogous to computer programming. Skill is described as a plan* consisting of a sequence of movements that become relatively fixed through overlearning and that must be fused together to make skilled performance. For example, the execution of a tennis serve is the result of hierarchically organized patterns (body position and action, arm position and action, ball toss, and so forth), each of which depends upon the others for successful completion. The various components are executed in a sequence of so-called behavioral units or subroutines.

The theoretical computer model also is used to describe the learner, in which the learner is viewed as a complex analyzer, an information processing system that accepts, rejects, compares, combines, and applies information received in the process of skill acquisition and performance. "Feedback" also is a term borrowed from the language of electronic computer programming and although different approaches and unique terms, such as "closed-loop operations," "input-output," and the like, are employed to describe what feedback is, in one form or another feedback provides the stimulus that elicits or shapes a desired skill pattern.

There are many and different sources of feedback, both intrinsic and extrinsic, but, as Clifton pointed out, whether provided from an external source, such as the teacher giving information, or an augmented source, such as an arrow hitting the gold, or intrinsic information from the movement itself, feedback provides knowl-

---

* Most theoretical discussions revolve around Miller, Galanter, and Pribam's[17a] TOTE concept, in which they propose that "a Plan is any hierarchical process in the organism that can control the order in which a sequence of operations is to be performed." More recently, Fitts and Posner[6a] described skill acquisition in hierarchial phases, progressing from the early or cognitive phase, in which the requirements of the task are intellectualized, through the intermediate phase, in which individual units become associated in patterns of response, to the final autonomous phase, in which component processes are unified.

edge, motivation, and reinforcement.[3] The successful use of some modes of feedback that are available at a conscious level depends upon the individual being attuned to feedback information and conceiving of it as being a new input to be reorganized. (Some sources of feedback are available at a subcortical level and do not have to be consciously attended to, e.g., postural adjustments in maintaining balance.)

The beginner or unskilled performer may not be able to utilize the same information as the skilled performer. In computer language she may be described as having limited use of her channel capacity whereas the skilled performer is able to select from the information she receives. The tennis player who is able to put together a number of good shots in a rally gets advance information from the opponent's position, teammates, court position, ball placement, and so forth. As she *monitors* these various environmental situations, each successive vital cue is registered, from the welter of cues available, and this information is used to *program* the next movement and to modify play as needed for the next action. In other words, skilled performers, although they may not have better techniques than do the less skilled, possess a greater ability to program their movements so that they are able to *put together a string of successive and successful movements* without being overhurried. Thus, skilled performance is characterized by words such as "smooth," "coordinated," "good timing," "consistent," "controlled," "efficient," "effortless," and similar synonyms.

Although the term "skill acquisition" is used primarily in reference to the beginner, even the skilled performer is a learner in the sense that she must learn new skills or may need to restructure old skills in order to improve performance eventually. The dovetailing or smooth articulation of the entire sequencing of subroutines of the total skill becomes largely a matter of what kind of feedback the learner uses, regardless of skill level, and the teacher provides in order to modify responses so that the required action occurs.

CAPITALIZING ON
PRIOR EXPERIENCE

One source of feedback to the learner is prior experience. The experienced and more skillful player is better able to select appropriate responses more easily than is the uninitiated, because she has a greater repertoire of skills and experience to draw upon. Actually, most new skills are put together from existing skills (memory storage, motor drum, engrams, neural images, perceptual traces), just as discoveries are made through what already is known by a recombination of old elements. Psychologists remind us that the words "invent" and "inventory" share a common derivation. Thus, the tennis player may be said to transfer some tennis skills to badminton because both games are derived from a similar inventory of skills. Many sport techniques, including the tennis serve, the volleyball serve, the badminton smash, and so forth, may be considered as being drawn from the skill information pool called the "overhand throwing pattern." Obviously, then, many questions of learning are intimately interwoven with problems of *transfer*. The question is not whether transfer occurs, but what conditions maximize the possibilities for positive transfer effects to occur.

One of these conditions favoring positive transfer is concerned with the similarities and differences between sport activities. If the *new* activity to be learned (e.g., badminton) involves motor responses and situations similar to another activity (e.g., tennis), the rate of learning and positive transfer effects are increased. However, because a well-learned skill is more easily applied to a new situation or a new activity, it is best to learn one activity well (*overlearning*) before starting a similar one. If both activities are new and similar, such as tennis and badminton, they should not be learned at the same time or in succession. Two different activities having little in common (e.g., skating and volleyball) may be learned together or in succession.

ANALYZING SKILLS

No single method of presenting skills is best for all learners. Some learn best by watching a demonstration, some by hearing a verbal description, others by thinking through the skill and giving themselves various directions. In the initial stage of skill acquisition it appears to be sufficient to demonstrate the skill, giving a general idea, gross pattern, or rough outline in order to help the learner acquire an approximation of the skill and strategy of performance required. The lay-up shot in basketball may be introduced by (1) demonstrating the *whole orientation* of the lay-up skill and the strategy of its performance—its execution from a give-and-go or a dribble toward the basket, its relationship to the cut-in process of taking out a guard or of moving into open and unguarded spaces, its follow-up with a rebound opportunity or a pass back to another cutting player, and so forth; (2) demonstrating the skill *similarity or relationship* (thus transfer possibilities) between the lay-up shot and, for example, the jump used for tossed balls or rebounding.

When the learner has been introduced to the general idea of the whole orientation required, the skill may be *developed in stages*. These stages may be described as the first stage of flexible fooling around or experimenting with the new skill, the second stage of precision involving a great many rehearsals, and the third stage of generalizing or adapting the skill to varying conditions—implements, playing surfaces, weather, opponents, related skills.

In *analyzing* the specific skill of the lay-up, the teacher selects a few essential principles from broad categories of the skill, such as initial position, direction of movement, and final position. The learner can easily remember the few principles when she is experimenting on her own. Learners instruct themselves in subtle ways and the teacher should not interfere with self-instruction by intricate explanations or by overstructuring the situation with fancy drills. The advanced performer, on the other hand, may profit from a more detailed skill analysis and often uses such explanations as cues or reminders of points to be emphasized.

In *arranging drills* in which the lay-up shot and its evasive action are practiced, a progression may be used in which the players become acquainted with the skill first, then try it against (1) a stationary opponent, (2) a reaching opponent, and finally (3) a challenging opponent who actually tries to break up play. Thus, the basketball offensive player learning the new skill would be introduced to the skill in a hierarchical order of difficulty—first in a mimetic or imitative situation, then against a stationary opponent, and then with an actively challenging opponent.

The general guideline that the early stage of skill acquisition should not be cluttered by overteaching does not imply that the teacher need not know every detail of the skill. The effective teacher attempts to shortcut the learning process and to correct performance errors without having the learner engage in blind trial-and-error experiences in the process of selecting appropriate movements and discarding inappropriate responses. If ineffective habits are allowed to be formed or to persist, they become more difficult to correct.

In *analyzing and correcting performance errors*, the teacher should attempt to determine the root of the difficulty rather than to correct each and every symptom. Beginners may have more than one performance error at a time or may change errors, or several faults may be combined. When a problem in performance appears rather consistently the teacher should be able to recognize important deviations from the desired performance and determine the root of the difficulty. She should observe the performer several times, analyzing the components that make up the skill, checking one action or body part at a time, checking the relationship of one movement to another, checking the mechanical aspects involved in the movement. When the major problem has been identified, the learner should be made consciously aware of it, which may be done by demonstrating the error and having the learner experience the difference between the ineffective and the effective movement. It is desirable to explain to the learner the necessity for changing performance, particularly if she is experiencing temporary success with what she is doing. Sometimes new situations or experiences will be needed in order to correct the performance error. Even in error correction, the accent should be on positive guidelines rather than on fault-finding.

MAKING PART—WHOLE CONNECTIONS

In order for the learner to proceed, largely under her own control, from what she can do to what she should do, it is important that she tackle tasks that make sense to her, that permit her to do what comes naturally. The teacher helps make sense out of what is being learned by showing relationships, pointing out situations where established or familiar skills may be used, indicating elements common to two tasks, organizing and arranging the elements of a situation into some meaningful wholes.

In general, practice on wholes or the largest manageable whole is better than practice on a part if the task is familiar, possesses a unity that involves continuity and timing, and is not too complex. If the whole task overwhelms the learner, a progressive-part-whole method, in which parts are chained together, is the preferred practice procedure. The importance of analyzing a whole task into its constituents is still vital. Even a so-called simple task consists of several sub-learnings. Simplifying the whole task by integrating component skills and by teaching the largest manageable unit or natural subdivision, rather than fractionalizing each of its parts, helps the learner grasp wholes that make sense and gives the greatest transfer possibility.

Perhaps an effective way of describing the largest manageable whole is to consider sport activities as being either closely knit or loosely organized. (In his early writings on motor learning at the University of Wisconsin, Clarence R. Ragsdale used the terms "closely knit units" and "loosely organized aggregates of units.") Thus, a whole may be a closely knit unit such as diving or the gymnastic event of vaulting. Sports such as tennis and basketball may be considered as loosely organized aggregations of units—tennis consisting of drive, serve, volley, and so forth, and basketball consisting of passing, catching, shooting, and so forth. Each of these simple wholes or natural subdivisions (sub-wholes) is developed into the more complex unit or whole game.

If skills are practiced in the drill situation in the same way they will be used in the game, players are more likely to recognize the situations in which certain skills should be used. Combination skill drills or game modifications can be used to practice meaningfully related skills and blend parts of the game as units of the whole. Team game skills performed in a team context, rather than as isolated skills, favor transfer of these skills to the game and enhance meaningfulness for the performer. For example, in basketball such skills as the pivot (as a maneuver to evade the opponent or to move into open spaces toward the basket), followed by a bounce or dribble (as part of a cut-in maneuver), followed by a lay-up shot, followed by a pass back to a teammate could be blended together in a practice drill. The part as one manageable unit then is related to the whole game in contrast to learning each of the skills isolated from its use in the whole game.

This type of consideration of actual play situations should be given to all practice situations. Soccer forwards practicing line play against a backfield should have a backing-up halfback line to work with them; goal shooting should be practiced against opposition; hockey forwards practicing a triangular pass should have an opponent to evade, and so on.

Principles of transfer and meaningfulness are ignored in such practices as using a shuttle-type formation drill in basketball, in which one player dribbles out, pivots in a full-circle turn, and passes back to the next player in her line. The player may learn how to do the drill, but it is not gamelike and the drill violates the use for which the pivot was intended.

ARRANGING SKILL PROGRESSIONS

Tasks should be arranged by their apparent difficulty, progressing from simple to complex. There is, however, some controversy about what constitutes a logical sequence or particular order of parts. Some research indicates that the order in which the skills of volleyball (set, spike, dig, serve) are learned has little bearing on learning and retention.[24] Some research shows greater transfer occurs from complex to relatively easy tasks, the difficult task being equivalent to direct practice on the easy one and including all its features.[19]

Perhaps the best guide to practice progressions related to skill difficulty is to be found in the situations in which skills are used. Some sport activities involve repetitive skills performed under fairly routine, continuous, and consistent conditions; whereas other sports are performed in more unstable or less predictable situations, such as those that require moving through space and responding to a moving object and other moving players. Such sport activities as diving, archery, golf, bowling, track and field events, and trampolining may be classified as repetitive, "habitual,"[12] or "closed."[21] Such sports as basketball, volleyball, tennis, and badminton may be classified as predominantly "perceptual"[12] or "open."[21] Although two theories perhaps are necessary to describe best the type of learning going on in either of these two categories, the complex skills involving continuity and timing in a habitual situation (e.g., gymnastics) should be practiced first and directly rather than through lead-up activities, whereas for those activities characterized by a changing environment (e.g., basketball) perhaps the practice should progress from the simpler to the more complex situation.[24]

Obviously, in practicing parts or wholes, simple or complex skills, the practice drill ought to make sense to the learner. She can understand what she is doing, be introspective about it, be encouraged to think of ways to accomplish desired objectives. She also can understand how to attack any particular kind of a problem restricting performance, not merely correct a difficulty. Explaining the *why* of an action, in contrast to merely describing the *how* or expecting more imitative performance, leads to more complete understanding by the learner and invokes the possibility of that sudden "Eureka, I have it" discovery which shortcuts endless repetitive practice. Probing questions that help the learner evaluate the success or lack of success in her performance offer more useful feedback than mere conversational or neutral remarks such as "Okay."

PATTERNING THE VISUAL-PERCEPTUAL FIELD

Many sports require something different from routine or habitual response. The term "open" skills has been used to designate skills that require a diversity of responses depending upon the cues and conditions in the environment, in contrast to "closed" skills that call for a rather consistent pattern of responses. Open skills, such as those that occur in the team sports and some individual sports (e.g., tennis and badminton), involve what may be described as timing, ball sense, visual perception, transit reaction, anticipation, ability to intercept objects, and so forth.

I described visual-perceptual ability as the ability to perceive, to analyze, to interpret, and to react instantaneously to visual cues in space.[17] When making a cut-in, the basketball play-maker must decide the time to do it and whether to pass-off to another cutting player or to go for the basket. Therefore, she must be able to visualize spatial relationships, to orient herself in space, to reject given plays in favor of others, to make quick and adaptive decisions based upon a changing rather than a relatively stable environment.

The skills in the open sports may be practiced in isolation because they may be regarded as too complex to practice in the game situation. The stimulus cannot be controlled in the game situation; the volleyball player cannot be expected to learn how to receive a serve in a game situation in which each serve she receives is a different type (low, high, fast, slow, and so forth). In such a situation the learner is expected to learn the skill by practicing it only one time. Such single trial learning is not only frustrating but is usually unsuccessful. It is still necessary for the players to experience the changing perceptual cues that may occur in the actual game situation. After the learner has established the basic response pattern through repetitive practice, the drill can proceed to one that involves the player moving through space and responding adaptively to the moving ball and to other moving players. The idea of a single set play or move *should not* be instilled. With word cues such as "now," sound clues such as a hand clap, or tactile clues such as might be provided by moving with the player, the teacher can involve the learner's senses in a way that helps her integrate what she sees, hears, and feels.

Focusing attention on a small area or part of the play (e.g., the classic cue of "keep your eye on the ball") also may not be desirable. If attention is distributed over a wider area, the performer may become more aware of various sources of information as she makes a decision about what to do. Although the beginner is not able to utilize the same information or process as much data as can the skilled performer, the teacher may filter specific information in order to help the learner become better oriented. Visual attention can be focused first on the source of the object (ball, players), then on the flight or movement of the object (speed and direction). When catching a fly ball, the center fielder should focus on the ball leaving the bat, monitor its flight in such a way that she can position herself to intercept it (remembering that the ball's arcs of rise and fall are the same), and stand so the ball drops in front of her, near her chest. This visual procedure is much more successful in getting the desired response than is simply running somewhere as soon as the ball is hit.

In those sports in which the perceptual need is great, concepts may be organized into simple whole image forms or models. By painting a picture of a skill and its relationships, the nonvisible can become visible. In tennis the concept of the "angle of widest possible returns" represents the wholeness or completeness of strategy, and establishes the relationships of the strokes of forcing drive or serve to those of a volley or overhead smash. The teacher may help the learner see these relationships by painting an image that shows continuous flow: "Visualize yourself making a forcing drive to your opponent's backhand, and then moving from a defensive position near the baseline through no-man's-land (backcourt) to an offensive position at the net near the center of the angle of widest possible returns." Thus, each stroke can be related as a whole figure to its environment or field rather than detached as a separate entity. Similarly, by painting a picture of the situation, the relatedness of things can be visualized in the mind's eye regarding such problems as which club to choose for a particular golf shot: "Your ball is 50 yards from the green, lying in the rough under a low hanging branch. What club should you choose and why?" Portraying (or "portraiting") the use of a skill and its related strategies should be the first part of any skill analysis. Even history and equipment can be made to come alive with simple yet related psychologic sequencing and refining of the powers of observation.

SPACING PRACTICE AND REST

Motivation to learn or the intent to learn and to use, maturity, intelligence, the ability to use insight or to see into situations are among the characteristics of the learner that enhance early skill acquisition and retention. At the same time, the fact that learning does occur within intent indicates a clear limitation of the role played by motivation in the learning process. With few exceptions, laboratory studies show that the longer one works at learning, the more he learns. In short, there appears to be no substitute for repetitive intensive practice over a prolonged period in the overlearning of skills that have to be automatized. Certainly champion performers, whose practice extends over many years, provide striking evidence that sustained and purposeful practice is essential to acquire skill and improve performance levels.

Practice, however, does not automatically improve performance. The old adage "practice makes perfect," therefore, is not necessarily true. Even the highly skilled performer, who subjects herself to long and grueling efforts in order to achieve higher levels of performance, experiences slumps in interest and effort. Obviously, determination of the optimal length of practice sessions involves numerous variables, including whether or not the practice is meaningful as suggested in the previous section. Some further guidelines may be formulated for helping the learner gain or regain a receptive attitude and a favorable disposition for initial skill learning and for continued skill practice.

First the teacher should determine how to space practice schedules for the individual learner. Although there are numerous interpretations of massed practice and distributed practice, in general, schedules of practice that approach continuous or relatively constant responses are called "massed"; practice sessions that are shorter and more frequent are referred to as "spaced" or "distributed."[8]

Various theories and hypotheses have been proposed to explain why short, frequent practice periods are favored over long periods of practice crowded into a brief span of time. Among these reasons are that mental rehearsal may occur during the rest interval or that memory processes continue and consolidate material after cessation of practice; fatigue may be a deterring factor of prolonged practice periods; rest allows errors to be forgotten and correct responses to be reinforced.

Current research indicates that the length of practice schedules has greater influence on performance than on learning, and that the learning of motor skills is relatively independent of the spacing of practice sessions, all other things being equal. Contradictory evidence regarding the superiority of one type of practice schedule over another does not warrant unequivocal acceptance of any particular theory.[20] Continued investigation may one day resolve the problems associated with arranging the work load of practice schedules. Meanwhile, some guidelines may be gleaned from the following generalized summary:

1. Spaced practice periods may be favored when:
   a. the learner is a beginner, inefficient, more easily fatigued because of making many inappropriate movements;
   b. the learner is not highly motivated or prone to loss of interest or to inattention;
   c. the learner is not intelligent;
   d. the learner is immature (age);

    e. the activity is complex or the frequency of error is likely to be high (reminiscence is more apt to occur and complex skills are retained at a high level over relatively long periods of nonpractice; learner may forget errors in rest period) ;

    f. the activity is not meaningful or is physically demanding;

    g. the foundation has been laid.

2. Massed practice may be more favorable when:

    a. the learner is advanced, or the material has been learned to a high degree of proficiency;

    b. the learner is intelligent;

    c. the learner is mature (age) ;

    d. the learner is highly motivated;

    e. the activity is meaningful (satisfying), insightful learning is possible, or the activity is not highly complex;

    f. a foundation is being laid, or in the first few sessions of an activity;

    g. the standard of mastery is high, peak performance is required, or immediate performance is necessary.

Sensitivity for the learner may be most needed during the learning of difficult skills. Although learners who demonstrate initial difficulty with a task may profit from extended practice periods, some rest is better than none. Generally a longer practice period should be followed by a longer rest period. Breathers that create teaching and learning fun should be provided, such as using many and varied experiences and activities to wake up and calm down. A stimulating atmosphere of learning induces renewed interest.

ESTABLISHING EFFECTIVE SPEED/ACCURACY PATTERNS

A ballistic movement is one performed with great rapidity or one that takes place over a short period of time, although ballistic skills are also capable of speed variations. Such activities as throwing, kicking, rapid walking and running, golf, badminton, and tennis are characteristically ballistic in nature, although there is some evidence that the tennis forehand is nonballistic.[12] Skills that are primarily ballistic should be practiced in a ballistic manner, because the movement and neuromuscular impulses are radically different at different speeds.[30]

In general, when learning new skills, speed should be emphasized at the expense of accuracy so that the learner will not establish the bad habit of tensing the muscles. The meaning of speed in this context is not intended to imply full or haphazard speed. Nor is it the intention to suggest that the manner of the teacher's approach to initial skill development is other than as careful and slow as the situation warrants. More specific directives to practice are as follows:

1. In skills in which *speed* is the predominant factor (e.g., javelin and discus throwing, sprint start), early emphasis should be placed on speed.
2. In those sport skills in which *speed* and *accuracy* are important (e.g., tennis, badminton, golf, bowling, batting, throwing, kicking), both should be stressed; however, an initial emphasis on speed transfers readily, whereas accuracy gained at low speed is quickly lost when speed is increased. Although early adjustments in speed set may be used for motivating the less skillful performers or beginners (they may be taught the movement pattern at slightly slower speeds initially), a speed should be used that produces a ballistic-type movement from the first (e.g., both serves in tennis should be ballistic).
3. In activities in which accuracy alone is of primary concern, it should be the directional set.
4. Performers should be encouraged to find their own optimal speed set for a particular skill rather than all be expected to perform at exactly the same speed. Once an effective speed pattern is established, the individual may use various adjustments in extent and force of the ballistic movement (e.g., the highly skilled tennis player may make adjustments in the speed of the first and second service).
5. Demonstrations should indicate the proper speed of the performance.
6. Team game skills involving rapid and accurate movements of several players should be practiced in situations simulating their actual use in the contest.

UTILIZING
KNOWLEDGE OF RESULTS

Feedback refers in many instances to knowledge of results, which is usually provided by giving the learner information concerning the nature of good performance, knowledge of her own mistakes, knowledge of successful results. In some sports (e.g., archery, bowling, basketball shooting) the learner can easily assess the extent of error or correctness of performance; however, there are advantages in providing additional knowledge of results. The amount of trial and error can be reduced by providing *verbal cues* that direct attention to correct stimuli and responses. Players may use techniques of predicting their own performance. The tennis player may declare the intent of her shot—"down the line," "cross-court." The player may be made aware of some progress through use of techniques such as progress charts, by recognizing the consequences of her action (as might be revealed in incidence charts), by identifying her own mistakes (diagnostic checklists might be used for this purpose).

Feedback that closely follows performance is more effective than when it is delayed. Using such techniques as spot bowling or providing a during-performance acknowledgement of correctness of performance, such as "Now you have it," promotes immediate reinforcement.

Although the ideal frequency of reinforcement appears to be random, in general it should be more frequent in the early stages of learning, less frequent later. Performance may be improved with some uncertainty, that is, by providing feedback unpredictably. The one good golf shot that keeps the player going apparently supports B. F. Skinner's thesis that it is the veritable ratio of payoff that produces results.

Television and videotape techniques, in which the learner sees a televised image of her movements, represent a method of producing what K. U. Smith called "dynamic feedback."[28] The learner may be said to have become locked or yoked with the image in a dynamic feedback circuit. Smith considers dynamic feedback conditions more effective in learning and performance than the static aftereffects of knowledge of results.

Obviously, the use of such techniques as videotaping provides the learner with an instant source of feedback of her performance and one with which she can easily identify in contrast to a demonstration provided by an expert. The feedback offered by such devices may be of most value to performers of closed skills (e.g., diving, trampolining, track and field events) in which precise timing and body orientation in space are crucial factors. Care must be exercised in the use of such techniques with individuals, particularly beginners, who may be upset or embarrased by viewing their own clumsy performances. Further discussion of tools such as instant replay, Polaroid graph-check sequence action, and so forth is presented in Chapter 7.

USING SENSORY AIDS

Verbal, visual, auditory, kinesthetic, manual, and mechanical aids may provide feedback to the performer as well as motivate practice simply by virtue of offering novelty and challenge. Research evidence does not indicate the unquestioned worth of such aids, nor conclusively point to one type as being superior to others. Individuals respond differently to different techniques and some skills seem to lend themselves to more effective use of some devices than others. Each sport also requires specific applications. The suggestions presented in this section are pertinent to an overall picture.

Verbal Aids. Detailed *verbal description,* as is used in extensive analyses, is more beneficial for the highly skilled performer, who has a skill vocabulary, than it is for beginners; it is more valuable for brighter than duller learners, and for more complex than simpler skills. Verbalizing the mechanical principles involved in the skill may facilitate an ability to analyze the skill, particularly at higher skill levels. In general, however, in the early stages of skill learning, teachers should not overteach. Preceding or interrupting performance with too many words may be of less value than letting the individual instruct herself in her initial approach to a skill.

Verbal cues (or guides) or colorful words that paint a mental picture of the act ("hold the bird as though it were a pinch of salt") seem beneficial in early practice and in complex unpredictable play situations where timing is important. Providing a basketball guard with repeated verbal cues, such as "pick her up now," "cut her off outside the circle," and so forth, may assist in timing and in tying skill sequences together. *Verbal mediation* (talking to oneself aloud or internally), aside from relieving tension and as a self-encouragement device, seems more valuable in the stable or "habitual" activities (e.g., archery, golf, track and field) than in those characterized by quick and adaptive responses to unpredictable situations (e.g., tennis, basketball). A tennis player may be told *not* to *think* or even to talk to herself during the volley. Such a directive also may be consistent with studies that suggest the favorable effects of inattention during performance or of directing attention away from the movement.

Kinesthetic Aids. Kinesthesis refers to conscious perception of movement, the "how-does-it-feel" directive to the performer. Researchers report contrary results in the methods of developing an awareness of this sense and whether stressing the feeling of movement actually enhances learning.

After reviewing studies of kinesthetic perception, Smith concluded: "It is possible that man cannot rely on his kinesthetic feedback to provide detailed information about his movements."[27] The evidence suggests, in fact, that one cannot consciously modify most movements performed in sport activities on the basis of feeling while the movement is in progress. The conscious awareness of the feel of a movement comes after that phase of the movement has been completed. Research findings suggest that if the performer consciously thinks of a movement in progress, it hinders her performance. Nonetheless, the evidence supporting some "value to proprioceptive sensing and adjustment" seemingly warrants sharpening the kinesthetic sensorium.[15] Some suggestions are:

1. Have performer close her eyes or perform the movement in a dark room concentrating on the feel or kinesthetic perception of the movement rather than on its outcome.

2. Use manual manipulation minimally but for special purposes such as the person who is seemingly unable to imitate demonstration or to translate verbal explanations and the low skilled individual who experiences limited eye-hand coordination and/or lack of strength. The limb may be guided through the movement pattern (e.g., the serve in tennis); however, the teacher should not overcontrol the learner's movements. Specific positions or aspects of the pattern that need attention may be etched by holding the limb or body part in the desired position (such as the ball impact position on tennis serve). The individual also may feel others perform the movement pattern (this works effectively for the backhand drive in tennis). These manipulations should be cooperative rather than a passive compliance or resistance by the learner or force by the teacher.

   In addition to being used for body positioning, speed and force of movement, manual guidance may provide understanding of spatial relationships and team play positions (e.g., a guarding player can be moved through her zone positions by standing behind her and placing your hands on her hips).

3. Have the individual use heavier or lighter equipment for warm-up swings—using weighted bats or swinging more than one bat, swinging a racquet in a press—to increase speed and power; practice with light balls then heavier balls to provide greater transfer.

4. Use verbal cues to give the individual the feel of an action (e.g., on the loop of the tennis serve say, "It feels as though

you are scratching your back."). Verbal cues used in this sense are stated in "feel" words and supplement rather than duplicate the verbal description provided by skill analyses.

Mental Imagery. Imagining (conceptualization or introspection) and performing are undoubtedly related. Thinking through an act or seeing it in the mind's eye can cause actual muscle movement.

Although the findings concerning the value of *mental practice* as a form of imagery are controversial, such practice generally prevents forgetting and benefits retention. It permits analyzing and reorganizing points of confusion, aids in attaining smooth and easy performance, and actually increases the level of skill (though not as much as actual physical practice). Some factors in the effectiveness of mental practice appear to be the level of skill and kinesthetic sensitivity. Other variables include the novelty of the skill and the ratio of mental practice to actual practice. Mental practice tends to be more profitable for the highly skilled performer or for those with prior experience than for beginners, perhaps because knowledge of the skill is needed in order to know what actions to rehearse mentally.

In using mental practice, teachers might direct performers to:

1. Utilize before-class, waiting-a-turn and between-class periods to rehearse mentally the newly learned skill or as a pre-performance review.
2. Concentrate deeply on the particular aspect for short periods of time, blocking out all other thoughts.
3. Think in terms of the feel of the movement as well as in general verbal terms and mechanical principles.
4. Read material about the skill or strategy analyses or word cues while mentally rehearsing the action.
5. Simulate the movement while thinking about it.
6. Acquire the habit of situational planning—mentally replaying the game or planning the day ahead, anticipating what to do if certain situations arise.

During actual performance of a movement, players should think ahead, that is, direct attention to the next response rather than pay too much attention to present acts or to precise details of specific movements. The skilled tennis player should not think of the movements as she executes a series of rapid volleys. Rather, she lets body action automatically take over while she watches the opponent(s) in the field of play, sorting out the most appropriate succeeding action. To consciously think of a movement in progress hinders performance. Thinking about a movement while doing it is too late, unless it is a slow, self-paced movement which most sport skills are not. Studies of kinesthetic perception and reaction time and high-speed filming analysis reveal that a performer makes many refinements and correct adjustments, integrating movements automatically during the movement in progress, without being conscious of doing so.

Visual Aids. There is controversy about the value of various visual aids and of the value of visual over other aids. Joseph Wood Krutch, distinguished critic, naturalist and philosopher, asking whether audiovisual aids are "anything more than concessions to the pupil's unwillingness to make the effort of attention necessary," suggested that they are at best "a surrender to delusion." He did contend, however, that the "mechanical means of communication are interesting in themselves."[13] Perhaps it might be concluded that the real value of visual aids is simply to motivate interest and further practice.

Insofar as research reveals, recall seems to be more closely tied to verbal symbols than to visual images, at least at the advanced skill levels.[15] At the same time, a gross visual outline by demonstrators or by manual guidance may be more beneficial than is verbalization in the early stages of learning when the individual may lack sufficient past experience to evoke verbal recall, although the value of a visual image of a successful performance as a guide to performance is not clearly supported by the research.

Some general suggestions for using visual aids include: select the aid that makes a contribution over others for specific purposes; plan in advance for its use; follow-up with discussion, evaluation, supplementary material, and, most of all, with actual practice of that which has been presented; evaluate the aid by testing knowledge or checking actual performance movement. Further suggestions for using specific aids follow:

1. *Demonstration* has been considered the best method of giving players an idea of the whole skill and a general impression of its timing. Demonstrations also may serve to inspire players to improve, to point out misconceptions or to draw attention to strengths and weaknesses in performance, to add clarity to something not easily explained in words. The skilled performer apparently benefits from demonstrations of those aspects that need changing or refinement. Research[18] indicates that demonstrations should eliminate distracting cues (clipboards, whistles, sun) ; should not be too hurried and should be repeated (two demonstrations are more effec-

tive than one) ; attention of performers may be directed to important points or analysis may be combined with demonstration for clarity; performers may be directed to use pursuit rather than saccadic (or jerky) eye movements and to avoid excessive eye movements (vertical or horizontal) and blinking; time for questions and summarization of important points should be provided.

2. *Motion pictures, still pictures, loop films, blackboard diagrams, bulletin board displays.* Motion pictures are best to give a general overview; to show continuity, rhythm, and timing of a whole skill; to show integral parts of the skill in slow motion; to reveal details that cannot be developed in demonstration. Still pictures, diagrams, and displays may serve to stimulate interest; to analyze in detail one's own form and discover performance problems; as reference material for study. Some brief suggestions for using such aids are:

   a. Aids should provide more precise knowledge or point out apparent differences between effective and ineffective performance.

   b. Posted material should be strategically located; be simple, interrelated, and well-organized; be accompanied with short, direct, stimulating titles and/or descriptions; be accurate, relevant, significant, attractive, and interesting (color, neatness, unusual textures, three-dimensional objects, drama).

   c. For blackboard illustrations or diagrams, materials should aid communication (sharp color contrast in board and chalk, clean board, few well-chosen, carefully spaced items) ; time may be economized and material made more readable by putting items on the board before class.

3. Picture representations of a task may provide the individual with some insight into complex skills. In one experiment, before learning the task subjects were given preliminary training on a paper-and-pencil pictured representation of the task. The procedure resulted in effective skill acquisition and better performance.[24] Another technique was the use of a pen-drawn graph of force to measure the pressure that sprinters applied, at the start of the sprint, to the sprinting blocks. Those performers who viewed the graphs immediately after each start and heard them explained performed better than those who did not.[24]

Such devices, as well as the simple look-at-yourself-in-the-mirror technique, do provide some immediate visual feedback of knowledge of results. Other technologic devices providing instructional assistance are presented in Chapter 7.

Perhaps the observations made at the outset of this chapter are most appropriate in synthesizing the concepts throughout this chapter. Just how teaching and learning interact and the uncertain relationship between learning and performance are complex problems that have tried theorists for many years. Teaching and learning obviously are not the same thing. In fact, teaching practices may be in contradiction to how learning takes place. There is, of course, ample evidence that the creative teacher can be distinguished from the technician just as the good sculptor can be distinguished from the hack-and-chisel brigade. At the same time, there are many gaps in knowledge about the nature and process of skill acquisition and the later process of skill refinement. The results of research are meager, sometimes contradictory, and do not lead to agreement on preferred approaches to be used by either the learner or the teacher. Teachers, learners, and the teaching-learning process cannot be regarded as discrete entities. They are complex, liquid amalgams that spill over, merge, and coalesce. There is no straightforward relationship between a specific teaching technique and learning. Whether the teaching technique is successful probably does not depend upon the technique itself but upon the way it is used. The effective teacher employs an approach or technique that she regards as appropriate for herself, the type of learner, the learner's level of ability, the skill involved, and so forth. Even then, the teacher may be successful without even knowing why. She may feel like the lady golfer, who, when she holed a ball from the edge of the green, said, "I wish I knew what I did right."

Just how learning and motivation interact also is a complex problem. Some sources of motivation may be derived from the material presented in this chapter. Further sources of multiplying motivation are presented in the following chapter.

REFERENCES

1. Adams, J. P. A closed-loop theory of motor learning. *Journal of Motor Behavior, 3,* 1971, p. 113.
2. Bigge, M. L. *Learning Theories for Teachers.* New York: Harper & Row, 1964.
3. Clifton, M. A. Pertinent theories of motor learning. Report of the 1968 Workshop, National Association for Physical Education of College Women, Asheville, N.C., August 1968, p. 13.
4. Cratty, B. J. *Movement Behavior and Motor Learning* (3rd ed.). Philadelphia: Lea & Febiger, 1973.

5. Cratty, B. J. *Psychology and Physical Activity*. Englewood Cliffs, N.J.: Prentice-Hall, Inc., 1968.

6. Cratty, B. J. A three level theory of perceptual-motor behavior. *Quest, VI*, 1966, pp. 3-10.

6a. Fitts, P. M., and Posner, M. I. *Human Performance*. Belmont, Calif.: Brooks/Cole, 1967.

7. Frost, R. B. *Psychological Concepts Applied to Physical Education and Coaching*. Reading, Mass.: Addison-Wesley, 1971.

8. Gagne, R. M., and Fleishman, E. A. *Psychology and Human Performance*. New York: Henry Holt & Co., 1959.

9. Gentile, A. M. A working model of skill acquisition with application to teaching. *Quest, XVII*, 1972, pp. 3-23.

10. Hilgard, E. R. (Ed.) *Theories of Learning and Instruction, the Sixty-third Yearbook of the National Society for the Study of Education*. Chicago: University of Chicago Press, 1964.

11. Kingsley, H. L., and Garry, R. *The Nature and Conditions of Learning* (2nd ed.). Englewood Cliffs, N.J.: Prentice-Hall, Inc., 1957.

12. Knapp, B. *Skill in Sport: The Attainment of Proficiency*. London: Routledge & Kegan Paul, 1964.

13. Krutch, J. W. *A Krutch Omnibus*. New York: William Morrow, 1970.

14. Lawther, J. D. *Sport Psychology*. Englewood Cliffs, N.J.: Prentice-Hall, Inc., 1972.

15. Lawther, J. D. *The Learning of Physical Skills*. Englewood Cliffs, N.J.: Prentice-Hall, Inc., 1968.

16. Melton, A. W. (Ed.). *Categories of Human Learning*. New York: Academic Press, 1964.

17. Miller, D. M. The relationship between some visual perceptual factors and the degree of success realized by sports performers. (Doctoral dissertation, University of Southern California), Los Angeles, Calif., 1960.

17a. Miller, G. A., Galanter, E. G., and Pribam, K. H. *Plans and the Structure of Behavior*. New York: Holt, Rinehart and Winston, 1960.

18. Mott, J. A. Eye movement during initial learning of motor skills. (Doctoral dissertation, University of Southern California), Los Angeles, Calif., 1964.

19. Oxendine, J. B. *Psychology of Motor Learning*. New York: Appleton-Century-Crofts, 1968.

20. Oxendine, J. B. Effect of progressively changing practice schedules on the learning of a motor skill. *Research Quarterly, 36*, 1965, pp. 307-315.

21. Poulton, E. C. On prediction in skilled movements. *Psychological Bulletin, 54*, 1957, pp. 476-478.

22. Robb, M. D. *The Dynamics of Motor-Skill Acquisition*. Englewood Cliffs, N.J.: Prentice-Hall, Inc., 1972.

23. Sage, G. H. *Introduction to Motor Behavior: A Neuropsychological Approach*. Reading, Mass.: Addison-Wesley, 1971.

24. Singer, R. N. *Motor Learning and Human Performance*. New York: Macmillan, 1968.

25. Singer, R. N. *Readings in Motor Learning*. Philadelphia: Lea & Febiger, 1968.

26. Skill learning and performance. *Research Quarterly, 43,* 1972.

27. Smith, J. L. Kinesthesis: A model for movement feedback. In *New Perspectives of Man in Action.* Roscoe C. Brown and Bryant J. Cratty (Eds.). Englewood Cliffs, N.J.: Prentice-Hall, Inc., 1969.

28. Smith, K. U. New horizons of research in physical behavioral science and rehabilitation: Dynamic feedback designs in learning and training. Report of the 1968 Workshop, National Association for Physical Education of College Women, Asheville, N.C., 1968.

29. Smith, Leon E. (Ed.). *Proceedings of the C.I.C. Symposium on Psychology of Motor Learning,* University of Iowa, Iowa City, Iowa, October 10-12, 1969. Chicago: The Athletic Institute, 1970.

30. Wells, K. F. *Kinesiology* (4th ed.). Philadelphia: W. B. Saunders Co., 1966.

5. Actualizing Potential
by Multiplying Motivation

When love and skill work together, expect a masterpiece.
John Ruskin

Skill (or ability) and performance are not the same thing, nor is performance always constant. Everyone is aware of instances in which the less skilled athlete wins over the athlete with superior skill. Examples may be brought to mind of the skilled athlete achieving peak performance or playing over her head, on some occasions. Although other factors, such as fatigue, may account for the difference between ability and actual performance, and for the variability in performance from one situation to another, motivation is the catalyst in actualizing performance potential. It is the key to bringing about more favorable and faster results, whether an athlete is learning a new skill, is involved in an arduous training program, or is striving for a peak performance. In short, performance may be said to be skill multiplied by motivation.

Motivation is, however, an individual matter. The question of why persons participate in sport is not easily answered, much less generalized (see Chapter 2). The reasons are as individual as are human motives. Even individuals seem to be motivated by different reasons at various stages in their development. The motives underlying an individual's mere participation in sport may differ, too, from those that push her to achieve her fullest potential. Many variables, therefore, play a part in determining the appropriateness of motivational techniques to be used. These variables may be within the personality and physiology of the athlete—drive, aggression, anxiety level, temperament, body image, self-esteem, self-derogation, pain threshold, constitution, and so forth—or they may be in her responses to such external variables as the social situation, structure of the group, and so forth.

No attempt will be made to summarize the theory of motivation or the various theoretical approaches. Some insights into the nature of the athlete are offered in a previous section. An attempt will be made, however, to describe some further concepts as they relate to athletic performance and to actualizing performance potential. The material that follows may be considered as being additional to and consistent with those theories and techniques described in the section dealing with facilitation of skill development. Some might just as appropriately have been classified under the heading of feedback. Knowledge of results, for example, is a commonly acknowledged principle of motivation. Or some of the following suggestions may be regarded as belonging to discoveries in *affective* education and sensitivity concepts. Regardless of origin or rightful relationships, these suggestions represent possible ways of multiplying motivation, the optimum level of which may be "somewhere between apathy and wild excitement," to borrow a phrase from Jerome Bruner.

IGNITE SELF-INCENTIVE

An individual may motivate herself (intrinsic motivation) or be motivated by influences outside herself (extrinsic motivation), but if she has minimal intrinsic motivation she can be exposed to the richest materials possible and numerous manipulations of environment yet will experience no change. Paramount in the psychology of improving performance is the idea that self-motivation is crucial. It is a crucial factor in retention of what has been learned and in striving for further attainment, and, when an individual is responding to incentives that are not manipulated by someone else, she may be less dependent and less resentful of the tasks to be accomplished.

A term commonly used in motivation theory is *level of aspiration*, referring to what one expects to achieve as opposed to what one would like to achieve. One way to motivate an athlete to improve performance in sports may be to allow her to choose her own desired level of performance, her own level of aspiration. Once the aspiration level is determined, she may be strongly motivated to achieve it. Of course, some individuals may set a level of aspiration below the level of performance they are capable of achieving. The hypothesis of "par" or "tolerance," proposed to account for this difference between performance and aspiration, suggests that some persons are content to achieve but do not really want to strive to exceed the standard they have set for themselves.

Several factors, such as past experience, the effects of success and failure, arousal level, and other personality factors, as well as social setting, are related to aspiration level. Some of these factors are discussed in the following sections. In general, success tends to raise subsequent aspiration levels and failure encourages the lowering of them. Implications of these findings are postulated. **Further** discussion in this section is designed to focus on ways in which aspiration level may be self-determined.

According to the Achievement Motivation Development Project of Cambridge, Massachusetts, personal changes and *goal-setting* occur when the individual recognizes a motive that is an improvement in her own self-image and that is consistent with (or better than) her cultural values and with the demands of reality.[22] The relevance of performance in sport to an individual's long-term goal may be crucial, although as yet unproved by research. Some approaches to personal change, which are consistent with achievement motivation theory, might include devices in which the individual describes what she really *expects to attain* and what she would *like to* attain. Some illustrations follow:

1. *The admiration ladder* in which the athlete designates a range of persons from most admired to least admired, places herself on a rung of the ladder, and answers such questions as: Why do I place myself on this rung? On what rung would I like to be? What will I have to do to get there?
2. *The individual report form* in which the athlete describes what she likes and dislikes about situations, how she would like things to be, and what she is doing about it.
3. *The obituary* or (if this is too morbid) *the newspaper personality profile* in which the athlete describes her accomplishments and what they might have been.

What an individual thinks about her body is important. The mental image she has of her physical appearance and capabilities for participation may figure in her choice of activities, influence whether she participates in any activity, and affect the performance levels she achieves. Janet Wessel provides *body image profiles* that are helpful tools in the assessment of one's attitudes toward oneself and physical activity in general.[41] The person records her assessment of her actual body image (real) and her body as she would like to be (ideal). A comparison of these scores is provided to help the individual locate the areas of greatest discrepancy. Words such as "coordinated-uncoordinated," "rigid-flexible," "weak-strong," "graceful-awkward," "flabby-shapely," and many others are provided at opposite ends of the continuum and the individual judges where she places herself along the scale.

Although self-image should be a positive perception, it should also be realistic and not just in one dimension. The individual should be pointed toward many environments, as psychologists have cautioned. There is evidence in the stereotype of the athletic superstar of what happens when one dimension crumbles—the individual crumbles.

Other self-programs in which the individual can show growth against herself might include progress records, graphs, statistics, scoring records, batting averages, strength indices, and the like. Or athletes may employ self-ratings and other devices to test their sport character. Competition at high levels brings a great deal of strain to bear on any character. Arnold Haultain, in his book *The Mystery of Golf,* stated it so amiably: ". . . few if any games so strip a man of the conventional and the artificial. In a single round you can sum up a man, can say whether he be truthful, courageous, honest, upright, generous, sincere, slow to anger—or the reverse."[12] The athlete may check herself on these dimensions or rate herself on the times she blamed her less-than-superb performance on bad officiating or on distractions caused by playing partners. On the other hand, she may check how many times she called a penalty on herself when it would otherwise have gone unnoticed or helped an official on a close call that hurt her team. Every sportswoman can bring to mind several instances of this type. Each of these is a test of the participant's character.

Perhaps the athlete may actually identify as her goal a *peak performance.* A peak performance in sport is in effect what happens in any peak experience, variously described as excitement, intensity of encounter, the most ecstatic experience in one's life, mystical, an epiphenomenon, over one's head, masterful, virtuoso-like, and so forth. It is not always a moment of winning or losing, but in such a moment the person's powers are at a height and she becomes more effortless, more daring, more whole, more self-actualized, to use Abraham Maslow's term, than at any other time.

Although the athlete may be startled by her unsuspected skill, this is not to say that a peak performance is without hard work and control. Although the peak performance may just happen, *the person makes it happen.* And, although the peak performance is far more likely to occur at the highest levels of skill, educators have been guilty of not giving all performers the opportunity to have a peak-performance experience. How to cultivate them is something else. As Reuben Frost pointed out, consistent performances at peak levels are the result of many things, including optimum physical development and condition, perfection of skills, proper self-concept, optimum state of arousal, and motivation from within—the individual must want to excel.[9]

What the athlete thinks about her physiologic capabilities is also important. Investigations in the area of *perceived exertion* indicate that if an individual thinks he is exhausted, he is, even if he is not physiologically.[4,5,8] The individual's perception of exertion during exercise may be used to indicate relative work intensity. Swimmers have been found to be 2-, 3-, 4-, 5-, 6-, or 7-day swimmers. If they were to swim one day beyond, alarm reactions were observed. There was a peculiar response style for each individual. *Not pushing* athletes to the "extra" day may help avoid peculiar reactions. The further implication is that the athlete is not different from the picture she draws of herself.

In summary, whether the potential of any individual athlete is actualized apparently starts from some sort of personal agreement with self. A fully competent athlete possesses skills of self-assessment and self-modification. She knows what is happening within herself and the environment. The question is, can an individual be taught to act in more personally effective ways? The proposed answer is that of providing opportunities for establishing self-identified goals and incentives, for selecting internal self-control actions (thought, images, physiologic responses), and for improving self-esteem by reducing negative self-thoughts. The transfer of responsibility to self might be regarded as a measure of success of any of the motivational techniques described on the following pages.

TURN ON
EXTERNAL INCENTIVES

Although internal motivation is favored over external, human beings are not passive responders to external stimuli. External incentives may come from persons, objects, or situations in the environment—material reward or promise of reward, verbal praise or reproof (punishment), force or threat of force, pep talks, words, music, and hypnosis.

Individuals are not all motivated in the same manner or all of the time by the same type of incentives. The athlete who displays a high level of achievement may be approached in a different manner from the beginner. For example, persons with high ability levels seemingly perform best with verbal inducement. Yet, for highly motivated persons, the effects of some of the external incentives (verbal inducements, knowledge of results, encouragement, music) might be irrelevant or ineffective during the skill-learning stage. Some experimenters suggest that those who already have a high level of drive do not need additional inducement.

Whatever incentive causes stimulation, it is apparently something to which the individual has not been accustomed. It is something new in the environment, something novel, intense, more challenging or demanding of effort. Any of the following techniques may be effective stimulants in this sense, although considerably more research is needed before refinement of their use can be made.

Psychologists are generally agreed that *reward,* in the form of praise, recognition, prizes, and the like, operates more noticeably in facilitating (or depressing) *performance* than *learning,* although both can be facilitated through appropriate application. Although rewards tend to engender enthusiasm and create pleasurable association with the task being performed, a potentially negative outcome of rewards, or of any form of external motivation, may be that they may create dependence—the reward rather than the behavior is important. Reward is considered to be better than punishment because it does not need to be administered continually and is longer lasting. The effect of rewards in encouraging better performance depends on the amount, frequency, and delay. Too-frequent use is disadvantageous. *Praise* and *reproof* are better motivators than is ignoring the person. Reproof or some form of punishment seems to be effective with some persons. Extroverts may be stimulated more by reproof than praise.

The athlete's initial *success* and fear of *failure* contribute to level of motivation. In the early stages of learning, or when tension is high, achievement and satisfaction are important because confidence is built with success. Success does not automatically increase motivation and failure decrease it, however. Although early failure has an inhibitory effect, as success increases the experiencing of some failure may increase motivation. Reich, in "Stress-seeking: The Unknown Factor of Human Personality," stated: "There is a margin of the human mind that can be stimulated by pain and inconvenience, but which is indifferent to pleasure. That is to say, that man's moments of freedom tend to come under crisis or challenge, and when things are going well he tends to allow his grip on life to slacken."[28]

When it is not too frequent, *defeat* may serve to improve motivation. The certainty of winning, the absence of risk, satisfaction with one's level of performance may, in fact, lead to overconfidence and the stultification of achievement (or deterioration of performance). Knute Rockne perhaps typified the reaction most coaches have about defeat in that he wanted his players to take defeat to heart, not laugh it off with the thought that, oh, well, there will be another game. Success in sports costs just that—taking failure to heart, analyzing why it happened, and desiring to overcome the reasons for defeat.

An important role of the coach is that of helping the athlete establish realistic goals so that success and failure can be regulated in some way. Some suggestions are to give constructive criticism, not mere praise; to avoid scheduling games that result in too many wins and too little or too weak competition; to avoid pre-game publicity that predicts certain victory or runs down the opponent; to avoid chalking up an excessive score against the easy opponent; to analyze failures rather than being defeated by them.

There is disagreement about the value of *verbal exhortation* such as pep talks, inspirational speeches, and the like in motivating athletes to greater effort, but there is also a scarcity of research on the topic. There is little evidence that the coach's language habits, in general, have been examined for their implications to motivation. Neither the point of view regarding the effectiveness of this technique as a myth nor the side that considers it to be an indestructable force can be said to have won the day. Until such time as such differences of opinion are resolved, it may be assumed that for some athletes and on some occasions *words* themselves may serve as facilitators or inhibitors of performance achievement. As James Young stated in *A Technique for Producing Ideas*: "Words are, themselves, ideas . . . in a state of suspended animation." Language is not just the vehicle of our thoughts. To a great extent, words determine the ideas, thoughts, and reactions one has.

In the sports world, there are makers of shrewd phrases and words that salt down important ideas and experiences for many players. Some suggestions also may be gleaned from sources and persons outside the realm of sports. The following illustrative examples are indicative.

As a thumbnail lesson in how to bypass the roadblock to regret, Arthur Gordon suggested two words to avoid and two to remember. The two words to avoid are "if only" and the two words to substitute are "next time." The words "if only" do not change things. Rather, they keep the person facing backward instead of forward. The idea of substituting the words "next time" is that the focus may be shifted by key words that supply lift instead of creating drag.[11]

William James' words were: "Try to be one of the people on whom nothing is lost."[15] In abiding by this bit of advice, the athlete could become newly aware of people, places, and things, less complacent and indifferent. She may begin to be much more observant—to notice personal idiosyncrasies of the opponent, to become acutely aware of all manner of things she had once overlooked that may be the key to self-improvement.

In a letter to his son, the father used a phrase which might suggest another word usage for coaches: "Life isn't 'having it made' . . . , it's 'getting it made.'" In the business of getting it made he pointed out that it is not just the great climactic moments that count, but also the little partial victories, the defeats, the deadlocks, the waiting. "If you're ever unlucky enough to 'have it made,' you will be a spectator, not a participant in life."[1]

The idea in using words as incentives is that they are part of the force that forms attitudes, and, when trying to stimulate through words, attention should be kept on the positive. The coach might monitor, by observing and recording, the effects of her own behavior and words, positive and negative, on the actions of the athlete. The coach plays a special role by the words she uses to define how competent or incompetent an athlete is. The more the athlete is treated as competent, the more she may come to exhibit the self-sustaining prophecy. By the same token, the coach who makes mild demands or insipid appeals can expect dull responses.

ILLUMINATE EMOTIONS

Motivation is a complex mixture of many things, and emotion is part of that mixture. It is a well-known fact that even in everyday life under conditions of emotional excitement a person can release great reservoirs of energy and perform seemingly impossible feats of skill, speed, power, and endurance. The sports world, too, is replete with examples of performers who rise to great heights of achievement on the emotional pitch and excitement of the moment. Many an underdog has beaten a more skilled opponent and many a team has caught fire and produced a victory over seemingly overwhelming odds in favor of the opponent. Perhaps more than any other endeavor, sports call forth unusual emotions. The pressures of competition, the crowd and its behavior, the importance of winning, the influence of the coach, parents, and friends, all these and more are among the conditions that set into motion such responses as self-confidence, poise, expectancy, and the like, as well as fear, hate, anxiety, anger, frustration, despair, grief, feelings of guilt, resentment, indignation, and similar emotions.

Although there is little doubt that motivation involves emotional reactions, there may not be general agreement as to the definition of emotion. Some psychologists suggest that emotion be called "arousal" or "energy mobilization" or "activation." Some equate the intensity of motivation with arousal; others take the view "that emotions may be differential along dimensions other than level of arousal."[31] Despite the theoretical questions and controversies regarding the properties of emotion, numerous psychology texts and books on motor performance devote attention to the role of *emotional arousal.*

The important concern of the coach is how to use and stimulate valuable emotional responses so that reservoirs of power can be called forth and how to avoid the harmful effects of misused emotions. Obviously, too, some understanding of the athlete is needed in order to deal with such questions as what part anxiety plays in an athlete's selection of a sport or in her performance, which athletes need to be aroused or calmed and how, when an athlete experiences the most anxiety. Consideration also needs to be given to the part that emotional level may play in a given sport or how it may vary from sport to sport.

As Oxendine pointed out, abundant evidence is offered on arousal-performance topics to support generalizations such as: optimum arousal level varies with the task, from person to person, and for the same person at different times; a positive relationship exists between a high arousal state and strength, endurance, and speed; a high level of arousal interferes with performance of complex skills, fine muscle movements, coordination, steadiness, general concentration; and, for all motor tasks, a level of arousal slightly above average is preferable to a normal or below normal level.[25] Oxendine noted, however, that although reflective explanations of the Yerkes-Dodson law offer rough guides of emotional arousal and performance, they are of little value in predicting performance. (According to the Yerkes-Dodson law, complex tasks are performed better when drive is low; simple tasks are performed better when drive is high.)

Although research showing the levels of anxiety generated by various sports is limited, except insofar as it deals with personality traits of those engaged in various sports, Oxendine offered some speculative suggestions as to the most *appropriate arousal level for different sports activities*[25] (see page 90).

Research studies in sports on how to use and stimulate valuable emotional responses and to avoid harmful effects of misused emotions are scarce. One general guideline appears warranted: techniques such as "psyching-up" and "mood-getting" are not effective when used on an entire group, because they should be compatible with the individual athlete's personality. The performance of an already overanxious athlete may be impaired by an extra dose of psyching-up. Some further guidelines for individual athletes may be gleaned from the following discussion of various emotional reactions.

Fear is an emotional reaction that may be considered only as a negative motivator. Yet, fear may become positive motivation of the most critical kind. When they are scared, adventurers, pilots, mountain climbers, and performers in all fields of endeavor seem to

Optimum Arousal Level for Some Typical Sports Skills

Level of Arousal:	*Sport Skills:*
#5 (Extremely excited)	football blocking and tackling performance on Rogers' PFI test running (220 yards to 440 yards) sit up, push up, or bent arm hang test weight lifting
#4	running long jump running very short and long races shot putt swimming races wrestling and judo
#3	basketball skills boxing high jumping most gymnastic skills soccer skills
#2	baseball pitchers and batters fancy dives fencing football quarterback tennis
#1 (Slight arousal)	archery and bowling basketball free throw field goal kicking golf putting and short irons skating figure 8's
0 (Normal state)	

From Oxendine, J. B. Emotional arousal and motor performance. *Quest, XIII,* 1970, pp. 23-32.

call up energy and resolution that normally seem to be lacking. Persons on the verge of panic, who muster up the strength to perform seemingly impossible feats, testify to the fact that there are untapped resources of improved performance. The person who is trapped under a car in a snowslide and escapes by lifting the car and the injured person who runs from a burning house carrying the baby to safety are examples of persons who achieved what they believed they must do in adverse situations.

How are such occurrences explained? Physiologically, when an unusual effort is required or when a person is threatened by danger or in times of an emergency, the adrenal gland goes into action. Its secretion stimulates action of the sympathetic branch of the autonomic nervous system, which in turn triggers physiologic responses of all systems of the body. Thus, the person is prepared for action —to "fight or flee." Whatever the factors may be that stimulate emotions, the physiologic processes are set in motion in order to restore the human organism to a state of equilibrium or homeostasis. Behavior, therefore, is linked inextricably to bodily responses.

Psychologically, how can such a training effect on the mind be produced to achieve maximum effort in sport performance? Can fear be a useful spur, be welcomed as a stimulus to courage? The mind's balance mechanisms parallel the body's basic system for maintenance of equilibrium. More than is realized, people have remarkable self-restorative powers. The human mind is provided with an array of resources designed to withstand stress, strain, and pain, and to overcome fear and self-doubt. Thomas, in his book *Science and Sport*, suggested that, in terms of the psychologic barrier of pain tolerance, the mind (or the soul) can be trained "to accept pain—to welcome it almost as if it were a friend who comes to say that maximum physical effort is at last being expended. . . ."[39]

The thought factor in achievement has been the subject of numerous books and essays. The theme of the book *Psycho-Cybernetics* by Maxwell Maltz, M.D., is that a person gets out of his servomechanism what he feeds in. If he wants to build confidence, he must think confidence. Whatever the validity of *Psycho-Cybernetics*, it had a marked effect on Hobie Billingsly, coach for the United States Olympic divers, who for seven straight years was voted coach of the year by the American Swimming Coaches Association. As one diver said of Billingsly: "The great thing he does is make you believe in yourself, even when you tend not to. He's given me confidence more than anything else."[27]

The power of thought in guiding emotions and thus achievement in sports, however, should not be too much a matter of exhortation on the part of the coach. Perhaps what is needed more is for the athlete to be taught to go it alone or even to be left alone, to trust her own thoughts, to propel herself forward. There are too many instances of the coach or parent standing on the sidelines giving comfort, support, or calling the next move. Dr. Ian Stevenson, in the *American Journal of Psychiatry*, wrote that "the loss of supportive persons seems often to contribute to recovery from the psychoneuroses." Perhaps permitting, even requiring, the normal athletes to go it alone will bring about a process of self-reorganization and self-awareness.

What is the optimum level of fear? Obviously this differs among different individuals and is related to constitution, temperament, self-esteem, pain threshold, level of competition, and so forth. Competition can become a fearful stressor at every level, even for those attaining international status. Anxious people are easily aroused and may perform simple tasks well, but in stressful situations their arousal level goes beyond optimum, causing them to perform poorly. For any individual, however, prolonged fear may interfere with the effectiveness of mental processes and skill endeavor as well as bring forth unwanted behaviors. Prolonged emotional excitement even of the positive variety is exhausting and leads to unwanted consequences such as muscular tension. Prolonged anxiety, anger, fear, or guilt can lead to serious emotional disorders.

Thus, the optimum level of fear appears to be the level at which it can be handled by the individual and used by her as a stimulus to go beyond her ordinary limitations. Wylie, author of such notable books as *The Young In Heart* and *Keeper of the Flame,* looking back on dread moments and recalling how he enjoyed himself most when he was scared, made the point that being able to handle fear means "being afraid at the right time." This is not the same as worry and anxiety, which are nagging, persistent, crippling restraints.[42]

How does a coach deal with fear that may be or may become an unwanted restraint? The following suggestions, gleaned from many sources, were offered by Reuben Frost:

1. Try to discover and treat the cause of the fear.
2. Approach the fearful situation gradually (fear of water, fear of falling).
3. Prepare participants for the situation (a definite plan, specific tactics).
4. Examine and analyze the reasons for the fear. Help the players recognize why they are apprehensive (previous injuries, unfamiliarity with the problem).
5. Encourage group interaction and "camaraderie" (talk together, sing together, etc.).
6. Suggest that experienced veterans help "rookies."
7. Improve their strength and skills.
8. Do something—action dispels fear.
9. Most fears disappear at the start of contest.[10]

A more detailed treatment of extinction of fear as well as other aspects of behavior modification can be found in Bandura's *Principles of Behavior Modification.*[3]

The term *aggression* often is used for the emotional responses known as anger, rage, hostility, indignation, and various other synonyms. Aggression, like fear, is both good and bad. It can hinder concentration, clear thinking, and rational behavior. On some occasions it helps in overcoming fears or in conquering difficult tasks, or it acts as a catharsis, serving to relieve pent-up emotions. If the cathartic theory of sport is valid, the sport expression of aggression renders the athlete more kind and friendly away from the contest, as Lawther contended. It would be a mistake to assume that fair play and sportsmanship mean gentle play or take it easy on opponents during a contest. Sportsmanship means observing the rules, being respectful toward the opponent, being impersonal in relations with the opponent, concentrating all attention on the action itself and appropriate cues to action.[16]

Most normal human beings experience unwanted **aggressive** responses at times to something or another. Sometimes physiologic conditions such as fatigue, illness, or hunger may increase aggressive tendencies. Often in the world of sports misplaced aggression is the response to such diverse and complex phenomena as fear of failure, injury to one's pride, shattered expectations, humiliation, anxiety, and the like. Not infrequently the coach who makes inconsistent or excessive demands, who criticizes the officials and players, or who exposes lack of control in other ways may be the culprit in situations in which aggressive behaviors get out of hand.

Many persons have explored what has come to be known as the violent world of athletics and have pointed out that, although sport activities can be a method of safely getting rid of aggressive tendencies, they are filled with hazardous possibilities for promoting aggressive behaviors. Psychiatrists, concerned about the dangers of violence in sport, have urged positive changes. Among the changes advocated are to de-emphasize winning as the sole purpose; to emphasize playing for the fun, enjoyment, and thrill of the game; to rechannel the outcomes toward molding character; to provide new incentives and rewards for winning and not limit rewards to winners only; to accept playing the games as potential therapy and catharsis.[38] Some further insights into behavioral engineering in sport situations may be provided by *The Development and Control of Behavior in Sport and Physical Education* by Brent S. Rushall and Daryl Siedentop (Philadelphia: Lea & Febiger, 1972) in which the theories and principles of B. F. Skinner and his operant psychology are employed.

Obviously, the same emotions that produce outstanding athletes are also part of the makeup of *the problem athlete,* although according to Tutko athletes are not strange or kooky, as many observers may be led to believe.[40] Results of tests indicate that athletes as a group are far above the average population in showing control and maturity. There are exceptions, however, and these exceptions may become difficult problems for the coach. Tutko reported that clinical work with athletes has revealed that when the athlete poses a problem he is participating for reasons other than the love of the sport, in the majority of cases. The athlete who is trying to compensate in one way or another for some important need by participating in sports may confront the coach with perplexing problems, and the coach may even contribute to the underlying difficulty.

Ogilvie and Tutko, in their book *Problem Athletes and How to Handle Them,* attempted to outline the most common problems, the factors causing them, and how the coach may be able to detect and work effectively with such problems. Some of the problems are labeled the rebellious athlete, the con man, the hyperanxious or the psyched-out athlete, the success-phobic athlete, the injury-prone athlete, the withdrawn athlete, and the depression-prone athlete.[23]

It is not difficult for any teacher or coach to call to mind some students and athletes who fall into these problem categories. The difficulty comes in being able to deal with such problems. It may be advisable in some instances to suggest that the individual seek professional help. For the most part, however, a coach's understanding of some basic principles of psychology and skill in treating the athlete as an individual human being will aid immensely.

PERSONALIZE PERSUASION

It often has been said that teacher motivation is the single most important factor in student motivation. The teacher who encourages experimentation and exploration, who shows facility in simplifying, elaborating, substituting, varying, and combining, who demonstrates pride and encourages this quality in others, who promotes encouragement and commendation among students—this teacher by her or his own preparation, attitude, and intensity produces conditions in which students can be as much as they are able. This teacher awakens students' capabilities.

The undeniable impact and value of an association with great teachers are nowhere displayed more prominently than in the development of athletic champions. Research studies, too, at least those concerned with boys and men's athletic programs, document the influence that a coach has on his players. A study by Snyder demonstrated the influence of the basketball coach in several aspects, including helping with personal problems; teaching pride, teamwork, sportsmanship and hard work; providing guidance and counseling of the players regarding their educational and occupational plans for the future.[37] The study gave evidence that many former players continue to seek out their coaches for advice. A study by Frost clearly illustrated the importance of the coach in directing the behavior and perceptions of those who come under his influence.[10] Frost gathered information from questionnaires and interviews with coaches regarding the best and worst games ever played by their teams, motivating factors, and what motivates peak performance. The replies emphasized, among others, some of the following factors as being closely related or necessary to obtain wholehearted participation and enthusiastic response: personal involvement of the teacher or coach, the player's own feeling of worth or need for security, the sense of achieving, knowledge of results, constructive criticism and encouragement, positive self-image, personal pride, peer approval, fun and enjoyment, confidence and self-discovery, a sense of responsibility and love of the game by both athlete and coach, the desire to win.[10]

Despite these research findings, many newspaper headlines and countless books are devoted to the thesis that, at least in the professional sports world, the athlete has no individuality or rights. He is merely an actor playing out a role in a vast entertainment enterprise. In such a setting there is no human interaction. Nor is there opportunity or need for any of that inspirational "gee-whiz" stuff between player and coach. Many persons suggest that close inspection of high school and college athletics reveals little difference from the dehumanized world of professional sports. The male coach as recently portrayed by many players on the collegiate level has the unmistakable ring of the drill sergeant who has little, if any, understanding or rapport with his players. As one football player, asserting that coaches cannot cope with individuality, remarked: "If you're not going around with fire in your eyes, frothing at the mouth, having epileptic fits about football, they don't want you. They claim to teach pride and poise, but except for one or two of them, they don't have any either."[19]

Whether this is really the case in men's athletics and whether the pressure to win makes any effective relationship between coach and player difficult, some lessons can be learned by those who coach athletics for girls and women.

Being a Model. The way in which the coach handles her own adequacy, her emotions and views winning and losing, is a potent source of education for the competitor and a model for the identification of her actions and values. Because values are communicated by example as much as by discussion, coaches must make a place for the theory that acknowledges the use of example and the directing of their own action in influencing the actions of others.

The learning of sportsmanship is not an automatic outcome of participation in sport. In fact, numerous studies indicate that the opportunity to learn sportsmanship and other desirable social values is lacking in many school sports for boys and men when winning is the major objective.[2,6,13,14,29] And it seems that with each succeedingly higher level of sport competition, the lower the sportsmanship-like behaviors. Motivation to learn ethical values is like motivation in any other area of concern. Incentives for the learning of values must be a part of the individual's makeup (basic motives), must be a part of the total learning situation, and must be identified, recognized and made a satisfying experience by the coach. The coach is capable of creating great personal development by whether she finds sadistic pleasure in combat and victory regardless of skill of the players or whether she discovers pride in skill accomplishment and self-respect in effort even in defeat. The coach also must assess her own ego-needs as a former sport star, her ability to act decisively and respectably in the stress of competition, and most important, she must know her players as people.

Knowing Players. Knowing players as people, as women, means knowing their *feelings about themselves* in competitive roles, about intensive practice, about winning or losing, about their motivations and backgrounds. Although limited information from research is related to women coaches, what is available suggests that coaches do not know their players as is commonly believed. Coaches of the team sports may misjudge their players to be "more outgoing, happy-go-lucky, venturesome, and controlled" than the players' personality profiles show them to be, whereas coaches of individual sports tend to overestimate the intelligence of the players.[17] As Malumphy suggested, understanding who the players really are "might help us in our role as model, and it might help to reaffirm and reassure them of their womanliness as well as their skill." She suggested further that coaches need only to support and to direct their efforts at maintaining the fine sense of proportion, concern, and sincerity that many women athletes already have regarding practice and performance demands essential for high level competition.[18]

Knowing players as people also means knowing what happens psychologically to the *players who are not selected* for the team. Athletic exclusion is a complex phenomenon and while skill ability may be the main criterion for selection of players, undoubtedly the criteria for selection include, if not emphasize, the coach's personal and emotional response to the candidate.[26] The experience of being excluded from the team at a time when the person has a high need for social approval and affiliation may represent potential problems—self-esteem may be subject to stress; defensive psychologic mechanisms may be resorted to; significant changes may occur in interest in school, athletics, and peer-group behavior.

Knowing players as people also means knowing *what becomes of the highly skilled performer* after she graduates or when she can no longer play. The outstanding performer must ultimately adjust to a life which may be different from that in which she experienced the sheer joy and excitement of being excellent, in which she may have been the center of attention, surrounded with adulation, the star, a unique idol.

Whether the male star athlete can cope with a life of comparative anonymity and obscurity has been the subject of concern to some. There is evidence that these superheroes do not adjust emotionally and psychologically, that, in fact, many of them desperately attempt to forestall the day of obscurity, and they demand, cling to, and trade on being idolized. Jack Scott, Director of the Institute for the Study of Sport and Society, wrote:

> The big-time college athlete gets spoiled. He gets a distorted perspective on things because he's not subject to the same academic and economic pressures as the other students. . . . People not only recognize him, they do things for him, defer to him, make life easy for him. . . . After a while, he gets to taking all these things for granted.[32]

Surely every coach can cite instances in which star players gave up the game at that point in their life when they ceased being motivated by victory, by adulation, and, perhaps most of all, by well-meaning parents standing on the sideline pushing them to achieve what the parents may have wanted to achieve themselves.

Perhaps coaches may help players cope with the aftermath of being temporarily enshrined as a sport star by not caring for their every need, not cheering their every word, not permitting them to live in a virtual cocoon away from the normal concerns of other typical students, but by treating them as individuals who matter outside their athletic accomplishments.

Just as it is important not to foster prima donna tactics or narcissistic tendencies in the athlete, it is also important to permit the athlete to have individuality. In this sense, coaches may need to examine what priority they give to *participatory democracy*. Should players call the plays in crucial situations rather than being coach-directed? Is it possible for players to become involved unless they choose their own captain, determine the format for team practice? Can a sense of unity and a sense of democracy arise from each player knowing that she has a unique role to play in a collective enterprise, from knowing that she is contributing the best that she is able to a joint effort, from knowing that she is playing the part expected of her alone within the context of a group? And if the coach, by virtue of her own special preparation, is in the best position to make decisions about, say, psychologic and physiologic needs of each individual, should she relinquish her role as decision-maker and relegate this leadership responsibility to the group?

Edward Olson, exploring some philosophic inconsistencies in suggestions offered for the free play of the athlete's individuality, provided a sensible rationale for bettering relationships between player and coach and for the pursuit of excellence in athletic performance.

> But the meeting of individual personality needs cannot be unilateral; it must be equal for all involved, the player and the coach alike. . . . The coach will establish, with the players' counsel, a set of rules that he believes are consistent with achieving top performance. As long as the players do not assume that the coach exists solely for their pleasure and personality development, the agreements will far outweigh the arguments.[24]

Drawing upon the works of authorities in counseling and psychotherapy, Murray Smith discussed coaching behaviors and emphasized that the key attribute of the superior coach, the one who motivates athletes and helps them to control themselves under the stress of competition, is intelligent and concerned attention to the athlete. The emphasis on the athlete requires building in more factors that operate toward friendship—genuine liking, warm acceptance, empathy. Smith underlined the importance of the coach being able to behave both in an authoritarian way (effective when goals of athlete and coach are shared and emotional arousal is controllable) and in an integrative way or one characterized by sensitivity to the athlete and a nonthreatening manner.[35]

Perhaps the meaning and value of a coach's relationship with players are best summarized in the expression of Willie Smith, head football coach at the University of Maryland, who called it a "marriage" that flourishes abundantly all the time, not merely during the season. When a coach gives of himself sincerely and the player realizes that the coach's interest in him as a person, a student, and an athlete is not just seasonal, then the coach is likely to witness something more than merely a performance of matching skills with the opponent. The reward of genuine caring and giving brings forth an "inner-giving," an extra desire and determination "emptied from within the performer."[36]

SPARK SOCIAL STIMULATION

Understanding the nature of social factors as well as personal factors in motivation is also imperative to the coach who regards the improvement of performance as something more than a push-button, routine affair. Obviously, sport activities involve social relationships; thus, how one interacts with and reacts to teammates, opponents, and audiences may be strong determinants to performance. In social psychology the term *social facilitation* is used to designate the effect of the presence of others on learning and performance. Experiments involving a study of the presence of others on learning and performance refer to a passive audience (does not encourage or discourage the performer), a verbal-remarks audience (makes encouraging or disparaging remarks), and a co-active audience (co-workers or teammates acting with or engaged in the same task as the performer).[31]

Research in social facilitation, like that in personality dimensions, has not provided any simple or surefire clues to performance behavior, and because numerous variables tend to confound the experiments the findings are contradictory. Although theory, methodology, and instruments for measuring such complex human behavior are not yet refined, some illustrations of research undertaken and observations made warrant consideration.

In general, research findings have supported the social facilitation hypothesis that an audience or co-workers enhance the performance of well-learned responses by increasing the individual's arousal or drive level but inhibit the learning of new responses. Although social facilitation research concerned with *complex motor performance and sport activities* is extremely limited, pertinent evidence supportive of social facilitation has been reported by Martens,[20] Martens and Landers,[21] Roberts and Martens,[30] and Singer.[33,34]

Because the social facilitation theory is based on the thesis of arousal, obviously the personality of the individual and related factors such as anxiety and skill-confidence influence the performer's reaction to an audience. Although the results of studies are contradictory, Sage offered a possible explanation, in keeping with Zajonc's generalization (an "audience enhances the emission of dominant responses") that wrong responses are dominant during early learning.[31] Thus, if an audience has arousal consequences for the performer, correct responses may be prevented in the presence of an audience whereas wrong responses are enhanced. Also, if one learner can benefit from the responses of another who may serve as a guide or model, as Zajonc stated, "the harmful effects of increased drive level might be diminished or even overcompensated for."[31] In short, it is possible that a highly skilled athlete with a high level of arousal, who is learning some new skill or performing a skill not yet well-learned, may do more poorly with an audience than a person of lower skill, who may not be anxious, and who may profit from the model or guidance of the highly skilled performer.

Research is very sparse and unclear concerning the effects of a verbal audience, either cheers or jeers, on sport performers. Empiric evidence, gleaned from amateurs to professional sport competitors, both male and female, leads to the general conclusion that spectators stimulate improved performances as well as cause complete disintegration of effort. Many factors may determine the effect of verbal remarks on the performer—the performer's experience with audiences, the type of audience (friend or foe), the personality of the performer (shy or show-off) the type of activity (easy or complex), the performer's estimation of herself, the respect she has for the judgment of the audience, whether her performance is being evaluated for critical purposes, and so forth.

An overall conclusion to the findings of research on social facilitation is that if the skill is not too difficult or just being learned most performers improve in the presence of an audience, because an audience increases the individual's arousal or drive which in turn enhances the "emission of dominant responses." The players who have highly developed skills, who are not easily distracted, and who are low in anxiety perform better in the presence of others, whereas highly anxious persons perform worse.

Some possible guidelines for the coach follow: During the initial stages of learning a skill, players may be isolated; however, if a player can learn from the responses of others, some form of group practice might be more profitable. The player should be provided with opportunities to perform in the presence of others as soon as possible after the skill has been learned, as frequently as possible, under many types of audience responses as possible (boos and cheers, evaluations), and for a variety of audiences (other outstanding performers and coaches, teammates, friends, mere observers). The information gleaned from the player's response to audience situations should be utilized as feedback for her improvement in further responses and as a basis for determining the extent to which she is prepared for competition. The presence of others could be used to spice up drills or training programs that may have become dreary, boring, and seemingly unproductive. Some nonthreatening audiences with whom she experiences self-esteem—success in her own achievement and in relationships with others—could be provided for the performer.

The findings from some research suggest that the efforts of a team may be dissipated if the team is too friendly, too close to one another socially.[7] Obviously, constant conflict among team members disrupts team effort, although some tension between the better performers and those who inhibit group effort may not be unhealthy. Teams must cooperate and concur, of course, which means having a "we" feeling, but the optimum condition for the best team effort appears to be when the group members are focused primarily on successful performance rather than on a need for affiliation.

In summary, actualizing performance potential and facilitating skill acquisition must be based upon appropriate motivation, even though it is not always possible to separate the techniques called "motivational" from those that are simply successful for some reason or another. Considerations that have been explored as leading to effort and performance results are those embodied in the athlete, the coach, and the environment or social situation. Self-esteem and the transfer of responsibility to self might be regarded as the measure of success of any technique. And, because motivation is very much a personal matter, techniques should be individualized for the athlete, rather than directed to anonymous groups, and should be something more than a permanent "addiction" for all coaches.

REFERENCES

1. Anonymous. Don't tell me I've got it made. *Reader's Digest*, April 1964, pp. 90-92.

2. Baley, J. A. Practical sportsmanship—a unique contribution of physical education and athletics. *The Physical Educator, 17*, 1960, p. 128.

3. Bandura, A. *Principles of Behavior Modification.* New York: Holt, Rinehart & Winston, 1969.

4. Borg, G. A. V. Physical performance and perceived exertion. *Lund Studies in Psychology and Education, 11*, 1962.

5. Borg, G., and Linderholm, H. Exercise performance and perceived exertion in patients with coronary insufficiency, arterial hypertension and vasoregulatory asthenia. *Acta Medica Scandinavica, 187*, 1970, pp. 17-26.

6. Coon, R. Sportsmanship, a worthy objective. *The Physical Educator, 21*, 1964, p. 16.

7. Cratty, B. J., and Sage, J. N. The effects of primary and secondary group interaction upon improvement in a complex motor task. *Research Quarterly, 35*, 1964, pp. 265-274.

8. Frankenhaeuser, M., Nordheden, B., Post, B., and Sjoeberg, H. Physiological and subjective reactions to different physical work loads. *Perceptual and Motor Skills, 28*, 1969, pp. 343-349.

9. Frost, R. Motivation for peak performance. Talk given to the Division of Men's Athletics at the American Association for Health, Physical Education and Recreation Annual Convention, Houston, Texas, March 24, 1972.

10. Frost, R. *Psychological Concepts Applied to Physical Education and Coaching.* Reading, Mass.: Addison-Wesley, 1971.

11. Gordon, A. Two words to avoid, two to remember. *Reader's Digest*, January 1968, pp. 53-56.

12. Haultain, A. *The Mystery of Golf.* New York: Serendipity Press, 1965.

13. Kroll, W., and Peterson, K. H. Study of values test and collegiate football teams. *Research Quarterly, 36,* 1965, pp. 441-447.

14. Lakie, W. L. Expressed attitudes of various groups of athletes toward competition. *Research Quarterly, 35,* 1964, p. 497.

15. Lansing, A. Words to live by. *The Arizona Republic,* date unknown.

16. Lawther, J. D. Sport Psychology. Englewood Cliffs, N.J.: Prentice-Hall, Inc., 1972.

17. Malumphy, T. M. Personality of women athletes in intercollegiate competition. *Research Quarterly, 39,* 1968, pp. 610-620.

18. Malumphy, T. M. Athletics and competition for girls and women. In *DGWS Research Reports: Women in Sports.* Dorothy V. Harris (Ed.). Washington, D.C.: American Association for Health, Physical Education and Recreation, 1971, pp. 15-19.

19. Mann, F. Players feel coaching pressures. *The Stanford Daily,* October 1, 1971, pp 1, 10.

20. Martens, R. Effect on performance of learning a complex motor task in the presence of spectators. *Research Quarterly, 40,* 1969, pp. 317-323.

21. Martens, R., and Landers, D. M. Coaction effects of a muscular endurance task. *Research Quarterly, 40,* 1969, pp. 733-737.

22. *The Need to Achieve.* Middleton, Conn.: Education Ventures, 1969.

23. Ogilvie, B., and Tutko, T. A. *Problem Athletes and How to Handle Them.* London: Pelham Books, 1966.

24. Olson, E. C. Individual rights for the coach. *Journal of Health, Physical Education and Recreation,* January 1970, p. 16.

25. Oxendine, J. B. Emotional arousal and motor performance. *Quest, XIII,* 1970, pp. 23-32.

26. Pease, D. A., Burlingame, M., and Locke, L. F. Athletic exclusion: A complex phenomenon. *Quest, XVI,* 1971, pp. 42-47.

27. Perrin, F. Dive for gold. *Creative Living.* Milwaukee: Northwestern Mutual Life Insurance Co., June-July 1972, pp. 9-11.

28. Reich, K. E. Stress-seeking: The unknown factor of human personality. *Sport Psychology Bulletin, 4,* The North American Society for the Psychology of Sport and Physical Activity, 1971, pp. 6-9.

29. Richardson, D. E. Ethical conduct in sports situations. Proceedings of the National College Physical Education Association for Men, 1963, pp. 66, 98-104.

30. Roberts, G. C., and Martens, R. Social reinforcement and complex motor performance. *Research Quarterly, 41,* 1970, pp. 175-181.

31. Sage, G. H. *Introduction to Motor Behavior: A Neuropsychological Approach.* Reading, Mass.: Addison-Wesley, 1971.

32. Shaw, D. Sport heroes: Do they adjust? *Los Angeles Times,* 1971.

33. Singer, R. N. Effect of spectators on athletes and non-athletes performing a gross motor task. *Research Quarterly, 36,* 1965, pp. 473-483.

34. Singer, R. N. Effect of an audience on performance of a motor task. *Journal of Motor Behavior, 2,* 1970, pp. 88-95.

35. Smith, M. New principles of teaching sports skills. *Proceedings of the First International Symposium on the Art and Science of Coaching,* October 1-5, 1971. Willowdale, Ontario, Canada: F. I. Productions, 1971.

36. Smith, W. S. One man's philosophy of coaching. *Journal of Health, Physical Education and Recreation*, October 1971, pp. 40-41.

37. Snyder, E. E. A study of selected aspects of the coach's influence on high school athletes. *The Physical Educator, 29*, 1972, pp. 96-98.

38. Sorochan, W. D. The violent world of the athlete. *California Association for Health, Physical Education and Recreation Journal*, September/October 1971, p. 24.

39. Thomas, V. *Science and Sport*. Boston: Little, Brown & Co. 1970.

40. Tutko, T. A. Some clinical aspects of sports psychology. *Quest, XIII*, 1970, pp. 12-17.

41. Wessel, J. A. *Movement Fundamentals: Figure, Form, Fun* (3rd ed.). Englewood Cliffs, N.J.: Prentice-Hall, Inc., 1970.

42. Wylic, I. A. R. I enjoy myself most when I'm scared. *Reader's Digest*, March 1963, pp. 77-80.

6. Exploring
Mechanical Principles

We must make greater efforts to . . . reduce the results to quantitative terms.

C. H. McCloy

Obviously, the teacher who is equipped with knowledge of mechanical principles is better able to analyze skills and to distinguish between principles basic to efficient movement and idiosyncrasies which characterize a performer's individual style than is the teacher who does not have this knowledge. An added consideration is that of the desirability of the learner to acquire such knowledge. Although research findings are somewhat inconclusive regarding the relative importance of verbalization in early learning, verbalization providing insight into the mechanical principles involved is believed to aid retention and to provide the more advanced performer with a frame of reference for her own skill improvement. And, although experienced sports performers display a variety of forms because they differ in physique and other qualities such as strength, underlying their utilization of the body's full potential is the effective use of mechanical principles. Certainly, at high levels of competition, techniques of improvement center around developing skills as mechanically perfect as possible.

The following section presents a brief discussion of some of the numerous principles concerned with controls over body movements with a few examples of their application to sports. This listing, however brief, may serve the coach and/or athlete to solve some performance problems or to analyze basic points of emphasis and continuities when attempting to develop higher performance levels.

The reader who is unfamiliar with the extent and importance of such principles should read in depth some of the excellent texts covering mechanical principles which are listed at the end of this chapter.[1-11]

FORCE AND MOTION

Production of Force—
Overcoming Inertia

A body at rest tends to remain at rest and a body in motion tends to remain in motion, with constant speed, in a straight line, unless acted upon by some force (Newton's first law). Examples of application are:

1. Overcoming inertia at the start of a motion requires the greatest amount of force.
    a. The crouch start in track, using the mechanically efficient large muscles of the legs and back, enables a runner to exert the horizontal force required to take off.
    b. The preliminary arm swing in the racing dive, the push-away motion of the ball from the body in bowling, and the rocking motion or off-balance receiving position in tennis enable a player to put the body in motion by a transfer of momentum from part to whole.
2. Overcoming inertia in order to change direction while in motion requires outside force applied in the direction of motion.
    a. A runner around a track oval or around softball bases leans toward the center of the arc to apply force to the outside of the arc.
    b. An ice skater continues to move essentially straight ahead until the blade is pushed to one side, causing the skater to move toward the opposite side.

Acceleration of Force—
Change in Speed

The greater the force applied to a body or object, the greater its speed (Newton's second law). Examples of application are:

1. A skater accelerates the rate of spin by bringing the arms close to the body.
2. A bowler gains momentum of the body through the approach steps, adding to it the momentum of the arm swing.
3. A volleyball spiker adds force to the jump by a preliminary run. A thrower obtains maximum speed in the throw by a run, hop, or by bringing more contributing parts of the body (transfer of weight, rotation, and arm action) into

the throw, which enables the momentum developed by the movement to be transferred to the object thrown.

4. A jumper is aided by a quick extension of the legs against the floor and a forceful arm swing.

Interaction of Forces— Action and Reaction

Every action (force) has an equal and opposite action (Newton's third law). Examples of application are:

1. The action of a gymnast contacting the bed of a trampoline and extending the legs rapidly causes the trampoline bed to react with greater depression followed by greater rebound than if this action is not used.
2. A runner pushing against starting blocks is propelled forward with a force equal and opposite the backward push.
3. A broad jumper swings the arms backward while the body is in the air to aid in swinging the legs forward.
4. A skier and a skater employ various actions and reactions of body parts to increase or decrease momentum in a given direction.
5. Objects striking a surface rebound at an angle equal to the angle of impact. A tennis ball carrying spin pushes backward (top spin) or forward (backspin) against the court. The equal and opposite force of the court is forward (top) or backward (chop) and the resultant of the two forces causes a lower angle (top) or higher bounce (chop) to the ball (see Projection, page 111, for further explanation).

Resultant of Forces and Conversion of Momentum

The magnitude and direction of force depend upon the resultant of the forces and the resistance and distance (duration) over which the force is applied. Examples of application are:

1. A high jumper or a basketball player on the lay-up shot converts the horizontal momentum of the run to vertical (upward) momentum by shifting the center of gravity (settling back) and forcefully lifting one knee.
2. A softball player utilizes the momentum of the catch to start the throwing movement.
3. After being hit a ball moves faster than the speed of the striking implement because of the reaction force produced by its push against the implement.

4. Force is magnified in throwing and striking (tennis, golf) by the accumulative effect of the body levers functioning in sequence from backswing to follow-through. Follow-through prevents slowing of the hand or implement and provides longer duration of contact with the object.

5. When spin or twist (tennis) or rebound (tennis and basketball) is involved, the ball moves in the direction of the resultant of the forces applied. The resultant forces of a chop stroke in tennis (force of the spinning ball pushing in a forward direction against the court and the rebound force of the court pushing backward against the ball) slow the ball and produce a higher bounce than that of the normal drive and a bounce that tends to move backward toward the player hitting the ball (see Projection, page 111, for further discussion).

Conservation of Momentum

When two or more objects collide with each other momentum is conserved. Examples of application are:

1. A golfer, softball batter, or tennis player contacting the ball in line with its center (center of gravity) produces linear (straight) motion and transfers momentum of the implement (and moving ball) to impart greater force to the ball (also see Conversion of Momentum, page 107).

2. Off-center contact of an object, resulting in rotary motion, imparts spin to the object, changes its direction, and reduces its speed (spin strokes in tennis and hooks and slices in golf).

Absorption of Force

Absorbing force involves increasing the distance and time over which the momentum (force) is reduced and increasing the area of the body receiving the force. Examples of application are:

1. A catcher uses a mitt to distribute the force of a ball over a larger area and gives with the throw to increase distance and time over which the force is absorbed.

2. When falling a skier throws the weight backward and uphill, body relaxed and flexed, absorbing force on legs, buttocks, back, and arms.

3. The base slider distributes force over as much area as possible.

4. When landing from a jump a jumper recoils downward

absorbing momentum by taking weight first on balls of feet, then ankles, knees, and hips in succession.

5. A volleyball server achieves more accuracy and absorbs more force by enlarging the area of the hand used for a striking surface.

LEVERAGE

In the production of force in sports, levers also are concerned. They are used to gain a mechanical advantage in order to convert a small force exerted over a great distance into a larger force over a lesser distance, or to gain speed which is also linked with gain in range of motion. Sport implements (bats, racquets, clubs) lengthen the body levers and increase the speed of the object being hit. Levers are used not only to move external objects but also to maintain body position or to move the body (see further discussion under Center of Gravity, below, and Projection, page 111). Examples of application are:

1. Most levers of the body are of the third-class type which are especially designed for speed and range of motion. A third-class lever has a long resistance arm and a short effort arm. The longer the resistance arm or lever (gripping a bat near the end of the handle, extending the arm in a throw or the leg in a kick, keeping the left arm straight in golf) up to a point, the greater the speed at the end of the lever. The shorter the resistance arm in proportion to the length of the effort arm (bent arm bowling delivery, batter's choke up on the bat, jump shot in basketball) the smaller the moment of force but the more immediate the action.

2. Total assembly of the system of levers working together provides a summation of forces that increases speed (throwing, kicking, striking movements employing sequential movements of the many segments of the body— the step forward, rotation of hips and shoulders, extension of the elbow, wrist, and fingers).

EQUILIBRIUM AND CENTER OF GRAVITY

Stability of the body is greater the lower the center of gravity, the wider its base of support, and the nearer its line of gravity falls to the center of the supporting base. Examples of application are:

1. A runner on her mark (get set position) leans forward, shifting the center of gravity toward the hands (nearer

the forward edge of the base of support) in order to
start quickly.

2. A tennis player in an active position of readiness places
   her weight well forward on the balls of the feet and as-
   sumes a more upright body position than that of a crouch
   in order to keep the center of gravity as high as possible
   and toward the edge of the supporting base.

3. In order to provide instability in a forward direction, a
   distance jumper puts the center of gravity well ahead of
   the feet at takeoff, making the base small in this direction.

4. A skier parries difficult terrain or avoids a possible fall by
   bending the knees and ankles to lower the body's center of
   gravity.

5. To stop quickly from a quick run (tennis, softball) a player
   widens the stride giving with the forward leg and moving
   the center of gravity backward and as low as is consistent
   with initiating following movements.

Stability of the body is maintained if the base of support is
widened in the direction of a force being given or received. Examples of application are:

1. Maintaining stability in the forceful motions of hitting a
   softball, tennis drive, golf drive, hockey drive, which are
   similar in weight transfer and length of backswing, requires a side-stride position that allows for the shifting of
   the center of gravity without the line of gravity falling
   outside the supporting base.

2. Maintaining balance in forceful motions of the overhand
   throw, tennis serve and smash, badminton clear and smash,
   which are essentially the same motions, requires a forward-
   backward stride in order to enlarge the supporting base in
   the direction of the force being applied.

3. In landing from a jump, balance is maintained by widening
   the base of support either forward-backward or sideward
   and lowering the center of gravity.

Greater force is transferred to a body or an object when the
force is applied in line with the center of gravity of the body or the
object. Examples of application are:

1. The jumper (basketball tie-balls or lay-up shot, volleyball
   spike) places the center of gravity over the feet in the
   desired direction of the straight upward jump.

2. In striking activities in which linear motion is desired (ten-

nis and hockey drives, volleyball serve, batting, putting, soccer kicking) contact is made in line with the object's center of gravity.

FRICTION AND RESISTANCE

Friction is the force opposing efforts to slide or roll one object over another. The coefficient of friction depends upon the speed and weight of objects and the nature and conditions of the rubbing surfaces. Starting friction is greater than moving or sliding friction (see Overcoming Inertia, page 106). In sports the effects of friction should be minimized in some instances and utilized in others. Some examples of applications are:

1. A golfer approaches and putts with a longer backswing for greens having long, wet grass (greater friction) than for hard, dry ones. A different type of play in tennis is necessitated on clay or grit, asphaltic combinations, cement, and wood court surfaces, each of which provides a different firmness and thus different rebounding force from slowest to fastest in the order listed.
2. A badminton shuttle falls more slowly (and almost straight downward) than does a tennis ball because of air resistance against the lighter shuttle, thus, requiring different timing of the strokes by the player.
3. More traction is provided by shoes with cleats, as used in golf, softball, track, which, by going into the ground, exert a firmer counterpressure of the ground against the feet than do shoes without cleats.
4. Hard waxes on skis for skiing on slushy snow lessen friction, thus providing a faster run. Tightening the grip at impact (golf, tennis) provides a firmer surface which aids in resisting the force of impact (also see Projection, below).

PROJECTION, SPIN, REBOUND

Projection

An object approaches the ground at approximately the same angle at which it was projected (arc of rise and fall describes a parabola). The projection angle depends upon the desired purpose (speed, distance, or both) and external factors such as air resistance which may modify the object's flight. Examples of application are:

1. Throwing: the softball or baseball throw for distance approaches the 45-degree angle, the optimum angle for maximum distance, because the horizontal and vertical components of force are equal in the absence of air resistance.
2. Basketball goal shooting: a 58-degree projection may be best because vertical drop is needed.
3. Projecting the body through space also necessitates an integration between speed and angle—a high jumper must project the body higher than 45 degrees in order to clear the bar; the hurdler loses time by elevating herself; the base slider loses time by leaping into the slide.
4. Flight path of object: air pressure increases as speed increases and the more air resistance the more the flight path of the object departs from a true parabola—a golfer projects the ball at a much lower angle than 45 degrees because of its speed and resultant air pressure. Because of its weight the flight of the badminton shuttlecock is affected considerably by air pressure, thus the badminton player uses a forceful hit on the high clear to achieve depth because the shuttle is light and force is overcome by air pressure long before gravity pulls the shuttle downward.

Spin

When force is applied off-center, an object is projected through the air with considerable speed, air resistance builds up on the side where the spin force is applied and is reduced on the opposite side, and the object moves in the direction of least resistance. Examples of application are:

1. Because the ball builds up air resistance on the top and consequently moves forward and downward faster, a top spin (forward) tennis drive is effective for deep drives, for ensuring accuracy of drives and in preventing opponent's offensive play at the net (the ball travels lower across the net than does the chop or backspin ball which, because air resistance is built up under and behind it, moves upward and tends to remain or float in the air longer).
2. Because a golf ball hit with the hook shot spins counterclockwise, it travels farther than one hit with the slice which spins clockwise.
3. Because a golf ball hit with the pitch shot carries backspin, it travels upward in a high arc and tends to stop or sit rather than to roll forward when it lands on the green.

Rebound

The force and angle of rebound vary with the angle of impact, the speed of the moving object, the object's elasticity, and the resistance of the rebounding surface. Examples of application are:

1. In the basketball lay-up shot, made without spin from the sides of the basket, the ball is projected to a spot above and to the near side of the basket because it rebounds at an angle equal to that at which it strikes (the closer to the basket the shot is made, the nearer the spot to the basket; the closer to the sideline the shot is made, the farther the spot from the basket).

2. The rebound of a ball carrying spin, as in tennis, is the resultant of the equal and opposite forces of normal rebound force and spin force; the rebound is in the direction of spin. Top or over spin causes a longer rebound. The ball pitches sharply toward the receiver at a lower angle than normal; or at the same height as that of a no-spin ball if it carries equal forward force; or higher than a no-spin ball if it carries greater force and thus it approaches the court surface at a higher angle. Backspin or underspin or chop causes a shorter rebound. The ball seems to stop, the rebound is more upward than normal or more backward toward the player hitting it if the ball is spinning rapidly; sidespin or slice causes a rebound to the side on which spin was applied and at normal rebound height if the forces are equal.

3. If the tennis surface offers great resistance (e.g., grass as opposed to cement) or if the ball has little elasticity (too soft to resume its shape), force is lessened and the rebound is slower and lower than normal.

ELASTICITY

The degree of restitution of an object and/or the striking implement (coefficient of elasticity or its ability to return to its original shape from the flattening effect of impact) affects the directional speed and angle of the object as it rebounds from the implement. Examples of application are:

1. Loose strings in a tennis racquet and improperly inflated balls modify the angle and slow the rebound of the ball because the force is dissipated as the ball pushes back the strings or pushes against the floor or the hand or the foot.

2. If a golf ball does not return to shape following compression (such as with some old balls or such as may be the case with the liquid center balls which require considerable force to compress), force is dissipated and does not contribute to speed.

The foregoing examples do not exhaust all the possible applications to sport skills of mechanical principles and laws that govern motion. They may serve to demonstrate the importance that efficient motion occupies in skillful performance and to illustrate a logical framework that both coach and athlete can use to analyze skills, to diagnose difficulties, and to select effective techniques for improving performance.

Other sources which may be sought for further tools of analyses are described in the following chapter.

REFERENCES

1. Broer, M. R. *An Introduction to Kinesiology.* Englewood Cliffs, N.J.: Prentice-Hall, Inc., 1968.

2. Broer, M. R. *Efficiency of Human Movement* (3rd ed.). Philadelphia: W. B. Saunders Co., 1973.

3. Cooper, J. M., and Glassow, R. B. *Kinesiology* (3rd ed.). St. Louis: C. V. Mosby Co., 1972.

4. Dyson, G. *The Mechanics of Athletics* (5th ed.). London: University of London Press, 1970.

5. Hay, J. G. *The Biomechanics of Sports Techniques.* Englewood Cliffs, N.J.: Prentice-Hall, Inc., 1973.

6. Johnson, W. R. *Science and Medicine of Exercise and Sports.* New York: Harper & Brothers, 1972.

7. Rasch, P. J., and Burke, R. *Kinesiology and Applied Anatomy* (4th ed.). Philadelphia: Lea & Febiger, 1971.

8. Scott, M. G. *Analysis of Human Motion: A Textbook in Kinesiology* (2nd ed.). New York: Appleton-Century-Crofts, 1963.

9. Steindler, A. *Kinesiology of the Human Body.* Springfield, Ill.: Charles C Thomas, 1970.

10. Wells, K. *Kinesiology* (5th ed.). Philadelphia: W. B. Saunders Co., 1971.

11. Williams, M., and Lissner, H. *Biomechanics of Human Motion.* Philadelphia: W. B. Saunders Co., 1962.

7. Harnessing Technologic Assistance to Analyze Performance

. . . one who knows just how to mix the pigments of his many disciplines in a proper proportion.

Arthur Steinhaus

Technologic hardware actually consists of a number of devices, including the traditional audiovisual media, as well as newer media, and new developments in the use of such devices. Movies, filmstrips, display boards, demonstrations, and so forth, whose function is primarily to impart visual information to the performer, have been discussed in Chapter 4. Some further categories of technologic assistance include television, programmed materials, computer-aided diagnostic and prescriptive devices, and a variety of self-instructional aids packaged in various multimedia forms.

POTENTIALS AND PITFALLS

The ability to capture, generate, transmit, duplicate, replicate, manipulate, store, and retrieve multimedia information has reached the point where the typical teacher (and coach) not only is hard pressed to comprehend the various media, but also realizes that there are dangers in the misuse and abuse of such media. As one reviews the literature dealing with technologic innovations in education, she is at once impressed with both good and bad assessments. These innovations are sometimes expected to do the entire job of teaching or to serve as a panacea for the treatment of all problems. They cost more than conventional methods and place heavy demands on the teacher because of the preparation needed. Despite these criticisms, they can be used imaginatively and serve effectively as "second teachers." They are, in fact, as inevitable as are the new approaches to learning. Teachers of physical education and coaches of sport activities should continue to be challenged by the possibilities that technologic aids provide for finding out how their own methods of instruction and the player's performance can be improved.

TELEVISION

Instructional television seems to serve two primary objectives: *instructor multiplication* and *image magnification*.[4] To the disappointment of enthusiasts, however, instructional television has not produced noticeable improvement in learning. Students apparently learn as much from live instruction as from television. Charles Silberman, in his book *Crisis in the Classroom,* noted, however, that perhaps one reason television has had marginal effectiveness is that it has not been used imaginatively, but rather "as a pipeline carrying the same dull curriculum via the same dull lectures."[16]

Television, insofar as the teaching of sports is concerned, has been primarily in the form of instant playback of a performance monitored on videotape. Instant reply of the performance on videotape can be an effective means of providing the performer as well as the coach an on-the-spot opportunity to analyze performance and improve perception. It has a built-in capacity for feedback—the knowledge gained reinforces learning and contributes to meaningful practice. The equipment consists of a videotape recorder (stationary or portable) and a playback screen (monitor) or television set. Many portable systems are available. The same tape may be re-used several times. In general, videotaping is considered to be a rather simple procedure. But, as with any other form of instructional television, failure awaits the user who has little understanding of this medium. It is not merely a new gadget. Videotape is not cheap film, and with any equipment one can count on exasperating mechanical flaws such as short-lived batteries, tape snagging during recording, handles or straps breaking, tape dropout. Editing presents problems, too, if one is a perfectionist. It is helpful to have a good engineering friend. In order to be used more effectively, one should plan specific objectives to be accomplished in any given session.

PROGRAMMED INSTRUCTION

Programs of instruction that teach by conditioning are not new, being rooted as they are in the history of education itself. B. F. Skinner, however, is credited with calling the attention of educators to the possibilities inherent in programmed instruction. Within the past decade programs and machines that teach have been used successfully at all levels of student ability and with a variety of verbal and manual skills, and, although programming depends for its effect upon some type of psychologic conditioning, some psychologists have demonstrated that programs can teach by "discovery" as well as by the usual kinds of conditioning.

The essential characteristic of programmed instruction incorporated in the many types of teaching machines and programmed texts is the idea of presenting the learner with a logically ordered sequence of small steps progressing successively closer to the desired objectives while providing immediate reinforcement or feedback after each step. What the program should consist of, in order for optimum learning to take place, is still a question unanswered conclusively by research evidence. Nonetheless, programming does offer some promising leads for individualizing instruction. By turning the skills teaching, the routine work, over to programs the teacher may be freed for guiding the process of discovery. At the same time, programs of autoinstruction ensure at least a minimum amount of practice, enabling the learner to work on her own and at her own rate without the constant aid of a teacher.[15]

The potential and use of programming in sport activities have not been fully explored as yet. Materials to be programmed have centered primarily on cognitive operations. A review of selected research on prepackaged sports skills instruction revealed that for some purposes programmed instruction may be at least as effective as traditional methods of instruction, particularly in those closed skills (e.g., gymnastics and golf) in which achievement is based on relatively constant performance criteria.[7] An interesting research finding is that, in several of the programmed instruction studies, instructors merely observed rather than took an active part in the students' learning experiences, despite the fact that programmed materials are used more effectively as a supplement to instruction than as a substitute for the instructor. The instructor needs to be thoroughly conversant with the subject matter and skillful in the construction of programmed materials. Materials should contain clear descriptions of the skills to be performed and the performance criteria for progression.[7]

Perhaps the new kind of learning choreography in which *performance objectives*—described variously as behavioral, operational, accountability, information objectives—which have generated a lot of interest, may be considered as a type of programmed instruction. For example, emphasis may be placed on organized sequential performance progressions with important skill goals identified at every level as contrasted to miscellaneous programs of practice. The performer knows what is expected and has the opportunity to pro-

gress at her own rate through tasks that increase in small incre-
ments of difficulty. For interesting discussions on behavioral or
performance objectives, the teacher is encouraged to read Mager[8]
and Plowman.[12]

Some specific situations in which programming is feasible are:

1. Knowledge areas such as strategies, rules, history and
   events, mechanical and physiologic principles;

2. Routine or regular practice drills of isolated skills—basketball goal shooting, tennis drives against backboard;

3. Activities characterized by a predictable step-by-step sequence of events, such as archery (stance, address, nock,
   draw, aim, release, hold), gymnastics, track and field
   events (Oxendine suggests a hypothetical program for
   teaching high-jumping techniques[10]);

4. Activities in which mechanical devices and machines may
   be available for practice drills such as tennis ball boy (program of drives down-the-line, drives cross-court, alternate
   drives down-the-line with cross-court, alternate drives with
   volleys, and the like);

5. Information that must be memorized such as basketball or
   volleyball plays or variations according to different situations confronting the player.

These suggestions, and others that the imaginative instructor
may devise, can assist the individual, particularly in the early
stages of learning new material, to proceed at her own rate through
a series of step-by-step sequences in a progressive cumulative manner. Thus, some of the hazards of learning plateaus, limited facilities, and large groups of students with varying levels of skill may
be avoided. Some programs may be arranged for prior-to-class
sessions and as take-home materials.

SELF-INSTRUCTIONAL AIDS

A variety of self-instructional aids are not programmed in the
manner of teaching machines or programmed textbooks. Some require new ways of using instructional talent and resources as well
as changes in allocating physical facilities and scheduling instruction time. The performer may plug in various forms of instruction
according to her individual needs.

Mechanical Training Devices. Mechanical devices such as
automatic tennis ball throwing machines, tennis rebounding nets,
suspended ball apparatus for serving, batting tees, and Golf-O-

Tron, which simulates actual playing conditions, are indicative of the many aids available for the development of skill beyond the typical group practice situation. They may facilitate learning because they offer novel conditions and because they allow individuals to concentrate attention on key movements and receive immediate knowledge of results. They may accelerate improvement more especially for the highly skilled performer.

Listening and Viewing Devices. Cooper transcribed the sounds made by competitive sports performers from a tape recorder to musical scores, and these sounds were used to help beginners learn supposedly correct movements at the proper rate and with proper emphases.[3] Numerous teachers use music to affect the performer's patterns of motion and rhythm (e.g., the waltz tempo coincides with the rhythmic 6-count of the tennis service). Although the value of such techniques is not conclusive, music or other induced sounds interspersed during practice sessions may improve motivation by stimulating a positive attitude and by decreasing boredom when skills must be repeatedly performed. Of course, noise can be a distracting condition which results in more errors or lessened precision when the noise is of high level and high frequency.

PHOTOGRAPHY

Photography in sports is a reality medium, sharper than words. Perhaps for this reason photography in sport is best in the hands of skilled amateurs who make the pictures frank, informative, and thoroughly tied to the sport. Instructional use of photography, however, requires not only knowledge of sports but of photographic techniques and instrumentation as well. Good beginner's books are available that cover camera, printing, film, photojournalism and provide good practical information (*Life Library of Photography*, Time-Life, 4200 N. Industrial Blvd., Indianapolis, Indiana 46254).

The variable-speed sequence-action Graph-Check Polaroid Camera is an easy-to-use instrument which does offer a relatively uncomplicated means of providing immediate feedback of performance for purposes of analysis. Images of eight sequential positions of the performer are recorded on one Polaroid print by this still camera. Such film techniques make it possible to produce a picture of the sequence of a total movement (such as the whole golf swing). Although filming for research purposes may be beyond the scope of the coach, the coach can collect films and utilize them for some analysis. Simple "eyeball" evaluations of film may show gross patterns—sequencing of movements, range of motion, angular positions of limbs—and irregularities that may decrease effective application of force. This technique also may be used advantageously in gathering data regarding position of impact (e.g., racquet contact with the ball in the tennis serve), and angular forces that contribute to or detract from ball speed.

Loop films and the more recent innovation of the 8mm *cartridge film loops* have been used extensively by coaches and many are available on the market. The cartridge film loop provides the advantage of isolating a specific skill or group of skills on a single loop. The cartridge may be easily placed in the projector to be reviewed by the athlete or coach as many times as desired.

Push-button motion analysis is available to coaches in many of the 8mm or 16mm *movie cameras* and projectors on the market. In many camera models, a power zoom lens delivers sweeping wide angles and close-up telephoto shots which can provide valuable playing cues, particularly in the team sports. There is a variety of films on the market to accommodate every lighting situation on the field or in the gym. Projectors equipped to stop action at a crucial instant in a play and keep the action going a frame at a time to show players in every detail enable the viewer to get the most out of a movie sport analysis program. Stop action may be operated by a remote control button or be coded to stop automatically. The Kodak Analyst Projector (Eastman Kodak Company, Department 640, 343 State Street, Rochester, New York 14650), for example, which was designed and perfected by coaches for coaches, enables the operator to flip a switch and repeat any part of a film as many times as desired. A variable-speed switch permits moving rapidly through unimportant footage or slowing down to dissect critical action.

CINEMATOGRAPHY AND RELATED TOOLS

Effective analysis of sports skills usually cannot be made during the actual playing situation, but necessitates isolating skills from the game and studying them in a laboratory situation. *Cinematography* and *electromyography* have been used increasingly and effectively as tools of analysis. The collecting and analyzing of data from films are laborious and time-consuming. Indeed, the average coach should be grateful that there are excellent materials made available through the diligent work of expert researchers in this area.[14] By combining anatomic data with principles of mechanics and data-collecting equipment, it is now possible to obtain a great deal of information about complex patterns of human motion, such as those which occur in sports activities.

Following the lead of Ruth B. Glassow at the University of Wisconsin and Thomas K. Cureton at the University of Illinois, who first stimulated work in this area of kinesiology, many persons have contributed to the development of kinesiology analysis of human motion. The following brief presentation is not intended to document the vast amount of literature in this area, nor is it intended to give a thorough description of the types of equipment and their uses for the purpose of providing the coach with a handy, practical tool. Although the techniques described have simplified analysis of motion and will continue to bring major changes in ways of quantifying human motion data, these programs are not presently practical for everyday use in the analysis of sports activities. Prerequisite to the complete understanding of these various instruments is at least a basic knowledge of anatomy, kinesiology, physics, and trigonometry. The purpose of this brief treatment is to provide an overview of the technologic means available to the teacher/coach and to present some of the language of areas of study pertinent to sports performance.

Within recent years the term "biomechanics," according to Nelson, has emerged as the most "widely acceptable as the descriptive label for anatomical and mechanical analysis of sport skills," although a variety of terms, including "anthropo-mechanics," "biodynamics," "biokinetics," "biomechanics," "kinanthropology," "kinetics," "mechanical kinesiology," in addition to the more traditional "kinesiology," have been used to identify that area of study defined loosely as the science of movement of the body.[9] The results of research in these variously related areas have been applied to such related disciplines as aerospace science, industrial engineering, medicine, rehabilitation, and sports.

Biomechanicians of sports, with the help of engineers and photographic and electronic technicians, have employed various techniques and instrumentation systems for recording and analyzing the data of sports movements. Stroboscopic-photographic techniques, which provide for multiple-image photographs of the body in motion, have been used to analyze the characteristics of rapid movement. More complete descriptions of movement have been provided by cinematography, which utilizes high-speed movie cameras for filming; film analyzers for obtaining angular and linear measurements and frame count; and the digital computer which has been used not only for the computational phase of movement analysis, but also for the simulation of sports movements observed in graphic displays. Combinations of techniques—cinematography, electromyography, electrogoniometry, and others—have provided even more information than is possible with one type of recording system. As

Nelson pointed out, unlimited potential for study is offered in the comparatively new techniques of "utilization of mathematical modeling, computer simulation and graphic techniques which make it possible to alter the biomechanical components of sport skills and observe the effects on the execution of the movement."[9]

Electromyography (EMG) is a method of recording, on graph paper or an oscilloscope, the force of muscular contraction during a movement from surface electrodes or from embedded thin wire electrodes placed as near as possible to the motor unit controlling the muscle. The advances in telemetry now make it possible to take readings of movement beyond the confines of the laboratory, although electromyography is still considered as being difficult to do and limited in the number of movements that can be analyzed by the equipment. The equipment and methods of interpretation of data are carefully presented in the works of Basmajian.[2]

Electrogoniometry, which involves wire attachments and laboratory set-up and thus limitations similar to those of electromyography, provides the advantage of obtaining fast and continuous recording of angular changes during a simple three-dimensional movement (e.g., elbow angle during the crawl, knee angle during the soccer kick). Ricci described this equipment and its use.[13]

High-speed motion pictures make it possible to analyze a vast number of motions under actual performance conditions and to deal with problems of friction, ball spin, and the like, because the time of impact of colliding objects can be measured. Several cameras may be used to obtain simultaneous records from different angles and thus permit data collection in three dimensions. Some researchers, Atwater for example, have effectively utilized and strongly advocated the three-dimensional approach in analyzing sports skills.[1] Plagenhoef described the techniques of cinematography and gave a detailed presentation of the problems, techniques involved, and advantages.[11]

COMPUTER-AIDED DEVICES

In recent years perhaps one of the most promising developments in the measurement and analysis of performance has resulted from *computer-aided devices.* Research investigators now use the high-speed computer to reduce drastically the laborious and time-consuming hand analysis technique which required the tracing of motion pictures frame by frame. Basically, the use of the computer to assist with the mechanical analysis of cinematographic records of human motion involves merely locating body joints on x and y coordinates of a film frame then feeding the location of these points to a computer that automatically calculates segmental and overall

body centers of gravity during movement. Angular and linear velocities of body segments also can be determined in this manner.
Thus, data from film frames can be put into a computer and stick
figures that duplicate the original frames are instantly available
in graphic form, displayed on a console screen. The system shows
continuous motion either of the entire body or of any desired segments.[6]

Currently, researchers are working on numerous refinements
and further possibilities of study across many disciplines.[5] Computer programs are being used to obtain massive amounts of information relating angular velocities and accelerations, forces, joint
moments of force, centers of gravity, and contributions of each
body segment to the total motion—data which now may be more
practical in their application to the teaching of specific sports. (See
Chapter 8 for description of studies concerning the lift-off thrust
in jumping.) In addition, special problems related to body or equipment impact, ball spin, aerodynamics, fluid dynamics, and so forth
may be computerized. This way of applying mathematical representation to the human body and of using it for analysis of events
and predictions of the future offers numerous possibilities for facilitating meaningful detailed studies in sport performance as well as
in all areas of human development.

What is the value of all this to the coach? Well, for one thing,
coaches would not be limited to guesswork based on personal data
—the "it worked for me" approach to performance. Then, too,
coaches may seek the aid of the biomechanician in order to help identify performance flaws and to indicate ways of overcoming them
just as they seek the aid of a physician, trainer, and psychologist.
Because greater emphasis is being placed on the direct application of
research in biomechanics, coaches may become knowledgeable ap-
pliers themselves. Too many coaches still dispute the findings of
research which they dismiss as purely theoretical. For example,
Atwater's research related to the overhand throw refutes much of
what is still being taught as absolute performance criteria by the
baseball coach. From a cinematographic analysis of throwing, Atwater found that subjects with the fastest ball velocity at release
were those with the most rapid sequential acceleration of trunk
and arm segment prior to release.[1] It is generally believed that the
thrower gradually accelerates the ball until release, whereas Atwater's study shows that the ball does not accelerate rapidly until
the last 0.10 second before release.

Eventually the pooling of research by experts in biomechanics
of sport, as well as by experts in diverse yet related disciplines of
neuroanatomy, mechanical engineering, biophysics, electromy-

ographic kinesiology, computer science, bioelectronics, and other areas, will lead to a much greater understanding and even programming of successful sport performance. Not only will the research tell the coach why a performer *was* successful but will show ways to improve future performance by devising better theoretical techniques and implementing them in the training program. Meanwhile, and until sophisticated techniques and instrumentation for film analysis become more practical for the coach to use, it may be possible to purchase or borrow prepared videotapes or slow-motion films. Thus, the coach could take advantage of this approach to analyzing sports skills.

REFERENCES

1. Atwater, A. E. Movement characteristics of the overarm throw: A kinematic analysis of men and women performers. (Doctoral dissertation, The University of Wisconsin), Madison, Wis., 1970.
2. Basmajian, J. V. *Muscles Alive—Their Functions Revealed by Electromyography.* Baltimore: The Williams & Wilkins Co., 1962.
3. Cooper, J. M., and Glassow, R. B. *Kinesiology* (3rd ed.). St. Louis: C. V. Mosby Co., 1972.
4. Ely, D. Facts and fallacies about new media in education. In *Revolution in Teaching.* Alfred de Grazia and David A. Sahn (Eds.). New York: Bantam Books, 1964, pp. 42-50.
5. Galton, L. A new way to display — and research — human development. *Backgrounder,* Purdue University Schools of Engineering, November 1968.
6. Garrett, R. E., Garrett, G. E., and Widule, C. J. Computer-aided research in kinesiology. Paper presented at the American Association for Health, Physical Education and Recreation Convention, Las Vegas, Nevada, March 1967.
7. Locke, L. F. Prepackaged sports skills instruction: A review of selected research. *Journal of Health, Physical Education and Recreation,* September 1971, pp. 57-59.
8. Mager, R. F. *Preparing Instructional Objectives.* Palo Alto, Calif.: Fearon, 1962.
9. Nelson, R. C. Biomechanics of sport: An overview. *Proceedings of the C.I.C. Symposium on Biomechanics,* Indiana University, October 19-20, 1970. Chicago: The Athletic Institute, 1971.
10. Oxendine, J. B. *Psychology of Motor Learning.* New York: Appleton-Century-Crofts, 1968.
11. Plagenhoef, S. *Patterns of Human Motion, A Cinematographic Analysis.* Englewood Cliffs, N.J.: Prentice-Hall, Inc., 1971.
12. Plowman, P. D. *Behavioral Objectives.* Chicago: Science Research Associates, 1971.
13. Ricci, B. *Physiological Basis of Human Performance.* Philadelphia: Lea & Febiger, 1967.
14. Roberts, E. An introduction to cinematography. *Proceedings of the C.I.C. Symposium on Biomechanics,* Indiana University, October 19-20, 1970. Chicago: The Athletic Institute, 1971.
15. Schramm, W. Programmed instruction today and tomorrow. In *Programmed Instruction.* Arthur Foshay, et al. (Eds.). Washington, D.C.: Office of Education, United States Government, 1964.
16. Silberman, C. E. *Crisis in the Classroom.* New York: Random House, 1970.

8. Analyzing and Assessing Athletic Potential

We don't know one millionth of one percent about anything.

Thomas Alva Edison

Within recent years, laboratory testing of sports potential
has greatly mushroomed. Large groups of athletes are processed
in laboratories and information which hopefully will enlighten the
coach and predict ultimate success of the performer is being
discovered.

PHYSIOLOGIC AND BIOMECHANICAL FACTORS

The new facts, skills, and techniques being uncovered, particularly in the field of running physiology, have provided better understanding not only of the performance levels in running but also of
methods of physiologic testing and their meaning to the individual.
A special feature section of *Runner's World* gives a broad picture
of tests being used by a number of specialists in exercise physiology
to uncover ways to make running safer and the runner faster.[11]
Assessments being made in laboratories throughout the country
include a variety of tests for evaluating the areas of cardiopul-
monary function: oxygen uptake (maximum oxygen consumption
rate), vital capacity (amount of air that can be moved in and out
of the lungs), maximum breathing capacity (strength and endurance of the respiratory muscles), hemoglobin content (capacity of
the blood to carry oxygen), stroke volume of the heart (pumping
ability of the heart), minute volume (amount of blood pumped in
one minute). Appraisals also are being made of other factors
affecting performance including body composition (bone-muscle-fat
relationships), body fluids (the problems of dehydration, overheat-
ing, circulatory strain, electrolyte imbalance), and certain aspects
of motor fitness such as strength, muscular endurance, and flexibility.

In most instances, however, the coach does not have easy access to laboratory facilities or the expensive equipment which may be desirable for assessing athletic potential. Although physiologists caution that most self-testing methods outside the controlled conditions and apparatus of the laboratory are inaccurate and often misleading, it is acknowledged that "physical feedback is too important to stay in isolated testing centers."[11] Some factors that can be self-tested fairly objectively and with reasonable accuracy are oxygen intake and percentage of body fat.

Oxygen Intake.   A self-test of oxygen intake, devised by Bruno Balke and provided by Jack Daniels in the publication *Runner's World,*[11] is as follows: run as far as possible in 15 minutes, record the distance in meters (1 mile = 1609.334 meters), divide the total metric distance by 15 to determine speed in meters per second, compute maximum oxygen intake using the formula (speed − 133) × 0.172 + 33.3. A level of 40 is considered a minimum standard of fitness, depending on age, although, as Daniels warns, the formula may underestimate or overestimate aerobic capacity for some people. Even casual joggers tend to score higher than 40, and increased aerobic training adds to this capacity as does lowered body fat.

Body Fat Level.   Average mature women have 25 to 30 per cent body fat which is usually about 10 per cent more than men have and which, when translated into extra weight, has a limiting effect on most types of athletic performance. Body fat is tested in the laboratory by weighing people underwater. Ned Frederick devised a mathematical method of measuring a runner's fat content which may be used in a simplified self-testing program.[11] Although he admitted that at best the method gives figures that vary about 2 per cent on either side of actual figures, it does provide an estimate of body composition. It is most accurate for individuals with average bone structure and proportions and least accurate for extremely lanky or portly persons. Anyone with more than 10 per cent body fat as calculated from Figure 1 might be expected to improve at least running performance by reducing fat level.

Sufficient data have not been accumulated to be able to decide the relative importance of various factors in the evaluation of athletic endeavors. Moreover, researchers may not be in agreement about the validity of certain measures. For example, the results of several investigations seem to be in general agreement that the use of such tests as vertical jump and reach, standing broad jump, and sprints designed to measure and predict leg power does not seem to be justified.[1] Some researchers have reported that the Harvard step test is a better predictor of performance than is the maximum oxygen intake test.[7] In the Harvard step test not only the speed of

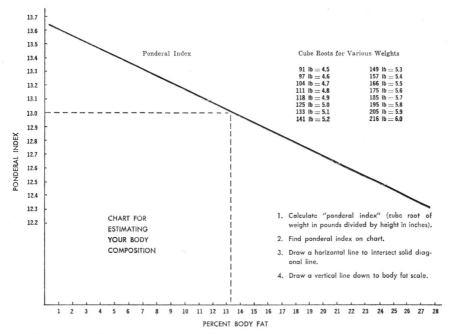

Figure 1. Chart for estimating body composition. (Courtesy of Frederick, N. Simplified self-testing plan. In "What goes on inside." *Runner's World*, Box 336, Mountain View, Calif., February 1973, pp. 10-25.)

recovery is important but also the ability to sustain the arduous effort of stepping for a period of five minutes. Poorly motivated subjects give up before the allotted five minutes.

The Harvard step test, which reportedly satisfies many of the necessary conditions for a good fitness test, is simple to use with large numbers and requires relatively little equipment. Because the 20-inch bench may be a limiting factor, however, A. W. Sloan suggested decreasing the bench height to 17 inches. For the Sloan modified step test the subject steps up and down (one foot at a time) at the rate of 30 steps per minute (up and down every two seconds) for a total period of five minutes, or until unable to continue the exercise. Following exercise the pulse rate is counted three times in 30-second periods (1 to 1½ minutes; 2 to 2½ minutes; 3 to 3½ minutes). The base of the neck is the easiest place to locate the pulse following exercise. The Fitness Index (F.I.) is computed by the formula:

$$\text{F.I.} = \frac{\text{duration of exercise in seconds} \times 100}{2 \times (\text{sum of pulse counts in recovery})}$$

The F.I. may be interpreted from the following standards: above 90—excellent; 80 to 89—good; 56 to 79—average; below 55—poor.

Some simplified means at the disposal of the coach may be used in order to assess such basic aspects of fitness as strength and flexibility, as well as factors such as balance, agility, coordination, and the like, which may play a role in superior performance. I found that balance, for example, is a differentiating factor between high- and low-skilled performers.[5] Scores on the Bass stick test of static balance, made by men and women champion and near-champion performers in basketball, fencing, gymnastics, volleyball, and swimming, were substantially higher than those made by low-skilled performers. Although it was not determined whether the superior athletes already had the ability to balance or whether they developed it in the process of training and competing, nonetheless, the ability to balance does characterize the skilled athlete. Measures of balance, therefore, would seem to have some merit as a predictor of athletic ability, particularly in those sports requiring balance. A test of static balance is easy to administer and requires little equipment. The performer stands on one foot placed lengthwise on a stick, 1 inch wide, 1 inch high, and 12 inches long, with eyes open and attempts to balance as long as possible up to six minutes (one minute at a time, then a rest). The test is repeated with the performer standing crosswise on the stick.

Textbooks that offer basic definitions, laboratory procedures, and methods for evaluating the multiple facets of fitness including physiologic parameters and sports competency that may be used by any coach in typical school situations are available.[2,4,10]

Another area of concern in the assessment of athletic endeavors and potential is that of the mechanical aspects of performance. The emergence of biomechanics of sports and the application of knowledges from fields such as biophysics, computer science, engineering, mathematics, and neuroanatomy are of considerable significance in providing more precise data and in gaining new insights into athletic potential. As one illustration Melvin Ramey, a civil engineering professor, is conducting studies in human ballistics with a Statos electrographic recorder which instantly produces a permanent graph of the lift-off thrust exerted during only one-tenth of a second.[6] The instrument is being used to answer questions such as: Why one athlete jumps farther than another? With this instrument, which is applicable to many sports and events in which running and jumping play a key role, research may aid the coach in predicting potential and in helping each athlete reach the potential. Precise measurements of each component and event will indicate the levels of strength that should be attained, how strong the take-off leg must be, or how much speed is needed on the run, or, on the basis of findings, some individuals may or may not be encouraged to train for certain events. Further discussion of computer-aided programs is presented in Chapter 7.

PERSONALITY PARAMETERS

Not all questions concerning the potential for superior performance can be answered by physiologic and biomechanical assessments. Some psychologists contend that personality ultimately makes the difference in performance potential. Studies of personality characteristics of athletes have been intended to help answer such predictive questions as: How will athletes react under the pressures of competition and can such reactions be predicted? How can the coach give careful guidance in directing the athletes' estimations of their potential and in improving skill performance? Will certain personality factors influence success in specific sport activities? What are the participants' attitudes toward athletic competition? By having some knowledge of the athlete's reason for participation and the personality factors that enhance or detract from effective performance, the coach may be better able to handle the athlete as well as to influence performance levels.

Kenyon developed a series of scales for assessing attitude toward physical activity.[3] He attempted to include independent scales that would determine attitudes toward social experience, health and fitness, pursuit of vertigo, aesthetic experience, catharsis, ascetic experience. The construction and use of such scales seem to be out of the range of most coaches and teachers. Kenyon himself stated that the use of such scales should be restricted to research purposes. The value of this research, however, may be in the definitions presented of the term "attitude," and in the difficulties and possibilities of measuring attitude on a broader scope.

An Athletic Motivation Inventory (AMI) was developed at the Institute for the Study of Athletic Motivation at San Jose State College. Thomas Tutko, codirector of the Institute, reported that several salient traits influencing athletic productivity have been revealed by the tests. The traits fall into two major categories: desire and emotionality. Desire is made up of the traits of drive, aggression, determination, leadership, and organization. Emotionality involves the traits of coachability, self-confidence, emotional maturity, conscience development, trust, guilt proneness, and mental toughness.[8]

Additional research cited in Chapter 2, Dimensions of the Athlete, will be of further interest to the coach in estimating what the vital personality components to high level athletic achievement may be. Such information as characteristics of pain tolerance, for example, may provide clues to predicting performance levels.

INTERRELATIONSHIPS OF SEVERAL ASPECTS

Miroslav Vanek, of the University of Charles in Prague, Czechoslovakia, although stating that the psychologic approach should be respected as the crucial key for performance capacity, acknowledged that the potential for superior performance depends upon several conditions, including equipment, condition, skills, techniques, tactics, and training methods.[9] Vanek presented Figures 2 and 3 to describe the interrelationships that are important for the realization of top level performance.

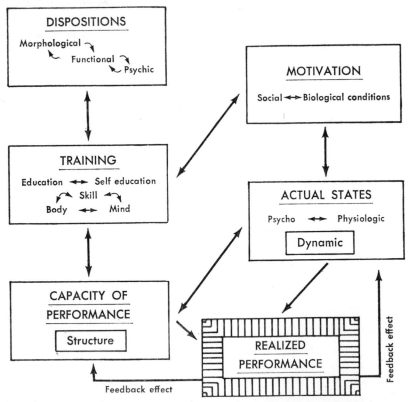

Figure 2. The important interrelationships for the realization of performance. The latter changes continually, depending on the influences of the various affecting factors, which are themselves inextricably bound together. The total is the realized performance, which also has feedback effects. (Courtesy of Vanek, M. Sport psychology, its use and potential in coaching. In *Proceedings of the First International Symposium on the Art and Science of Coaching.* Willowdale, Ontario, Canada: F. I. Productions, 1971, pp. 45-53.)

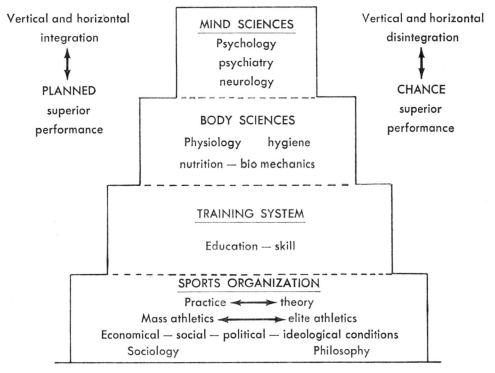

Vertical and horizontal
integration

↕

PLANNED
superior
performance

MIND SCIENCES
Psychology
psychiatry
neurology

BODY SCIENCES
Physiology   hygiene
nutrition — bio mechanics

TRAINING SYSTEM

Education — skill

SPORTS ORGANIZATION
Practice ⟷ theory
Mass athletics ⟷ elite athletics
Economical — social — political — ideological conditions
Sociology   Philosophy

Vertical and horizontal
disintegration

↕

CHANCE
superior
performance

Figure 3. Pyramid of the planned superior performance. The center of attention is usually the training system, but if it is not related to the basic structure then the potential is only for chance performance. (Courtesy of Vanek, M. Sport psychology, its use and potential in coaching. In *Proceedings of the First International Symposium on the Art and Science of Coaching.* Willowdale, Ontario, Canada: F. I. Productions, 1971, pp. 45-53.)

CAUTIONS TO BE EXERCISED

In any testing program designed for training and counseling individual athletes, caution should be exercised in the administration of tests and in the interpretation of such measures. The results from a number of valid personality measures and tests rather than from a single test should be employed. Biographic data, questionnaires concerning mood, and so forth, together with measures of personality, may be used to complement each other. It is imperative that the athlete be provided the option of participating or not participating in psychologic testing programs. "Informal consent" means that the athlete is *informed* of the nature and purpose of the testing program and her *consent* is obtained. Obviously, there is a need for trained experts, such as sport psychologists, to deal with some testing programs. Furthermore, the results of the testing programs conducted on superior athletes should not be used as a rigid classification of physical and personality requirements to be expected of all athletes. Athletes must be considered individually when attempting to improve performance potential. Prediction of an individual's limits of achievement is at best a guess, particularly when the unknown factor called "the will to achieve" is so unpredictable. Finally, it must be acknowledged at the end of this chapter, as it was in the beginning of the book, that endless research may never answer the question of why people compete in sports and why some excel. Because of the basic spirit of sport, the spirited answer to "Why?" will always be "Why not?"

REFERENCES

1. Considine, W. J. A validity analysis of selected leg power tests, utilizing a force platform. *Proceedings of the C.I.C. Symposium on Biomechanics*, Indiana University, October 19-20, 1970. Chicago: The Athletic Institute, 1971.

2. Corbin, C. B., Dowell, L. J., Lindsey, R., and Tolson, H. *Concepts in Physical Education with Laboratories and Experiments.* Dubuque, Iowa: Wm. C. Brown, 1970.

3. Kenyon, G. S. Six scales for assessing attitude toward physical activity. *Research Quarterly, 39*, 1968, pp. 566-574.

4. Mathews, D. K. *Measurement in Physical Education.* Philadelphia: W. B. Saunders Co., 1973.

5. Miller, D. M. The relationship between some visual perceptual factors and the degree of success realized by sports performers. (Doctoral dissertation, University of Southern California), Los Angeles, Calif., 1960.

6. Ramey, M. R. Force relationships of the running long jump. *Medicine and Science in Sports, 2*(3), 1970, pp. 146-151.

7. Shephard, R. J. Values and limitations of muscular strength in achieving endurance fitness for sports. *Proceedings of the First International Symposium on the Art and Science of Coaching.* Willowdale, Ontario, Canada: F. I. Productions, 1971, pp. 33-43.

8. Tutko, T. A. Some clinical aspects of sport psychology. *Quest*, XIII, 1970, pp. 12-17.

9. Vanek, M. Sport psychology, its use and potential in coaching. *Proceedings of the First International Symposium on the Art and Science of Coaching.* Willowdale, Ontario, Canada: F. I. Productions, 1971, pp. 45-53.

10. Vitale, F. N. *Individualized Fitness Programs.* Englewood Cliffs, N.J.: Prentice-Hall, Inc., 1973.

11. "What goes on inside." *Runner's World*, February 1973, pp. 10-25.

9. Preparing the Athlete — Training and Conditioning

A man prepared has half-fought the battle.

Cervantes "Don Quixote"

Champion performance is not something that just happens. As any good coach would explain, the secret of champion athletes is that they are developed by being properly motivated, by receiving guidance and instruction from experienced teachers and performers, and by systematic conditioning through well-planned training programs.

A well-planned training program is something that takes not only year-round participation but many years of building. Obviously the novice should not merely copy the training schedule or style of a champion. The coach, therefore, should understand the individual athlete and her needs, provide realistic goals—attainable yet challenging—within the individual's skill level, and offer a training schedule tailor-made for the individual. Just as individuals differ, so, too, does each sport have its own unique skills and effort demands; thus, training programs vary accordingly.

Although new experiments and ideas are constantly being developed, there are no magical formulas, undisputed systems, significant secrets, or sacred how-to-do-it steps in training that produce outstanding athletes. There are, however, some basic guidelines, some fundamental concepts that remain fairly constant for most individuals and for sports in general.

FEATURES OF A TRAINING PROGRAM

It is generally recognized that the best means of training in any sport or event is through practice of the sport or event itself. Merely practicing the activity, however, does not make sufficient demands on the physiologic systems to the point where they can give maximum support to the performance (exceptions would be swimming and running in track events). Practice of the activity must be supplemented with artificial exercises that develop the physiologic systems contributing to the overall effort. Conditioning programs usually involve the basic elements of muscular strength and endurance, circulatory-respiratory endurance, flexibility, and speed.

Muscular Strength

Muscular strength is the capacity of a muscle or group of muscles to exert maximum force against a resistance; this is accomplished by a single muscle contraction (measured by instruments such as dynamometers and tensiometers). Muscular strength in the context of sports means the ability to exert force. The ability to develop force and velocity is basic to the production of power and acceleration. In addition to producing propulsive movements of the limbs, muscles have other functions in sport (e.g., to protect other body parts by absorbing force). Muscular strength also is a factor in muscular endurance which refers to the ability of the muscles to perform work without undue fatigue. Research evidence indicates that muscular strength is a contributing factor to motivation, skill, and the efficiency of the oxygen transport system, all of which lead to improved performance.

There should be no doubt about the necessity of developing strong muscles for sport performance. The female athlete needs strength in order to handle her body weight with ease (thus skill and endurance are enhanced) and to decrease the possibility and severity of injury. Unfortunately, the words "strength" and "muscle" have held negative connotations for women, even for some of the most highly motivated sportswomen. Therefore, certain misconceptions regarding the meaning of strength and muscle need dispelling.

Although leverage, total number of fibers acting at a given time, and size of the individual fibers can affect muscular force, the degree of muscle hypertrophy (increased size) tends to be a concern for women, to the extent that they may believe strength means big muscle mass. Such concern need not be. In the first place, there are inherent differences between male and female musculature, and even the "Mr. America" physique is built only after many years of highly specialized body building exercises. Second, size may be related to things other than muscle. Size of the upper arm, for example, may not be a matter of a strong or overdeveloped biceps. Only a small proportion of the upper arm may be the biceps muscle. The total bulk of the upper arm consists of other muscles, blood vessels, nerves, tendons, and bones and may include considerable amounts of fat both internally and subcutaneously. And, although there is a link between muscle size and strength, increase in muscle size does not automatically result in increased strength. Some persons gain great strength without great increase (hypertrophy) in muscle size. Actually, the athlete should attempt to gain in strength rather than size, because an increase in body mass or the development of too much bulk may detract from cardiorespiratory training, and thus it would have an adverse effect upon endurance.

Muscular strength/endurance may be increased not only by the sport itself but also by the use of progressive resistance exercises that produce *overload* in the specific muscles to be developed. Overload means that muscles are loaded beyond previous requirements; progressive resistance means that as muscles become stronger they are worked against correspondingly greater resistance. Sixty per cent and upward of maximum muscular effort will increase muscle strength (60 to 70 per cent seems to be the threshold for causing muscles and central nervous system [CNS] to adapt). Overload in resistive exercises is applied by increasing the amount of resistance—by lifting heavier loads or applying greater force; by increasing the rate of work—by doing the exercise in a shorter period of time; by increasing the duration of work—by lengthening the exercise period while maintaining the rate; by increasing the duration of exercise periods—by shortening the rest intervals between exercise periods.

Vigorous basic exercise programs designed to condition for strength and generally recommended for workouts include *isotonic, isometric,* and *isokinetic exercises.*

In *isotonic* or *dynamic* strength exercises, the muscle is contracted under constant tension. The muscles change their length and movement of body segments takes place through the joint range of motion. An example of an isotonic exercise is pushing against or lifting a movable object such as weight training equipment (dumbbell).

Isometric or *static* exercises (*iso* means same; *metric* means length) designed to develop strength are those in which the muscles are contracted and held in the tensed position without shortening or lengthening, and without movement of the joint. Isometrics are used to increase strength in specific muscles and at particular joint angles. An example of an isometric exercise is pushing against an immovable resistance such as a wall (e.g., lateral arm press) or another body part.

Isokinetics is a new mode of strength building, based upon a constant load principle, in which the muscles work at maximum force throughout an entire range of motion with the speed of movement being controlled mechanically. The more rapid the acceleration, the more resistance. Although the beneficial effects of this method of training have not been determined, some advantages of this method are said to be that it eliminates soreness in joints; eliminates injuries due to overwork; requires no spotters; more nerve fibers are involved, thus training time is reduced; and no warm-up is needed. Isokinetic resistive exercise machines are available (Medimetrics, Inc., Specialists in Bio-Medical Instrumentation, 7460 Lorge Circle, Huntington Beach, California 92647).

There are various schools of thought as well as conflicting evidence regarding the relative merits of the various training exercises. As noted by Dr. Gordon Cumming of the Cardiac Laboratory in Winnipeg, the best way to achieve strength gains, rate of gain, and maximum limit, and the relative benefits of strength training with weights (isotonic) or with isometric exercises are controversial and scientific evidence is very inadequate.[7] Kroll gave evidence that strong muscles fatigue faster than do weak muscles.[16] Shephard reported that, since muscular development is specific, there is danger that strength and bulk may be accumulated in regions of the body not specifically related to sports. Another possible disadvantage noted is that the average weight training program does not lead to appreciable training of the cardiorespiratory system.[27]

Some persons believe that too many broad claims have been made without adequate evidence about the effectiveness of a single short *isometric* contraction and in relating gains in strength to lessened fatigue, increased cardiovascular endurance, speed of muscle movement, reaction time, coordination, and so forth. McGlynn suggested that it is possible that the increased muscle speed from isometric training could interfere with the individual's present skill pattern, because little is known about the effect of isometric training on various kinds of movement (controlled, rapid, ballistic).[17] Because of evidence that those who already are near their theoretical maximal strength gain little from isometric exercises, McGlynn considers it vital to determine the individual's pretraining strength and the increase in strength as training progresses. He also cautioned coaches against excessive and irresponsible training programs that could interfere with normal growth patterns, and strongly suggested a reevaluation of the influence of isometric training on strength and fatigability in the skeletal muscle.

Weight lifting (progressive resistance program that utilizes isotonic muscular contractions) is common in training programs and is based upon the premise that it increases muscle strength and delays fatigue, thus increases performance level. Barbells, dumbbells, iron boots, ankle weights, sandbags, or specially improvised weights are used as the resistance. The weight to be lifted depends upon the muscles used and the purpose of the exercise. Research evidence does indicate that weight lifting will produce muscle hypertrophy (increased size) and will lead to gains in strength. Some results of research have shown that weight lifting by young people can result in injuries to the vertebral column, the pectoral muscles, and the ligaments and tendons of the knees.[25] Furthermore, rapid and repeated lifting of weights carries some risk of injury because of the possibilities of fatigue and accidents.

Other literature suggests that weight lifting has become the most popular and perhaps the safest and most effective method of training for both female and male athletes. The easy adaptability to individual capabilities and needs, predictability of results, improvement in speed and flexibility, increase in muscular power and circulorespiratory endurance, reduction in incidence and severity of injuries, a convenient and quick way of regaining size and strength following injury, illness, or surgery have been variously cited as being the advantages and benefits from lifting weights. (See Appendix for sample exercises and weight training programs suitable for girls and women.)

Some physiologists maintain that if the performance of a skill is met with resistance by strapping additional weight to the body there will be more skill development because of the greater activation of nerve pathways leading to the muscles. Some training programs incorporate the use of weighted objects, for example, swinging a tennis racket with the press on the racket, throwing a weighted ball, or swinging a weighted bat. Numerous types of add-on weights such as vests, belts, ankle weights, iron boots, and sandbags are available, or they may be improvised from army cartridge belts, canteen bags, and the like filled with lead, shot, sand, or whatever is suitable. Although this method of performing the activity itself under resistive conditions (functional overload) may have the advantage of incorporating strength gains within the actual movement patterns of the sport, there is little research related to its effectiveness in performance. Some persons contend that such a method interferes with coordination and proper timing. In one study on women, it was reported that training with ankle weights actually hindered their times in the 100-yard dash.

Although there is lack of agreement about the best method for building strength, there is general agreement regarding certain procedures and guidelines to be followed in training programs:

1. *Baseline data* (initial measurements and scores) should be

recorded and a record of progress posted regularly in order to evaluate improvement and to determine further needs. Plagenhoef provided a listing of the maximum joint moments of force for a large number of sports motion patterns and exercises.[22] The maximum joint moments for a specific skill indicate the level of *muscular demands of the sport.* Thus, if it is known at which joints the maximum moment of force exists, such information may be used to plan readiness for participation, to design preseason training programs, and to design rehabilitation exercises following an injury.

2. Exercise programs *should not be used as a substitute* for practice in the skill or activity itself. The type of training program should be designed around the *specific requirements of the sport,* because the results of exercise are specific. Whenever possible, those exercises that work out the muscles and joint actions most used in the sport specialty should be selected.

3. A training program should not be exhaustive or call for too many exercises—*a few selected exercises* can be more effective and less monotonous. Whatever the exercise combinations of repetitions are, principles of *progressive resistance* should be followed, the work load being gradually increased as the body makes the needed adjustments. That is, the exercise program should allow the body to adapt without too many "growing pains." In order to prepare the body for body building exercises, a few preliminary repetitions against light resistance are recommended for *warm-up exercises*—enough to stimulate blood circulation but not enough to induce fatigue.

4. Exercise programs should be typified by both variation and continuity; that is, *systematic and frequent* training programs are much more beneficial in terms of continuous improvement and lessened fatigue or soreness than are haphazard short-term crash programs. The training season should be long enough to derive benefits—at least 12 weeks are generally required to produce effective results. Generally, during the *first two weeks, one set* of eight to 10 repetitions against moderate resistance should be used; during the *third* week, *two sets* of each exercise, gradually working toward *near-maximum* effort; after six weeks, *three sets* of each exercise using the first two sets to work up to six to eight repetitions at *maximum* effort in the third set.

5. Each exercise should be performed in a controlled steady rhythm through the *full range of movement,* with a brief pause between repetitions and a few minutes of rest between sets of repetitions.

6. *Pre-game* exercise workouts should be avoided, because the

resulting fatigue hinders reflexes and increases susceptibility to injury. *New exercises* that may produce unaccustomed exertion and muscle soreness should not be practiced during the playing season.

7. Weight training, generally, should be done during the *out-of-season* or preparation period when the athlete is not participating in the sport, with abbreviated workouts maintained during the in-season. During the in-season three sets of a 10-repetition maximum-effort exercise performed twice weekly may be effective for maintaining nearly maximum strength.

8. In weight lifting exercises, a weight should be selected that can be *handled without strain* and that will permit completion of a recommended number of repetitions—generally, begin with a dumbbell weight that can be lifted five times, ten times for a barbell or weighted shoes. To keep the exercise adequately resistant, weights may be added as the individual becomes stronger. *Breathing* should be *continued* rhythmically during the exercise, inhaling as the weight is lifted and exhaling as it is lowered. If breathing cannot be continued, the glottis should be left open to prevent a buildup of pressure in the lungs. Generally, lifters inhale before they start a repetition, hold the breath during the lift so the rib cage can be fixed, and exhale at the top or coming down. Blood flow may be interrupted and dizziness occur if the breath is held throughout the exercise or if the weight is suspended overhead, or wherever, for an abnormally long time. *Collars* holding the weights on the bar should be checked to make certain they are *secure and tight.* Spotters should be assigned.

9. Training periods should be performed with *complete attention* and concentration. Areas should be free of distracting sounds and sights, and possible aids to concentration such as mirrors for observation can be added.

Flexibility

Flexibility is variously described as range of motion in the joints, mobilization, freedom to move, suppleness, elastic tone, flexion. Regardless of the appropriate definition, it is generally regarded as an important factor in sport performance, thus warranting inclusion in a conditioning program. Herbert deVries, of the Medical Center Leisure World Foundation, dealing with flexibility as applied to some problems of muscle distress in athletes, called flexibility an overlooked but vital factor in sports conditioning. He pointed out that some athletes seem to have as much power as they need but are unable to apply it well because of stiff, unyielding muscles. Furthermore, flexibility exercises may be used to relieve and prevent muscle soreness.[9] After a careful review of the literature Holland indicated that numerous researchers agree that flexibility is a *specific* factor, varying considerably with each joint, and insist that flexibility should not be viewed as though it were a general factor of performance.[11] Although there are insufficient data to warrant generalizations about the relationships of flexibility to variables such as sex, age, body type, warm-up, and so forth, the literature does support the tenet that range of motion is modifiable—improving flexibility is, of course, the practical concern of the coach.

There are two components of flexibility: dynamic flexibility and extent or passive flexibility. Dynamic flexibility involves the speed with which maximum-range joint movements can be made. Dynamic (fast stretch) exercises include almost any bobbing or bouncing exercises done repetitively and aimed toward gradually increasing joint motion. Extent flexibility involves the maximum range of joint motion in which a static position is held for a period of time. Extent (passive) exercises involve slow, controlled stretching which puts the muscle in its longest state. And, although there are insufficient data regarding comparative effectiveness of either dynamic or passive flexibility exercises in improving joint mobility as well as in longer retention of better flexibility, both are considered effective. It seems, however, that passive stretching exercises are more favored than the bouncing type of stretch because of the lessened possibility of muscle soreness in the unconditioned person, and because they do not oppose what the athlete is trying to do by causing a reflex contraction. Also, passive stretching exercises are believed to relax the muscle tissue and, in fact, are used to relieve and prevent muscle soreness.[9]

Passive stretching exercises for general flexibility include almost any form of bending and reaching in various positions, in which the major joints are stretched through their full range of motion and the position is held for about a minute. If flexibility is to be increased, the overload principle must be applied, gradually causing the muscles and connective tissues to stretch through the full range of motion to just beyond what is called the "stretch pain" or "discomfort stage."

Calisthenic (sometimes called "freehand exercises") programs are also designed to increase flexibility as well as to improve muscle tone, strength and endurance, and cardiorespiratory endurance generally. Examples of basic calisthenic exercises are push-ups, sit-ups, chins and dips (considered as increasing flexibility in the shoulder joint more than do push-ups), squat jumps, back-ups or arching, and so forth. Such exercises may be used in simple warm-ups or in circuit training endurance programs, described in the following section, with the training dose and target time designed specifically for the individual athlete's needs.

Following a thorough warm-up of the muscles through passive stretching exercises and general conditioning exercises, the athlete may proceed to dynamic or active stretching exercises if she so desires, although there is doubt as to whether any additional flexibility will be gained.

Circulatory-Respiratory Endurance

Endurance or stamina refers to the muscular and circulo-respiratory condition that enables the person to support sustained effort without experiencing undue fatigue. Endurance is affected by muscular strength, performance skill, and efficiency of the circulatory system—strength enables the athlete to perform longer, skill makes her more efficient so that less energy is consumed, and good circulation provides for the necessary amount of oxygen and for the elimination of waste materials. Fatigue, which is the result of an accumulation of waste products (lactic acid) and lack of an adequate supply of oxygen to the working muscles, impairs the ability to maintain a high level of performance and interferes with skill. And it is often said that the availability of oxygen can be a decisive factor in who wins in sports, particularly when the sport demands that the player have a high aerobic capacity or when it makes the player depend heavily on aerobic metabolic pathways.

Cardiorespiratory endurance involves aerobic and anaerobic power. *Aerobic* power is Vo_2 capacity or maximum oxygen uptake, or, more simply stated, it is the ability of the heart and lungs to pump oxygen from the atmosphere to the exercising muscles that are conditioned to use the oxygen. Continuous large muscle exercises or events lasting over one or two minutes call for a well-developed oxygen transport system (aerobic power) in order for oxygen to be delivered during the event. Such events, for example, may be distance runs, swimming, cycling, and so forth.

Related to the ability to transport and utilize oxygen is the physiologic capacity to sustain heavy effort for a period of time even though the consumption of oxygen is not adequate (an oxygen debt occurs) to meet the exercise demand. This ability is referred to as *anaerobic* power. Events such as short dashes, jumps, and throwing, which call for a single all-out effort, require high anaerobic power. In sports such as hockey, basketball, tennis, and the like, which call for repeated spurts of all-out effort, oxygen delivery (aerobic power) during the event may be only moderately important, but rapid and complete recovery is important to the ability to sustain repeated spurts of maximal effort. Energy for such activities, therefore, is considered to be supplied in part by aerobic and in part by anaerobic sources.

Although there is some controversy regarding the relative benefits of aerobic and anaerobic training programs, both are considered as being important in a complete endurance training program. Aerobic training may be induced by a few minutes of continuous effort. Aerobic training does not require maximum-exertion training, although anaerobic work has been shown to improve aerobic power. Anaerobic training is achieved by short bouts of activity at maximum intensity. More specifically, special programs of training that increase the normal work load to the point of placing some stress (overload) on the physiologic systems are the following:

1. *Circuit* training is designed to develop cardiovascular-respiratory endurance as well as flexibility, strength, and muscular endurance in essential muscle groups. It is an efficient training method in terms of gains made in a short length of time. It can be used by one person or a group and does not require elaborate equipment. *Circuit* is the term used to designate the total series of exercises (usually eight to 12 exercises). *Station* refers to each exercise in the circuit (approximately eight to 10 different stations). *Dose* means the number of repetitions performed at a station in a given time (usually eight to 10 repetitions to begin with). *Lap* means completion of all the stations (usually three laps constitute a circuit training program). *Target time* designates the time in which the circuit must be completed before progression to the next, more strenuous level.

The athlete moves through the circuit or series of varied exercises, numbered consecutively, as rapidly as possible, usually repeating the circuit three times. Each exercise is performed for a recommended number of repetitions and is to be completed regardless of the time it takes.

Circuit training is strenuous, therefore it is essential that the program be progressive and exercises be selected and arranged carefully in order to minimize fatigue. Gradually and progressively over a period of several weeks, speed and frequency are increased until the athlete can perform the circuit repeatedly, rapidly, and without a rest period between circuits and exercises. Perhaps one circuit may be accomplished the first week, two the second week, and three the third week.

Any series of exercises suited to the athlete and the sport may be designed. Janet Wessel and Christine MacIntyre suggest such exercises as sit-ups, push-ups, jumping jacks, side leg raises, jumping rope.[29] Some general all-round exercises recommended by Homola are push-ups, squat thrusts, bar chins and dips, sit-ups, back arching, barbell squats, rope climbing, heel raising, running.[12]

Circuit exercises are designed to develop cardiovascular-respiratory endurance; however, the circuit must be designed on resistive training to incorporate strength. It is the increase in strength that increases speed of movement. Whenever the athlete can complete the circuit in below average time, vest weights may be used or pounds added to the barbells in order to increase resistance. Authorities generally agree that, in the use of barbells or dumbbells, the best program for building strength is three sets of each exercise with six to nine repetitions in each set.

A circuit that includes some elements of the sport the athlete is engaged in permits practicing the skill and benefits specific endurance. The basketball chest pass against the wall may be included in a circuit for basketball players, jumps for volleyball players, racket swinging for tennis players, and so forth. The athlete may be motivated by keeping and posting records of completion of target time and by using competition based on speed of completion.

2. *Interval* training produces a great deal of strain on the physiologic systems supporting sustained effort. Basically, it is a method of training that involves running for a selected distance, alternating short periods of exertion with rest intervals. It is a frequently used method of training for swimming and track athletes. The speed of runs usually is held as constant as possible and strenuousness is increased by shortening the rest intervals or by decreasing the time of the runs. After determining initial work load, the work period should gradually increase overload until the activity is sustained for at least 10 minutes, preferably from 20 to 30 minutes, and heart rate is increased to 120 to 150 beats per minute or about double its resting rate. Various types of interval training include:

1. Paarlauf—teams of runners do continuous relays, one running while the others rest.
2. Fartlek—long period of running, usually done over rough country, at a cruising pace interspersed with peak efforts of speeding up.
3. Pyramid—lengths of runs and rest intervals vary in any session according to changes in runner's fatigue.
4. Resistance—running against greater resistance than normal, e.g., up sand hills, through water, pulling weights.

5. Tempolauf—short runs of maximum effort of 20 seconds or less, interspersed with short recovery periods of about five seconds.

6. Repetition runs—pace or run is more precisely determined than in other interval methods and a more complete recovery period is allowed between runs.

Those interested in pursuing the physiologic aspects of interval training should consult Astrand's *Textbook of Work Physiology,* which covers most of what is known concerning length of intervals, duration of recovery, and so forth.[1] Interval training programs, however, may be planned from activities other than running—any activity that involves the total body in a sustained effort and challenges heart and lung endurance, for example, the sport itself, running in place, jogging, bench stepping, bicycling, swimming, rope jumping.

In 1968, with the publication of *Aerobics,* Dr. Kenneth H. Cooper, a Major in the United States Air Force, seemingly revolutionized ideas about endurance fitness. Recognizing that women have specific needs and capabilities (the total aerobic capacity of most women is smaller than of most men), he and Mrs. Cooper wrote a book on aerobic exercise programs designed for women.[5] The aerobics exercise program, as noted previously, means promoting the supply and use of oxygen. The program involves doing a certain number of specific exercises (walking, running, swimming, cycling, rope skipping, stair climbing) four or five times a week, long enough to push the heart rate to 120 to 150 beats a minute.

Rope skipping should not be overlooked as a conditioning activity for girls and women, because it has been shown that it contributes to physical work capacity.[14] *Jogging,* a sport in itself, is also a fun method of fitness training designed to moderately overload the circulorespiratory system, thus bringing about an increase in endurance. An excellent case is made by Roby and Davis for the physiologic benefits as well as pure pleasure of participating in "jogging," a term used to include all speeds of running although it implies a slower pace than high speed competitive running.[26] A jogging and running session should be started with a warm-up and ended with a tapering down to a slower run, then a walk. The ideal foot strike technique to use, in order to avoid landing shock and to alleviate other problems, is to drop from the heel to the ball of the foot rather than from ball to heel to ball. The body parts (head, arms, hips, knees, feet) should be pointed straight ahead and excessive body sway should be avoided.

3. *"Model* training" is the term sometimes used to designate

training that duplicates the physiologic and psychologic stresses the athlete is expected to encounter in competition. The book *Champions in the Making*, which spells out the research evidence and opinions of athletes and coaches about how to succeed in track and field, provides this practical work formula: "To achieve maximum results, the work load must follow competitive situations."[15] Throughout the book the emphasis is placed upon "keep it simple— learn by feel." The authors firmly believe that duplicating in practice the physical, organic, and psychologic disturbances one is confronted with in competition obeys the laws of practical reasoning as well as mechanics. The authors, Bud Spencer and Payton Jordon—both track record holders, one of whom became a coach, the other a sports writer—follow the maxim: "The only way to learn how to run is to run." "There is no other solid way. You can stretch its pure simplicity with fancy padding and embellishments, but it will always boil down to the simple ingredient: run, run, run, or jump, jump, jump, or throw, throw, or hurdle, hurdle. It does not matter if the athlete is of Olympic caliber, a college fun runner, or a prep school boy of high hopes."[15]

Their "quality work system" is designed to acquaint the athlete kinesthetically with the feel of actual competition and is varied to avoid the monotony of a rigid work schedule. Standard practices such as calisthenics, springs, and laps are considered as preliminary warm-up preceding the practical work of the day in which the athlete attempts to work as near meet conditions as possible.

Speed

Whether or not speed of body movement can be developed extensively by training has been a matter of conjecture. Some researchers indicate that some persons have kinesiological advantages that enable them to be superior in some events requiring speed and power. They are born, not made, so to speak. Certainly, an individual's heredity (nerve impulses, tension level, body type, levers, and so forth) has much to do with the total speed factor. And it appears that there is great specificity of movement speed not only in terms of the task required (e.g., stopping and starting quickly, dodging, changing directions, alternating from low to high speed as contrasted to straightaway speed) but also in terms of the athlete (e.g., an athlete can have slow arms and fast legs).

Nonetheless, speed is considered to be a vital factor in sport success not only in sprinting speed in track and field events and other activities such as baseball, basketball, and tennis, which involve anaerobic sprints, but also in any activity in which the ability to sustain a good pace is needed. Although speed training in its widest application is still a much overlooked factor in training programs, research now indicates that the speed capability of the total muscle structure can be developed to a higher level than previously presumed possible.

George Dintiman of the Virginia Commonwealth University provided an excellent summary of recent findings in such significant areas as agility, ergogenic aids, explosive power, flexibility, reaction time, strength, stride, and warm-up and in their overall effect upon the improvement of sprinting speed.[10] Although conflicting evidence is uncovered in some areas (e.g., the effect of some ergogenic aids on improvement of sprinting speed), in general it may be concluded that strength, flexibility, explosive power, endurance, and reaction time ultimately contribute to speed.

Supplementary training programs which have been used to improve sprinting speed include weight training, use of body weights, isometrics, circuit training, wind sprints, stair sprinting, and hopping and jumping exercises. Such programs are designed to develop leg strength, leg endurance, explosive power, and, in the case of hopping and jumping activities, to simulate the sprinting action or to involve similar muscle groups. Dintiman suggested that wind sprints (probably the most common approach and frequently poorly conducted) should be replaced by a form of sprint interval training in order to improve sprinting speed, local muscular endurance, and cardiovascular endurance.[10] He suggested further that more attention should be given to the improvement of stride length because it is one of the most beneficial means of increasing speed of movement.

Dintiman described two relatively new approaches to improve the rate and efficiency of leg movement and to strengthen the muscles involved in the sprinting action. A sprint-resisted training program is one in which sprinting action is simulated while the body is placed under increased internal resistance through incline running or weighted clothing. Sprint-assisted training programs, used as a supplement to flat surface sprint training, include downhill running, towing, and treadmill running designed to improve the rate of leg movement per second without a decrease in stride length. Both approaches are believed to have something to offer in improved sprinting speed.

It has been found, in many instances, that speed drills in which the athlete moves as fast as possible in a given time, using movements as specific as possible to the performance movement, would be helpful in improving the ability to sustain good pace in an endurance type of activity. Other recommended practice procedures emphasizing the mental and emotional aspects of speed include mentally rehearsing the "feel" of speed, using action words such as "go" or idea cues such as imagining being a bullet fired out of a gun, relaxation drills to consciously release unnecessary and inhibiting muscle tension.[20]

Thomas suggested that speed training schedules should be devised around the following subdivisions:

1. Improve power-to-weight ratio (strength, hypertrophy, fat).
2. Develop mechanically advantageous techniques (levers, force).
3. Train the central processing mechanisms of the stimulus-response component.
4. Maximize the awareness of signals (keen senses, strength of signal).
5. Increase the preparatory tension before movement (muscles and nerves).
6. Decrease resistances to movement (fat, joint stiffness).[28]

Methods of Training

What is the most desirable overall method of training? There appears to be rather general agreement about using what is termed "mixed" or "complex training" for all sports and for general training programs rather than using only specific patterns of maximum effort training. James Counsilman, head swimming coach at Indiana University, although confessing that there is still much that is not known about training methods, suggested the mixed program, with some aerobic work, using interval training, repetition training, sprint training, some fartlek, and some over distance. Counsilman made the point that he has had swimmers on different types of training programs—short rest interval to high quality repetition training—and they ended up with almost the same results. The concept stressed is that athletes have to be treated as individuals. Not only do individuals vary in capacity but each individual varies from time to time. The coach must know the athlete, predict his adaptation energy, and find ways to make him work hard to put a physiologic stress on himself.[6]

Lloyd Percival, Director of the Fitness Institute and Technical Director of the Coaching Association of Canada, although pointing out that the major emphasis should be as specific as possible to the precise need of the sport with less emphasis on the methods contributing to general conditioning level, advocated the mixed training program. According to his evaluation of tests on many Alpine skiers, from low to high level competitors, the primary needs and approximate training emphasis and order were suggested as strength and power development (40 per cent), agility/mobility training and anaerobic conditioning (25 per cent), aerobic condi-tioning (15 per cent), tension control and flexibility training (20 per cent). Using the example of hockey which is primarily an anaerobic activity, Percival suggested that there is an advantage in increasing aerobic power as much as possible (about 20 per cent of the conditioning program), combining continuous with interval work in order to achieve better general endurance as well as to provide variety.[20]

As in developing endurance, it is suggested that the most suit-able method of developing strength is a mixed or complex approach including isotonic (with a variety of methods regarding repetitions and rest periods), isometric (especially the circuit stations sys-tems), and isokinetic or constant load principle (especially applied to simulated sports movements).[21]

Gordon Cumming, of the Cardiac Laboratory in Winnipeg, offered some observations regarding the improvement of aerobic power of athletes: since no training program has been shown to be better than another, a well-rounded program of interval, tempo, and distance work seems most effective. Furthermore, although the actual optimal levels of aerobic power for various sports have not been determined, any well-trained female athlete in any sport should have a minimum power of 50 ml/kilogram of body weight. Full development of aerobic power may take a long time, and, be-cause there is a biologic limit, the athlete may reach a plateau where further extensive training will not increase aerobic power.[7]

ADDITIONAL TRAINING CONSIDERATIONS

Seasonal Work Patterns

Most patterns of work intensity, although variable and flexible, revolve around three basic seasons: *Off-season* is a period of body building and maintaining tone of muscular and cardiorespiratory systems by means of conditioning programs. *Pre-season* is the period of increasing intensity of work load. It is generally the season in which the greatest amount of work should take place and a purposeful application made of the prior conditioning toward the actual goal. The athlete works on segments of the sport, doing them repeatedly until the desired objective is achieved, then putting the parts together into the whole competitive event. Here is where some degree of the pressure of competition is applied. An attempt is made to duplicate as nearly as possible the physiologic and psychologic stresses the athlete will encounter in competition. *In-season* is when the athlete should be at her peak. Improvement is concerned with refinements in economy of effort and feeling for the event. The work schedule may be lighter and varied, and the pressures of uniform routine lessened in order to stave off boredom or to relieve tensions. A brief vacation period may be taken. In short, quantity of work load changes to quality of work on form and performance details. The fun of competition becomes a reality, although the fun of competition and individual progress are interwoven all along the way. Research indicates, however, that some strength-producing activities should be interspersed with practices during the season, not just prior to the season. Otherwise, there are significant strength losses. For that matter, it is not possible to store strength or endurance, since they are transient; however, exercise gains are more quickly recovered with less effort once they have been established.

Staleness

Every athlete at one time or another seems to experience a period of what may be called "staleness," "stagnation," "dead spot," "overstress," "the choke," "the ragged edge," or various similar synonyms. In such a period, performance decreases or it becomes difficult to make further improvements. Increased effort may cause further aggravation and a whole host of other syndromes appear— worry, fatigue, headache, insomnia, irritability, joint and muscle pain, digestive difficulties, and so forth. In fact, staleness in athletes has been likened to the mental disorder known as depression. Some of the ways in which staleness and depression are shown to be similar include loss of appetite, loss of weight, difficulty sleeping, lessened tolerance for work and pressure, constipation and other physiologic changes including higher heart rate and greater accumulation of lactic acid.

Variability in performance may occur, of course, simply as the result of changes in the environment—different playing areas, altitude, equipment, and the like. The good athlete learns how to adjust and to adapt to such variances. But staleness, although it may be expected, is more difficult to predict and to correct. One of the problems is that in today's competitive sports programs the athlete is being stressed more, both physiologically and psychologically. Another problem is that, since stressors are accumulative, it is difficult to sort them out. Sometimes the stress comes from overworking physiologically, although athletes probably rarely approach the physiologic fatigue point. Sometimes stress comes from pushing the athlete into another athlete's pattern of training or performance. Sometimes the stress comes from the athlete's total life situation—daily habits, friends, even overambitious coaches, or what is known in the jargon of the athletic world as the OAP (overanxious parent). Sometimes the stress may be simply the result of too much talking about stress.

Sport physiologists and psychologists seem to agree that staleness is primarily emotional-psychologic and that the optimal prescription for remedy is an individual thing. Through experience with the stress tolerance of individual athletes and by monitoring changes from baseline data, the coach may avoid, or at least diagnose, staleness. Forbes Carlile, swimming coach and lecturer, Sydney, Australia, who has written much about the measurement of and observable symptoms associated with stress and staleness, suggested that the electrocardiogram (ECG) and the Cameron heartometer are excellent objective guides in detecting staleness. These instruments may be sensitive in detecting cardiovascular status or the state of training of the individual, thus performance capability and deterioration, although some persons contend that they are not reputable instruments and question their sensitivity. Such instruments, whether effective or not, are frequently not readily available. However, the coach could at least gather some relatively simple baseline data on a few physiologic factors (e.g., resting heart rate, exercise heart rate for a standard work load, weight) in order to assess the direction of changes and their significance.

When staleness occurs, sometimes what is called for is a temporary change or an abrupt stop in the training program or sometimes even an entirely different method of training. Sometimes recovery days involve rest and relaxation, a change of activity and scenery, or whatever helps to promote new vigor and a fresh mental outlook. The rest may not necessarily come from complete withdrawal from the work program, but from taking it easier. Generally, the nature of *mixed* training is such that there is enough variety to stave off training boredom. Some mixed programs also may include tension control methods (relaxation drills and breathing control). Sometimes special attention to nutrition is called for. Sometimes all that is needed is for the coach to show renewed interest and understanding.

Regardless of the method used in dealing with staleness, it is an individual rather than a collective matter. A coach's effort to psyche up a group may be of little consequence or even dangerous. Moreover, the concern is not just to avoid staleness or fatigue but to develop optimum achievement and zest. An absence of the negative is no assurance of the presence of the positive.

Nutrition

The athlete who really cares knows the importance of regular sleep habits, suitable diet, and other off-grounds behaviors. Regimented training rules without individuality do little to improve the quality of training programs. Some common sense principles, however, may call for a reminder or reinforcement now and then.

A well-balanced diet is the best nutrient—there are no magic foods or drugs that produce super performance. The best procedure, psychologically and physiologically, probably is to let the athlete follow her own desires and normal diet. The education of the athlete, concerning what is good nutrition, however, is very important and often missing. It cannot be assumed that the athlete knows the nutritional requirements of a well-balanced or ideal diet. Merely getting sufficient calories from a mixed diet does not guarantee nutritional balance. Most books on the physiology of exercise, as well as other authoritative sources, deal with nutrition. The whole subject of athletic nutrition is explored in depth in the *Proceedings of the First International Symposium on the Art and Science of Coaching,* held in Toronto, Canada, October 1-5, 1971 (Willowdale, Ontario, Canada: F. I. Productions, 1971). A handbook for coaches, *Nutrition for Athletes,* published by the American Association for Health, Physical Education and Recreation, suggests a good basic diet with recommended menus, theories, and practices concerning nutrition and athletic performance, problems related to eating and drinking before, during, and after athletic events, and claims made for dietary supplements.[19] Basic nutritional needs of the athlete are briefly summarized here.

Selection of foods from each of the *four food groups* is a recommended daily nutritional guide:

1. Milk—two or more servings; cheese and other made-from-milk foods may supply part of the milk.
2. Meat, fish, poultry, eggs, cheese, with dry beans, peas, nuts as alternatives—two or more servings.
3. Vegetables and fruits including green or yellow vegetables and citrus fruits or tomatoes—four or more servings.
4. Breads and cereals, enriched or whole grain—four or more servings.

The *composition* of various foods and nutrients and generally recommended *caloric intake* for athletes are:

Carbohydrate/starchy foods include fruit (fresh, preserved, dried), cereals, bread, corn, potatoes, rice, spaghetti, macaroni and the like, and honey, jams, corn syrup, and other sweet foods. The recommended intake of total calories is 35 to 45 per cent, with highest intake starting 48 hours before competition. Foods with high nutritional value should be emphasized over non-nutritional sources such as white sugar products, soft drinks, pastry, candy, and the like.

Fats include milk, cream, meat, fish, butter, margarine, vegetable oils, and ice cream. The recommended intake of total calories is 35 to 45 per cent with total fat intake consisting of 60 to 70 per cent unsaturated fat (vegetable oils, margarine, fish, and the like) and low saturated fat intake starting 48 hours before competition.

Vitamins include vitamin A found in vegetables (leafy green and yellow), butter, enriched margarine, liver; vitamin B in lean meat, whole grain breads, spaghetti, macaroni; vitamin C in citrus fruits, tomatoes, raw fruits and vegetables; vitamin D in fortified milk, sunshine, fish liver oils; vitamin E in vegetables (green leafy), whole grain flour. *Minerals* are found in vegetables and in lean meats and eggs (iron and sulfur), iodized salt (iodine, sodium, chloride), milk (calcium). Recommended intake is two servings daily of cooked vegetables and at least one serving daily of fresh.

Certain *food fads,* such as the precompetition meal of a big steak, should be avoided since the body cannot metabolize the protein and fat in time to be useful. In effect, the athlete carries the weight of the big steak. Evidence indicates that meals eaten near the time of actual competition do not affect performance, although the athlete should eat lightly and sensibly. Many athletes eat more than they need.

Although individuals differ in their psychologic and physiologic response to food, in general, foods that probably should be avoided the day of competition, and perhaps the day prior to competition, include gas-forming foods (cabbage, cauliflower, onions, kraut, dried beans, candy, soft drinks); greasy or fried foods (pastries, potato chips, buttered popcorn, gravy, nuts); spicy foods (chili, hot dogs, pickles, mustard); very cold foods; and hot or fresh bread. Just prior to competition or during halftime or rest periods an orange may be the best food if something is desired, because it contains a readily available simple sugar and may prevent thirst and clear the throat.

There appears to be no need for the athlete who is getting a well-balanced diet to increase the *intake of vitamins and minerals* or to take protein tablets. Such dietary needs are better met and more effective when taken in natural food forms than in synthetic form. However, great interest has been shown in various synthetic supplements and certain studies do support possible values to performance and recovery, especially in activities demanding high endurance, hard training, and excessive stress. Certainly some dietary practices are a matter of ritual and have been shown to have definite psychologic, as well as possible physiologic, effect. In some instances the reason that research shows intake of supplemental vitamins/minerals/nutrients to be helpful may be because the athlete's diet, in fact, is inadequate. There is need for further research in this area. Meanwhile, indiscriminate use of food supplements is ill-advised, and, in fact, could be harmful. Consideration also should be given to the possible detrimental effect of the athlete becoming psychologically accustomed to the need for some kind of pill. If it is necessary to make up for deficiencies, it is recommended that such supplementation be on a long-term gradual basis, not a one-shot, high-dose approach. Careful attention should be given to the individual athlete and medical advice sought in this matter.

There is some evidence that *nutritional manipulation* can be effective in the development of superior performance, although such procedures should be used with medical supervision. Per-Olaf Astrand, Swedish physiologist, in some special research into increasing glycogen to maximize energy levels in endurance events (such as cross-country skiing, playing soccer, marathon running), offered some insights into glycogen storage. As a rule of thumb he suggested that anyone involved in heavy exercise for one hour or more should have extra carbohydrates (corn, bread, potatoes, rice) in the diet for a few days before competition, then not exercise heavily the day before competition so as not to deplete the high content of glycogen in the muscles. For the high jumper and sprinter, of course, storing glycogen would not be advisable; glycogen, being a heavy fuel, would make them heavy.[2] Although suggesting that resting a day prior to competition with some increased carbohydrate is good, Astrand emphasized that the regular diet should not have high carbohydrate content because the enzymes specialize on carbohydrates and lose some ability to utilize free fatty acids which the muscles also must be able to do. Further, carbohydrates should be of mixed type, not one big dose of simple sugar, in order not to be digested all at once.[2]

There is some evidence that during severe training some athletes have problems of *low hemoglobin*. How it can be remedied is not known. Attempts to increase hemoglobin by giving high doses of iron have not been successful. Some coaches have found that a normal training program can be maintained and beneficial effects derived from training at high altitudes, the optimal altitude being 5000 to 6000 feet. Although training at high altitudes has been shown to produce an increase in hemoglobin and in the number of red blood cells, the athlete has to be at the higher altitude for a long period of time, which may be quite impractical as well as cause other problems. In general, it is believed that athletes get enough iron from a properly balanced diet, although women may need additional iron because of the loss of blood in menstruation.

Contrary to popular opinion, limiting *fluid intake* several hours prior to competition may lower rather than improve performance level, and drinking water before competition does not interfere with performance. In fact, during actual competition in hot climates, extra water is demanded to prevent dehydration and to allow effective dissipation of heat. In general, the athlete should be allowed to take water as desired. *"Drying out"* as part of a program of weight reduction poses serious health hazards, particularly during vigorous physical activity. The best concept in weight control is that there is no quick or easy method of losing weight safely.

Ergogenic Aids

The coach's arsenal would be incomplete without some knowledge about ergogenic (work-producing) aids, aids thought to enhance performance above levels anticipated under normal conditions. Ergogenic aids are classified by Morgan as *substances* (drugs, hormones, alkalies, oxygen, nutrition, water, and the like) and various motivational *methods* or *phenomena* (information feedback, mental practice, hot and cold applications, physical warmups, hypnosis, music, social facilitation, and so forth).[18] Some of these aids or ergogenic effects of various phenomena are discussed throughout this text.

The use of *hypnosis* is described in some athletic training books and is explored in depth in other sources.[18] It has been used to aid the athlete's strength and endurance, to increase aggressiveness, to help in overcoming psychologic inhibiting barriers to performance potential, and for therapeutic purposes. Although hypnosis is a method to be used only by those well qualified to do so, literature dealing with its use warrants the attention of all coaches. Of course, yoga and other forms of autohypnotic suggestion and relaxation are methods within the domain of anyone and have been found by some persons to be useful methods for controlling the nervous system.

There is considerable controversy surrounding the use of such ergogenic aids as drugs, hormones and steroids, alkalies, ultraviolet rays, and so forth. Sport psychologists and physiologists make a plea for looking at ergogenic aids in a positive context and far more broadly than in the past but warn that giving a blanket prescription of medicine has never worked. Medical men know the importance of individual medical diagnosis. Coaches and physical educators as well should learn.

The use of *drugs* by athletes for such avowed purposes as improving performance, overcoming pain, recovering from fatigue, gaining in strength and weight, and so forth is well documented in numerous popular articles and books. Without doubt the use and abuse of drugs are on the increase in the world of sports as in other walks of life and there is growing concern as to what to do about it. A myriad of materials for drug abuse education which testify to this growing concern is available.

There are, of course, important ethical and legal considerations regarding the use of drugs which warrant the concerned attention not only of sports governing bodies, but of the athlete and coach as well. Most importantly, however, is the matter of the welfare of the athlete. Unfortunately, some individuals seeking superior performance may not do what good health or conscience dictates, particularly if society itself seems ambivalent in its attitude toward drug use.

Perhaps what is needed more than legislation and governing bodies to control the use of drugs, which may in a sense offer added enticement to some individuals, is a psychologic antidote to the deadly attention to some prescription that offers a surefire shortcut to paradise and peak performance. Since most persons want a share of those exciting moments of heightened awareness, an affirmative alternative to taking the trip on drugs is to discover how one might heighten sensations, "turn on" in other ways—something that outshines drugs in achieving an effect on the mind and does not blur the experience of a competitive effort or vanish as normality returns. Finding substitutes for drugs is of course an individual matter, but such an approach is worthy of attention and may in fact offer a startling alteration to destructive life styles. Some related aspects of motivation are described in Chapter 5. Perhaps further answers may be found in the book *Drugs and the Coach,* recently published by the American Association for Health, Physical Education and Recreation, which is an attempt to "put it together" from the perspective of the coach. The book is geared to the person experienced in youth leadership but with little or no background in drug counseling. Special emphasis is given to the coach as a counselor who can relate to youth on drug matters.

But what about the question, do drugs actually enhance athletic performance? Amphetamine (e.g., Benzedrine), the most commonly used drug, is a powerful stimulant that abolishes or reduces the sense of fatigue. At one time amphetamine was easily obtained and frequently used, particularly as an appetite depressant for weight

control. Although the Bureau of Narcotics now lists it as a dangerous drug, its use by athletes who feel it helps them get keyed up
for the event is believed to be on the increase. The research evidence, however, *does not* support the belief that amphetamines
enhance physical performance. It shows that the physiologic effects
can be harmful, even deadly, in events requiring performance over
a long period of time because the athlete may fail to recognize and
to react to the danger signs of exertion and heat stress. Furthermore, those who use drugs to "turn on" continue to take the drugs
even when not competing, and the use of "uppers" is often accompanied by the use of sedatives or "downers," thus setting up an
undesirable cycle of stimulation and depression.[18]

The inherent dangers of other drugs such as cocaine (and its
derivatives Procaine and Novocain), ephedrine, and digitalis pre-
clude their use by athletes unless prescribed by a physician for
proper medical reasons.

Other substances reputed to have ergogenic effects also have
potentially harmful physiologic effects, aside from the legal and
ethical considerations involved in their use. Steroids, which have
the properties of functioning androgenically (stimulate male characteristics) and anabolically (stimulate increased growth and
weight, accelerate bone maturation, virility), have been used by
some athletes. The use of anabolic steroids appears to be rather
common among weight lifters, wrestlers, weight-event athletes in
track, and football players, on the premise that gains in weight and
strength do result. Although studies are confusing and contradictory, major investigations have not confirmed claims that steroids
improve weight or strength and motor performance or work capacity. Moreover these drug products have been recognized as
extremely dangerous and have been condemned as ergogenic aids
by sports governing bodies.

Whether or not the drug problem is widespread or exists for
the female athlete in the same dimensions that it does for males is a
matter only of conjecture at this point. Athletes of either sex,
however, live in the same sports world and drug culture and are
not immune to similar influences. The use of hormones by the
female athlete and the effect of birth control pills, which also contain hormones, have not received intensive investigation. Obviously,
for the female as for the male, the use of male hormones may result
in an increase in muscle mass and may endanger health, particularly
if she has not attained full growth. For females the side effects
attributed to steroids are most often irreversible. Recently a rather
questionable practice involving the use of hormones by female
athletes was reported in the popular literature. It was reported

that women athletes in the Olympic Games of 1972 took the sex hormone Norethisterone in order to skip a menstrual period so that menstruation would not interfere with performance.[3] Although there is variation among female athletes, research indicates that for the majority of girls and women performance is *not* significantly affected by the menstrual period. Considering the undesirable side effects attendant on the use of steroids, the supposed beneficial effects seem most insignificant.

Studies have not adequately verified the claimed benefits to performance of these extremely dangerous drugs or of some *other presumed aids* that pose no particular health risks (e.g., glycine, wheat germ, sunflower seeds, molasses, and so forth). For example, the claims that taking supplemental glycine would aid endurance and muscular strength, accelerate the effects of training, and prevent staleness have been discounted. The findings reaffirm the conviction that a well-balanced diet should meet the body's demand for high-energy-fuel food.

The possibilities of preparing an athlete for a super performance are being explored in other ways and pose further questions regarding the ethics of such practices. In one experiment a Swedish physiologist tested subjects on a treadmill, determined their maximum energy capability, then extracted approximately one-fifth of the blood from their systems.[4] In daily repeated treadmill tests the subjects at first showed lassitude, but after two weeks their energy capabilities were back to normal. A month after the blood was extracted and stored, it was returned to their bodies. The returned blood transfusions, which in effect produced an oversupply, resulted in a startling rise in energy, and physical performances soared to levels 20 per cent above previous maximums. The body eventually readjusted its blood supply and energy to normal.

Because it is virtually impossible to detect "blood doping," as the process has been called, the possibility of its use to create a super performance is obvious. The significance of this finding, as with similar experiments such as hormone injections for female athletes and controversial medication, has tremendous philosophic import. One is compelled to ask: How sporting is sport? Furthermore, is the aim in sport that of creating supermen or superwomen, or, for that matter, of super performance that is not truly related to the athlete's ability?

Warm-up and Cool-down

It is theorized that procedures used to warm up the player immediately prior to competition prepare her for optimum performance. Warm-up apparently is useful, although there are misconceptions about its real benefits. The effects of warm-up on flexibility, for example, require further study. Nonetheless, it may be assumed that stiff joints hamper the production of power. In those power-producing activities in which the joints may be taken to the extreme range of movement (e.g., high jumping, long jumping, throwing), warm-up or mobilizing exercises may enhance ability to move most effectively.

There is some doubt about the value of warm-up exercises in endurance or stamina-demanding events. Warming up in order to raise the level of organic function may expend too much energy that is needed for the actual event, if the warm-up period extends to the time of the event. If it does not, cooling down occurs and physiologic functions will return to where they were without warming up.

In terms of skill, warming up does seem to permit the performer to make needed adjustments to such factors as the condition and characteristics of the weather, implements, surfaces, equipment, and so forth. If the warm-up involves specific forms of movement used in the sport (e.g., swinging a racket or bat) practice effect may be achieved as an added advantage. Results of one study showed that, by applying the principle of overload to baseball-throwing warm-ups, the velocity of throwing was significantly improved, and after the first few throws accuracy of throwing was improved.[13]

Psychologically, warm-up probably is valuable in that the performer develops a feeling of well-being, reassurance, relieves some tensions, and may even show off a little of her skill, which sometimes may even demoralize the opponent (gamesmanship or one-upmanship is not being condoned, however). If the astronauts assure themselves that all systems are "go" by warm-up, why not the sports performer?

The evidence that warm-up prevents injuries is somewhat nebulous. Factors other than warm-up may be more involved in the injury. However, warm-up is necessary if the competitor has already suffered an injury and the warm-up may help accustom the body to the injury or make her less conscious of the pain.

Cool-down is strongly recommended. Gentle exercise following strenuous exercise greatly facilitates recovery by washing out fatigue products such as lactic acid from the vicinity of the working muscle cells and by eliminating oxygen debt. Jogging is one form of gentle exercise frequently used to cool down.

Some Further Female Considerations

As emphasized throughout this text, females can and should participate in vigorous sports. Basic features of a training and conditioning program do not have a gender (i.e., principles of circuit training, interval training, and so forth apply to both males and females). However, a more complete discussion of the physiologic capabilities of the female, including some sex-linked structural and physiologic differences that may alter the application of principles for the female, is included in Chapter 2 in Physiologic Explorations. Chapter 10 is of particular relevance to the design of programs best suited to the female athlete. Some facts are merely underscored here for added attention.

Females, on the average, do have certain limitations in trainability and do require that certain sex differences be acknowledged.[8] In terms of *strength* training, women appear to respond with a reduced or slower rate of improvement than do men. The physiologic cost of maintaining *heat balance* is greater for females than for males, thus the possibility should be considered that females may have greater limitations of performance in hot weather than do males. *Anatomically* (bones, muscles, tendons, ligaments) women are regarded as being more delicately constructed than are men, and on this basis they have been shown to have a higher incidence of inflammation of tendons, foot deficiencies, and knee injuries, particularly from sports involving overstrain and requiring explosive efforts (e.g., short runs and long jumps). The evidence does indicate that at least some activities may not be as well suited to the female's body structure as to the male's.

The best general guide to training programs and competition is, of course, the individual athlete. Such is the case also in regard to whether females should compete during the *menstrual* period. They should neither be prohibited from nor be required to participate, but rather be allowed to do so on a voluntary basis. Certain cautions concerning possible iron deficiency in females as a result of menstruation and the inadvisability of using hormones as aids to improved performance have been noted previously. Further attention is directed to the following changes that may occur and that may indicate the need to refer the athlete to a physician for medical attention concerning endocrine function: premenstrual dull heaviness in pelvis and lower back, swollen and sensitive breasts, headache, nausea and vomiting, tension, depression and full-of-energy or premenstrual tension-type spurts of energy; light or heavy menstrual flow; emotional instability and temper tantrums;

easy bruising, aches and pains, always in one place or another; acne.[24]

REFERENCES

1. Astrand, P., and Rodahl, K. *Textbook of Work Physiology.* New York: McGraw-Hill Book Co., 1970.

2. Astrand, P., et al. Seminar: Maximizing energy levels for training and competition; general athletic nutrition. *Proceedings of the First International Symposium on the Art and Science of Coaching*, Toronto, Canada, October 1-5, 1971. Willowdale, Ontario, Canada: F. I. Productions, 1971, pp. 189-208.

3. Beating the period. *Parade Magazine*, October 1, 1972, p. 15.

4. Blood sport. Scorecard Section, *Sports Illustrated*, Robert W. Creamer (Ed.), November 15, 1971, pp, 13-14.

5. Cooper, M., and Cooper, K. H. *Aerobics for Women.* New York: M. Evans, 1972.

6. Counsilman, J. Handling the stress and staleness problems of the hard training athlete. *Proceedings of the First International Symposium on the Art and Science of Coaching*, Toronto, Canada, October 1-5, 1971. Willowdale, Ontario, Canada: F. I. Productions, 1971, pp. 15-32.

7. Cumming, G. Limiting factors in developing physical performance in sport. *Proceedings of the First International Symposium on the Art and Science of Coaching*, Toronto, Canada, October 1-5, 1971. Willowdale, Ontario, Canada: F. I. Productions, 1971, pp. 427-449.

8. deVries, H. A. *Physiology of Exercise for Physical Education and Athletics.* Dubuque, Iowa: Wm. C. Brown, 1972.

9. deVries, H. Flexibility, an overlooked but vital factor in sports conditioning. *Proceedings of the First International Symposium on the Art and Science of Coaching*, Toronto, Canada, October 1-5, 1971. Willowdale, Ontario, Canada: F. I. Productions, 1971, pp. 209-221.

10. Dintiman, G. Techniques and methods of developing speed in athletic performance. *Proceedings of the First International Symposium on the Art and Science of Coaching*, Toronto, Canada, October 1-5, 1971. Willowdale, Ontario, Canada: F. I. Productions, 1971, pp. 97-130.

11. Holland, G. J. The physiology of flexibility: A review of the literature. *Kinesiology Review*, published by the Council on Kinesiology of the Physical Education Division. Washington, D.C.: American Association for Health, Physical Education and Recreation, 1968, pp. 29-62.

12. Homola, S. *Muscle Training for Athletes.* West Nyack, N.Y.: Parker Publishing Co., 1968.

13. Huss, W. D., et al. Effect of overload warm-ups on the velocity and accuracy of throwing. *Research Quarterly, 33*, 1962, pp. 472-475.

14. Jones, D. M., Squires, C., and Rodahl, K. Effect of rope skipping on physical work capacity. *Research Quarterly, 33*, 1962, pp. 236-238.

15. Jordon, P., and Spencer, B. *Champions in the Making.* Englewood Cliffs, N.J.: Prentice-Hall, Inc., 1968.

16. Kroll, W. Isometric fatigue curves under varied intertrial recuperation periods. *Research Quarterly, 39*, 1968, pp. 106-115.

17. McGlynn, G. H. A reevaluation of isometric strength training. *The Physical Educator, 29,* 1972, pp. 99-100.

18. Morgan, W. P. (Ed.). *Ergogenic Aids and Muscular Performance.* New York: Academic Press, 1972.

19. *Nutrition for Athletes: A Handbook for Coaches.* Washington, D.C.: American Association for Health, Physical Education and Recreation, 1971.

20. Percival, L. Question clinic and commentary on part 1. *Proceedings of the First International Symposium on the Art and Science of Coaching,* Toronto, Canada, October 1-5, 1971. Willowdale, Ontario, Canada: F. I. Productions, 1971, pp. 145-188.

21. Percival, L. Question clinic and commentary on part 3. *Proceedings of the First International Symposium on the Art and Science of Coaching,* Toronto, Canada, October 1-5, 1971. Willowdale, Ontario, Canada: F. I. Productions, 1971, pp. 463-493.

22. Plagenhoef, S. *Patterns of Human Motion, a Cinematographic Analysis.* Englewood Cliffs, N.J.: Prentice-Hall, Inc., 1971.

23. Rarick, G. L. Competitive sport for girls: Effects on growth, development and general health. In *DGWS Research Reports: Women in Sports.* Dorothy V. Harris (Ed.). Washington, D.C.: American Association for Health, Physical Education and Recreation, 1971, pp. 48-52.

24. Rasch, P., and Morehouse, L. *Sports Medicine for Trainers.* Philadelphia: W. B. Saunders Co., 1963.

25. Robson, H. E. Weight training injuries amongst some competitors at the 6th Empire and Commonwealth Games, Cardiff, 1958. Proceedings of Symposium on the Risks of Weight Training and Lifting in Young People. *British Journal of Sports Medicine, 5,* 1970, pp. 58-59.

26. Roby, F. B., and Davis, R. P. *Jogging for Fitness and Weight Control.* Philadelphia: W. B. Saunders Co., 1970.

27. Shephard, R. J. Values and limitations of muscular strength in achieving endurance fitness for sports. *Proceedings of the First International Symposium on the Art and Science of Coaching,* Toronto, Canada, October 1-5, 1971. Willowdale, Ontario, Canada: F. I. Productions, 1971.

28. Thomas, V. *Science and Sport.* Boston: Little, Brown & Co., 1970.

29. Wessel, J., and MacIntyre, C. *Body Contouring and Conditioning Through Movement.* Boston: Allyn and Bacon, 1970.

10. Taking Care of the Athlete — Injury Control, Recognition, Care

The very nature of competitive sport, since it intensifies activity, emotion, and the elements of risk, gives assurance that the possibility of accident is greater than it may be in the usual activities of daily routine.

The field of control and treatment of athletic injury is complex and requires special training, which is the work of athletic trainers and doctors of sports medicine. Coaches usually are not equipped with the knowledges or skills of the competent trainer. For that matter, the number of physicians who are knowledgeable about the factors contributing to sports injuries and preventive measures is small. However, some safety measures may be taken and information should be known by even the average "garden-variety" coach, who in most instances does not have the easy accessibility and guidance of a physician or trainer. The coach can and must take the responsibility for determining requirements related to health, skill, rules, conditioning, equipment and facilities, and emergency measures.

CONTROLLING INJURIES

The most important factors in minimizing the risk of injury are proper conditioning, adequate skill and playing techniques, and properly fitted protective equipment. In addition, the identification of the factors that cause injury may also be an important way to help to prevent injury-producing situations. These factors and some further potential hazards are described on the following pages.

Knowing and Applying Sound Principles of Body Mechanics

Inadequate conditioning is a recognized factor in a high percentage of athletic injuries. The incidence of injury can be reduced by strengthening the muscles. Strong muscles are thicker and more elastic and better able to withstand sudden stretching or stress than are weak muscles. Attention should be given to exercises designed specifically to strengthen the muscle groups most liable to injury in a given sport. Conditioning programs are presented in Chapter 9. Exercises for conditioning, however, can be misused or misunderstood. In some instances exercises may predispose the athlete to injury. For example, a common malpractice is that of performing sit-ups with legs straight and against resistance such as a partner holding the legs down. Other commonly abused exercises include deep knee bends or the duck walk (which may strain and weaken the knee ligaments) and leg lowering and leg raising when the performer does not have adequate strength. Flexibility exercises such as bobbing and bouncing, which involve the development of momentum, may cause too much muscle strain.

Obviously, it is necessary for the coach to have a knowledge of kinesiology in order to understand and to apply those principles of body mechanics that create more accident-free situations. Some basic mechanical principles are outlined in Chapter 6. The kinesiological principles of injury prevention have been outlined by Wells.[11] In addition, coaches should avail themselves of some of the excellent books dealing with muscle training, the prevention and care of athletic injuries, and safety procedures in sports.[1,5,6,8,10] The following small sampling of illustrations may serve to point out that basic principles of movement and safety are applicable to almost any sport.

Alignment of the body segments should be maintained in order to preserve the strongest anatomic position. Undue pressure can be put on the back or even injury occur simply by poor position. The legs offer the key to support. Bending at the waist without bending the knees (whether propelling an object, sitting, or moving one's body) is an unnatural position and can induce a painful pull in the muscles. Movement should be smooth rather than jerky, because jerking increases manyfold the pressure of any task. Muscles should be contracted (tensed) rather than relaxed in order to resist forceful extensions (throwing, hitting, lifting) or sudden, unexpected pushes, pulls, and blows.

Injuries usually occur when the total force is concentrated on a small area. The principle of giving with the force, or "riding with the punch," basically means flexing or bending the arms and knees, taking several steps in the direction of movement, rolling, or making other accommodations in body positioning that enable the body to absorb shock through the muscles rather than to cause undue stress in the joints. In landing from a fall or a jump or in a slide, the body weight should be distributed over as wide an area as possible. A roll or somersault or slight twist of the body to take the force of impact on the upper arm and shoulder may be needed in order to diminish momentum (e.g., making a reaching "dig" in volleyball). Falls or landings should be made on the heavily padded part of the body (e.g., in the slide in softball the side of the thigh should be used rather than the "tail" bone). An extended arm, wrist, elbow, or knee should not be used to break any fall.

A joint may be injured if it is forced beyond its normal range of motion. The safety adage, "It is not the blow that does the damage, it is the position of the joint," makes evident that some practices invite injury—fixing the foot, locking the knees, and making uncontrolled changes of direction that shift the body weight against the ligaments.

Proper technique is a must in running, stopping and starting, dodging, and other evasive maneuvers used in most sport activities. In running, for example, the toes should be pointed in the direction of movement. When quick changes of direction are made, the toes should be in alignment with the knee and with the direction of movement in order to avoid vulnerable angle positioning of the knee—if the knee points inward, so should the toes. During play the knees should be slightly bent with the muscles of the thigh and leg slightly tensed. By maintaining continuous tension in the thigh muscles, the knees are protected more by the tightened tendons. The weight should be forward over the balls of the feet in order to permit the legs to rotate with the body weight and to prepare for further action in any direction.

Knee injuries are common among athletes and almost always of a serious nature, because when a knee joint is injured it may never regain strength and integrity. Because most injuries to the knee occur on the inside (medial) portion of the joint, it is important to use good foot posture and exercises to strengthen the muscles passing over the inside of the knee. Leg curls, leg extensions, straight-leg raises, foot lifts, toe flexion, and pigeon-toed heel raises are exercises that help lessen the knee's vulnerability to injury.

Using Skillful and Sporting Playing Techniques

Skill, which reinforces a player's courage and sureness, is often a determining factor in injury prevention. The player who lacks proper skill may either barge ahead blindly or vacillate with lack of certainty in key situations, setting up the condition for inevitable injury. The athlete also should be careful not to exceed the effort accustomed to or suddenly change the type of exercise or activity. Trying too hard, straining, pressing, and hurrying result in tension and unnecessary muscular contractions which cause fatigue.

As Vince Lombardi noted, *fatigue* makes cowards of us all. Certainly numerous injuries occur when fatigue occurs and causes uncoordinated haphazard movements. This usually happens during the final stages of the game when emotions are running at high pitch. The last run down the ski slope frequently proves to be the last. The villain may be fatigue.

Strictly enforcing and obeying the *rules* and practicing good sportsmanship are necessary to control injury as well as to enjoyment of the game. When players clash with the rules, they frequently clash with each other. Sometimes it is the officials, by loosely applying the rules, who create hazards. Players and coaches who exert pressures on or deceive officials or who play to the limits of the letter-of-the-rule, rather than observe the spirit of the rules, introduce elements of danger as well as dislike into the game.

Using Proper Protective Equipment

Adequate protective equipment such as knee guards, padding, and other necessary safety devices often is needed to fully protect vulnerable areas from blows. The important concern is that the equipment does not restrict movement so as to interfere with coordination or to throw an extra burden on ill-prepared joints. Joints that are not supported or shielded from blows by protective equipment do become subjected to gradually increasing stress and are vulnerable to sudden injury.

There are disagreements about the value of such protective equipment as artificial supports—ankle straps, wrist bands, taping —although protective *taping* and preventive strappings are part of a complete injury prevention program. Physical harm, however, can be inflicted on the player by a haphazard tape job. It is also possible for the athlete to have a false sense of security because she is taped. Post-injury taping must also be practiced skillfully.

Some coaches (perhaps women in particular) are so enamored with techniques of taping that they tape every available appendage. Excessive and even unnecessary taping seems to be a kind of psychologic thing for some players as well, who come to believe they cannot play unless they are "all taped up." Such a practice seems designed more to prove that they have become real big-time coaches or champion players than to protect against injury. For example, some coaches believe it is necessary to tape automatically the wrists and fingers of volleyball players, when a better practice would be to develop the player's needed skills and strength. Taping should not be used as a substitute for proper conditioning and skill; its primary purpose is to prevent further injury.

Proper taping procedures may be found in numerous books dealing with kinesiology and athletic training, some of which are listed in the previous section. In addition, there are books devoted
ques.[2]

:o Injuries

zards. The coach should gather as
bout the nature of injuries peculiar
gh the causative factors of injuries
iny particular sport or activity, the
ie referred to a trainer or physician
ns and know how they can be pre-
e time, such data may be helpful in
programs. For example, Ken Fore-
n's Long Distance Running Sub-
hletic Union of the United States,
from a variety of sources revealed
ow a rather predictable pattern as
rents are concerned.[4]

ustain foot problems, including blisters,
having exceptionally long toes not infre-
of the second metatarsal. Medial displace-
ciated with long arch strain, is a common
io are forced to train on streets or other
er from severe inflammation of the flexor
ondyle of the humerus. This becomes a
particular   lem for girls who use a ¾ or side arm delivery.

Tendonitis of the wrist flexors is a common problem for shot putters. Painful hyperextension of the profundus and sublimis tendons commonly occurs when young girls begin to put the shot. The latter problem often can be eliminated, or corrected, by a protracted period of squeezing against a firm sponge ball. Because the brass shot is relatively small, frequent traumatic abduction, hyperextension of the index finger occurs when the implement slips off the hand during the ballistic flip at the instant of delivery.

The female athlete seems to be highly susceptible to soft tissue injuries. Hurdlers frequently bruise their shins, knees and gluteal muscles while working over the hurdle barrier. The hamstring pull is a common consequence of early season sprinting. Perhaps the underlying causative factor here is a marked imbalance between the agonists and antagonists due to minimal long term training by a majority of girls and women. In recent years achilles inflammation, with the classic edema and squeaky tendon, has become a major problem.[4]

Such findings led Foreman to recommend strongly that, for hamstring pull as a consequence of early season sprinting, early season stair running be eliminated and training sessions be conducted on soft surfaces in running flats.[4]

Numerous analyses of football injuries that have enabled coaches to help prevent injury-producing situations have been made; however, there is a need for further studies of body motion forces that cause injury in other sports, particularly in women's gymnastics.

Ruling Out Other Potential Dangers

Overcrowded *facilities*, which may create safety hazards, and inadequate time for conditioning programs and for scheduling events also may invite injury of players. The *length of the season* for any sport should be clearly defined and limited to a period consistent with the welfare of the athlete and the conduct of other sports programs within the school year. The time should not be so long that excessive demands are made on the participants nor should it interfere with the academic program of the sponsoring institution. The *athlete* can pose potential dangers to herself as well as to others. Crash diets or other drastic weight reduction measures can cause permanent harm to the body. Fads and superstitions, often characteristic of athletes, may interfere with appropriate training habits and practices. Personality factors such as proneness to injury, intense emotional reactions, immature behavior leading to self-inflicted punishment, and the like are certainly injury-producing behaviors. Personality inventories may help to assess the athlete's motivation in sport and her emotional reactions and thus be important in controlling injuries. The individual athlete, however, must be taught to assume a greater degree of responsibility for her own safety and welfare.[9]

RECOGNIZING AND CARING FOR INJURIES

The coach cannot assume that an athlete's good performance is assurance that she is in good health or free of injury. Just as athletes are known to fake injury, so are they known to transcend the limits imposed by injury in order to continue playing. At the same time an athlete may not realize the nature or extent of an injury or perhaps even care because she is so intensely involved in the activity. It is necessary for the coach to observe the athlete closely and to educate her to be observant.

Techniques of Physical Inspection

Both coach and athlete can utilize simple routine techniques of physical inspection in order to be on the alert for the familiar signs and symptoms of disorders that normally might be overlooked. Possible indications of injury which should be easily recognized are signs such as a dazed appearance, a limp, an expression of pain, a deviation in the player's typical personality. It is necessary also to be wary of what may seem to be normal. For example, the athlete who has continual or recurring back pains or repeated discomfort seemingly from merely a strain or a sprain, even if the pains are not severe, may, in fact, have a seriously disabling back injury.

Procedures in Case of Injury

When an injury does occur, it is a sound legal as well as therapeutic measure to follow certain approved standard procedures for taking care of the athlete. It may be advisable to have appropriate authorities determine whether or not the procedures to be followed comply with legal requirements.

Procedures such as the maintenance and utilization of charts for conditioning and weight control and having first aid equipment, stretchers, blankets, and the like at the scene of competition, should be matters of routine. Other standard procedures that should be followed when an injury or accident occurs are to:

1. *Determine the nature and extent* of the injury. Immediately, calmly, and with great care, examine the athlete. Observe eyes, neck, trunk, limbs, facial expression, breathing, position of the head, neck, trunk, limbs. Gently feel (palpate) the affected part with the fingers, noting any variation from normal position, size, shape, color; presence of lumps, depressions, swelling, fever, and the like. If medical help is needed, intelligently describe the injury to the physician.

2. *Obtain information* from the athlete or, if she is unconscious, from those witnessing the accident, if possible. Such information should include type of pain (sharp, dull, throbbing), site of the pain, evidence of any ripping, popping, or snapping, exact cause of injury, evidence of any previous injury to the same part or area.

3. Give the necessary *first aid treatment* prior to removing the athlete from the playing area after an assessment of the injury has been made; however, first aid often is administered, depending upon the injury, as the athlete is being examined. Removal of the

athlete is considered a part of the first aid procedure. If it is necessary to move the athlete, determine whether her condition warrants medical sanction before moving her. Use a stretcher if the athlete is unconscious or unable to move under her own power or with assistance.

4. *Report* the injury with all pertinent information on a standard accident report form, which should include: date and place, sport, injury, how injury occurred, emergency procedures followed, names and signatures (if possible) of two witnesses.

Muscle Injuries

Simple complaints such as muscle soreness or lameness and slight muscle injuries such as bruises and the well-known charley horse (muscle spasm) seem to be difficult to avoid and, in most instances, can be treated by simple first aid measures. There is evidence that the typical delayed muscle soreness, which frequently follows a hard workout, is the result of spasm, and that relief is obtained by treating it as a muscle spasm.[3] Local fatigue causes incomplete relaxation of some of the motor units, causing an insufficient blood supply to certain areas within the muscle. When there is muscle soreness, the muscle involved, how it became sore, and what the activity was should be determined. Then the muscle should be put in its longest length (static stretch) and held in that position for a minute or two, and the stretch repeated after a short interval of rest. The bouncing type of stretch which induces a reflex contraction should not be used.

Muscle spasm and a ruptured or torn muscle are not the same thing. The more serious injury of torn muscle, partial separation, or severe contusion is associated with such immediately recognizable symptoms as pain, disability, black and blue discoloration. Obviously, a medical doctor should be called immediately. Until the severity of the injury can be determined by a physician's examination, emergency first aid treatment should be rendered by applying cold (cold pack or immersion in a pan of water) to constrict capillaries, reduce swelling, and relieve pain. If "home treatment" is deemed all that is needed, cold should be applied continuously or as frequently as possible. If the injury appears to be serious, cold treatments should be repeated for 24 to 36 hours but not longer than 48 hours, because cold retards circulation and thus healing. Some quick sources of cold are Gel-packs which are chilled by storing in a refrigerator; chemically treated ice bags which become cold when opened; ethyl-chloride spray; or make-shift devices such as crushed ice in plastic containers or wrapped in a towel. After 36 to 48 hours, when pain and swelling have subsided, heat is usually substituted for cold since heat stimulates blood circulation, thus healing injured tissue. With the application of heat, usually light exercise and massage are used. Moist heat is more effective than is dry heat and may be administered by a hot water bottle or a moist cloth kept hot by a heating lamp or an infrared lamp. A complete guide to care of specific types of injury (e.g., of skin, muscles, joints, head, trunk, leg, foot, arm, hand, and heat-related problems) is Brown's *Complete Guide to Prevention and Treatment of Athletic Injuries*, which was written primarily for the coach who must be his own trainer or who must supervise the injury care program.[1]

Rehabilitation of injured muscles, such as may be done through weight training programs, should be started as soon as possible. The return of function depends upon the restoration of muscle strength, endurance, and range of motion. Therapeutic exercises yielding the greatest gains are those in which the muscles are contracted slowly with maximal intensity holding the contraction for a few seconds—greater gains in strength are made through the use of a heavy weight lifted a few repetitions than of a light weight lifted many repetitions. Any exercise should be done rhythmically and should not be executed to the point of exhaustion (see Appendix for sample exercises and weight training programs suitable for girls and women).

Fractures

The only way to identify fractures (partial to complete separation of bony parts) accurately is by x-ray films. Whenever there is the possibility of a fracture, the athlete should be referred to the physician immediately. There is little that the coach or trainer can do except to render first aid. It is important, however, that the coach understand the signs of gross fracture in order to know what first aid measures should be used. Excellent books are available and they should be studied carefully. The following brief statements from *Modern Principles of Athletic Training* by Klafs and Arnheim offer an example of the kind of checklist the coach should utilize in determining signs of gross fracture:

1. Determine the mechanism of injury (What sport? How was she hit? How did she fall? Did she feel sudden pain? Often immediate pain subsides and numbness occurs in 20 to 30 minutes.)

2. Inspect the area of suspected fracture. Is there deformity? rapid swelling? discoloration? (Discoloration may not appear for several days.) Is there abnormal movement of the

part sometimes giving the impression of an extra joint?
By palpation determine the presence of direct point ten-
derness, particularly over bony structures; indirect tender-
ness; irregularity in the continuity of the bone. On
moving the body part, determine if there is a grating sound
apparent at the fracture site.[6]

If a fracture is suspected, as in other unexposed injuries, pressure and ice should be applied in all cases with the exception of a
compound fracture (bone extends through the outer layers of skin,
resulting in an open wound). The athlete should be treated for
shock and the area of the suspected fracture splinted properly when
it is necessary to transport the athlete. Hemorrhaging of a compound fracture (open wound) should be controlled by applying a
sterile dressing to the wound. Immediate and professional care
should be secured. Professional care also means that, for any injury, the athlete should not return prematurely to competition that
might interfere with the healing process or invite further injury.

The reader who desires more detailed information regarding
prevention and care of injuries and physical restoration of the
competitor should consult a comprehensive text on athletic training.
One such text directed more specifically to girls and women is *The
Female Athlete* by Klafs and Lyon.[7]

REFERENCES

1. Brown, B. J. *Complete Guide to the Prevention and Treatment of Athletic Injuries.* West Nyack, N.Y.: Parker Publishing Co., 1972.

2. Cerney, J. V. *Complete Book of Athletic Taping Techniques.* Englewood Cliffs, N.J.: Prentice-Hall, Inc., 1972.

3. deVries, H. Flexibility, an overlooked but vital factor in sports conditioning. *Proceedings of the First International Symposium on the Art and Science of Coaching,* Toronto, Canada, October 1-5, 1971. Willowdale, Ontario, Canada: F. I. Productions, 1971.

4. Foreman, K. What research says about the female athlete. Report made at the Pacific Northwest Sports Medicine Seminar, Seattle, Wash., March 19, 1972.

5. Homola, S. *Muscle Training for Athletes.* West Nyack, N.Y.: Parker Publishing Co., 1968.

6. Klafs, C. E., and Arnheim, D. D. *Modern Principles of Athletic Training* (2nd ed.). St. Louis: C. V. Mosby Co., 1969.

7. Klafs, C., and Lyon, M. J. *The Female Athlete.* St. Louis: C. V. Mosby Co., 1973.

8. Morehouse, L. E., and Rasch, P. J. *Sports Medicine for Trainers* (2nd ed.). Philadelphia: W. B. Saunders Co., 1963.

9. Ryan, A. J. Prevention of sports injury: A problem solving approach.

Journal of Health, Physical Education and Recreation. April 1971, pp. 24-29.

10. *Sports Safety.* Safety Education Division of the American Association for Health, Physical Education and Recreation and the United States Public Health Services. Washington, D.C.: National Education Association Publication-Sales, 1971.

11. Wells, K. F. *Kinesiology* (5th ed.). Philadelphia: W. B. Saunders Co., 1971.

11. Some New Priorities and Coaching Extras

Great issues develop from small beginnings.

Norman Vincent Peale

Functions that will become increasingly important as programs of competitive sports for girls and women become enlarged include those which may be considered as ancillary to actual coaching. Some of these coaching extras, described on the following pages, include: spectator control, legal aspects, and relations with the public. In addition, the structures that guide and govern programs for girls and women are considered.

SPECTATOR SPORTSMANSHIP AND CROWD CONTROL

Patsy Neal, an outstanding sportswoman and coach, in her book *Sport and Identity,* captured rather poignantly the meaning of spectator sportsmanship.[11]

> I think only an athlete can fully understand what it feels like to work for years to make a team—to give up things in order to be at peak in performance—to pray that the mind and the body will be coordinated for that supreme effort that makes the difference between a good night and a poor one—and possibly only an athlete can comprehend the obscenity of having a spectator or a group of spectators be critical of the worth of years of effort when the spectator has had no real part in the agony or the glory.

> For a spectator to feel he or she has the right to make a judgment concerning the quality of play on the court or the field, or to be the judge who can lessen a man's achievement through catcalls and boos, is to me one of the most depressing facets of our society today. Probably the *least* qualified individual to judge excellence is the spectator. . . . [11]

But, somewhere, somehow, sometime, the concept of sportsmanship changed. Attendance at almost any competitive sporting event leads one to assume that perhaps audiences in general consider booing as one of the fundamental civil rights. In fact, within the context of what has come to be known as "battle games," sport may serve a crucial biologic purpose in that it provides a vicarious release of those potentially destructive aggressive energies frequently sublimated in other walks of life. Certainly the stadia and grandstands are filled with virulent as well as timid fans who alike vehemently yell "kill 'em," "murder the bum!"

Booing and similar invectives shouted at the opponents, however, may be the less bizarre and disruptive problems created when spectators enter the sport scene. The spectator problems, in fact, may be impossible to eliminate in men's athletics programs even though the seriousness of such problems appears to be increasing. Incidences of misconduct, such as attacks on players and officials, vandalism, rowdyism, and riots, have become critical problems in the world of sports.

Some causes of spectator problems have been delineated as being: lack of anticipation of and preventive planning for possible trouble; lack of proper facilities; poor communication resulting in lack of information; lack of involvement of one or more of the school administration, faculty, student body, parents, community, press, law enforcement agencies; lack of respect for authority and property; attendance at games of youths under the influence of narcotics; increased attitude of permissiveness; school dropouts; recent graduates; and outsiders.[6] A significant number of the respondents (88 per cent) in one survey declared that the conduct of the coach on the bench greatly influenced crowd behavior.[13] The problem probably is amplified when sport announcers point up the tensions involved and use instant replay to dispute the referee's decision.

In an attempt to deal with this pressing problem in programs for boys and men, organizations studying the causes of spectator brawls have developed policies and procedures to be followed in controlling crowds. The National Council of Secondary School Athletic Directors developed the publication *Crowd Control,* which points out that improving sportsmanship and avoiding misconduct necessitate three phases of action: education, involvement, and enforcement.[7] Several approaches to the solutions of crowd control and safety control problems concentrating on treating the causes of the problems are recommended in the document cited, including such suggestions as developing written policies and guidelines, providing adequate facilities, teaching good sportsmanship throughout the school and community, informing the community, involving law enforcement and supervisory personnel, preparing spectators and contestants.[7] Among other meaningful miscellaneous suggestions were to impose severe penalties on faculty and student leaders guilty of poor conduct; to publish the identity of offenders at games and notify their parents, if possible; to enforce rules and regulations consistently; to avoid overstressing the winning of games; to discontinue double-headers and triple-headers.

PUBLIC RELATIONSHIPS

Among the highlights of professional preparation conferences is the recommendation that persons in coaching need particular competencies in public relations and courage to withstand pressures from noneducational emphasis. Various professional conferences have identified the need to clarify the role of a participant in extramural sports to the many groups of the public—administrators, colleagues, students, community, and so forth.

Positive relationships with all school personnel may be established by involving administrators in all aspects of the program; being courteous and prepared with appropriate facts when making requests; cooperating with other faculty and offering to help with their programs; being involved in the total school and in policymaking areas; being flexible and innovative, particularly in such matters as use of existing facilities; employing a variety of techniques to reach people and to communicate the value of the program.

An effective program of public relations also involves other considerations such as: *financial soundness* and *equitable budgeting* for all sports; *harmonious* and *professional relations* among coaches, players, other faculty, and the community; the best possible *education, health protection,* and general *well-being of the participants;* proper *care of property and equipment;* evidence of *constructive and commendable behavior* in both players and coaches; *communication* with all news media, athletic associations, school administrations, and other appropriate personnel; *thorough preparation* related to facilities, officials, game schedules, spectators, and the like.

LEGAL ASPECTS OF COACHING

Where does the law fit into coaching? The National Safety Council reported in 1972 that of the 62.5 per cent of the accidents that occurred in the school, physical education, athletics, and recreation accounted for 40 per cent of them. Obviously, coaches are engaged in work in which there is considerable legal risk. In view of legal hazards of the profession to which they belong, as well as the trend of increased litigation in injury cases and changing immunity interpretations, it is imperative that coaches know the law, eliminate every possibility for injury, and exercise careful supervision.

The need for exposure to the legal aspects of physical education and coaching has been emphasized in numerous articles, books,[2] and conferences, and has led to the development of courses within the professional preparation program[4] that deal with such legal aspects as tort liability, negligence, attractive nuisance, governmental immunity, liability insurance, and so forth.

Litigation of particular concern to the coach centers around such matters as negligence and personal rights of the athlete. Negligence is established if it is shown that the coach failed to act as a reasonably prudent person would in the same or similar circumstances. Types of behavior and actions that may lead to an allegation of negligence generally result from failure to exercise due care and precaution in relation to: adequate *preparation;* appropriate *skill;* suitable *curriculum; situations* that may involve or create unreasonable risk; dangerous *equipment,* devices, or instrumentalities; *inspection* and repair of equipment and devices; the giving of adequate *warning* and proper representation; the entrusting of *competent* supervisory personnel; the performance of one's *duty;* and the exercise of control.

Although there are no simple, concrete answers for avoiding a lawsuit, Koehler offered some guidelines that should help to deter the possibility of a suit or litigation.

1. Teachers of physical education should be properly qualified or certified. A coach or teacher should know the extent of his abilities and/or qualifications and not overextend himself into areas of less competencies.
2. Instruction in physical education should occur within the rules and regulations of the state and its agencies, the profession, and course outlines.
3. Personnel in physical education should be aware of the dangers and hazards in activities, that they might be able to anticipate and foresee such dangers.
4. Physical education instructional methodology should include techniques of: (1) supervision; (2) ability grouping; (3) equipment selection; (4) proper first aid; (5) equipment and facility inspection; and (6) what constitutes a safe environment for conducting activities:
    (a) Supervision—Group size, nature of activity and participants.
    (b) Ability grouping—Age, size, health and skill ability level.
    (c) Equipment selection—Fit, quality, safety factors.
    (d) First Aid—Training, standardized procedure, report forms, follow-up and referrals.
    (e) Inspection—Equipment and facility defects, report forms, procedure and repair.
    (f) Safe Environment—Nature of activity, numbers participating, safety engineering (area design, location, and hazard free).[10]

Should a litigation for negligence result, there are some legal defenses:

1. no duty — the defendant had no duty or responsibility toward plaintiff;
2. no breach of duty;
3. assumption of risk—a plaintiff who, by his conduct, assumed risk of injury from an unknown danger;
4. contributory negligence—the injured person, by his own negligence or by the negligence of another legally imputable to him, proximately contributed to the injury;
5. vis major—irrespective of motive an act does occur in an unexpected manner, or by chance; this has been defined as an accident and is meant to imply the lack of purpose to create the result.

In addition, Koehler described some factors that may strengthen the defense:

1. Don't assume undue risk . . . in areas where certification, qualifications or competence is in question.
2. Foreseeability . . . have knowledge of dangers that exist in activity and use reasonable care against foreseeable danger, e.g., equipment, over-crowding, spotting and safety practices, techniques for skills or performances.
3. Standards or norms in methodology; the extent to which the mode or method is commonplace in the profession throughout the state or nation.
4. Teaching outlines, and/or guides; teaching accord with the standards established in the profession by leaders and expressed through teaching outlines and guides, etc.
5. Stare Decisis; precedent of previous cases under the same or similar circumstances.
6. Insurance; this affords not only financial protection, but also legal counsel and guidance.[10]

STRUCTURES SETTING DIRECTIONS IN SPORTS PROGRAMS FOR GIRLS AND WOMEN

Many organizations have influence on and provide direction to sports programs for girls and women. It is imperative that those who coach be knowledgeable about and involved in these organizations if they are to help determine policies that influence the course of athletics for the female competitor. A brief discussion concerning the organizations that formulate policy governing sports programs for girls and women and that are most instrumental in developing programs to improve teaching and officiating, and in disseminating information regarding sport opportunities, rules, and the like follows.

The Division for Girls and Women's Sports of the American Association for Health, Physical Education and Recreation was the first of these organizations. The early counterparts of DGWS directed their attention to specific sport situations. For example, a committee was appointed in 1899 to study modifications in basketball rules for girls. In 1916, the Women's Athletic Committee was formed by the American Physical Education Association (now the AAHPER) to develop rules and serve in an advisory capacity for the rapidly expanding sports programs. In 1923 the National Amateur Athletic Federation of America (NAAFA) was established and later that year the Women's Division of that organization emerged. In 1940 common concerns of the Women's Athletic Committee (of APEA) and the Women's Division (of NAAFA) brought about the merger of the two organizations under the name of the National Section for Women's Athletics, later called National Section for Girls and Women's Sports, and in 1958 it became the Division for Girls and Women's Sports.[3]

The 1960s witnessed considerable growth of interest in and organizations for competitive sports for girls and women. Sport federations began to appear in the early 1960s, at first in track and field and later in basketball, gymnastics, and baseball. These specific sport federations and other advocates of the federation emphasis, such as the National Collegiate Athletic Association, the National Junior College Association, the National Federation of State High School Athletic Associations (NFSHAA), the armed forces and "open" competitions, grew out of the belief that their interests should be represented in planning for international competition. Today DGWS has representatives on the governing boards of these various sport federations. For example, the National Federation of State High School Athletic Associations, to which DGWS sends a representative, formulates and carries out policies, develops rules, and provides information as the appropriate regulatory body for girls' interscholastic sports. Thousands of schools are represented through their State High School Associations. Rule books, official manuals, handbooks, and information on all aspects of high school athletics may be obtained from NFSHAA.

DGWS has provided service also to student Girls Athletic Association (GAA) and Women's Recreation Association (WRA) sport organizations in schools and colleges since 1962 when services to the Athletic and Recreation Federation of College Women (ARFCW) were incorporated and the National Girls' Athletic Association (NGAA) originated. In 1971 the ARFCW changed its title to College Women in Sport (CWS). DGWS assists CWS and NGAA by guiding, not dictating, their programs of sport and dance activities used for recreational, performance, or competitive purposes.[8]

The National Institute on Girls' Sports, held in 1963, was

sponsored jointly by DGWS and the Women's Board of the United States Olympic Development Committee. In 1965 the Study Conference on Competition, held in Washington, D.C., produced *Guidelines for Intercollegiate Athletic Programs for Women.*

DGWS also has representatives in numerous other organizations that are national[5] and international in scope in order to keep informed of their developments and to inform these organizations of DGWS policies and actions. Among such organizations are: the International Olympic Committee (IOC), which establishes the rules and regulations for all open international sport competition, and the United States Olympic Committee (USOC),* a member of the IOC. The IOC also recognizes one organization in each member country as the governing body for the particular sport in that country and DGWS has representatives on many of these governing bodies. Each governing body has jurisdiction over eligibility, regulations, and means of selecting athletes for international open competition (Olympic Games, World Games, Pan-American Games). For example, the United States Volleyball Association (USVBA) is the sport's governing group, designated by the International Volleyball Federation. A joint committee of the USVBA and the AAHPER, which is part of the USVBA development program, engages in procedures for improving instruction in volleyball in schools. The DGWS has a representative to the USVBA and to the joint AAHPER-USVBA. Organizations to which DGWS liaison representatives are appointed are:

AAU Basketball Committee   AAU Swimming Committee
USOC Basketball Committee   USOC Swimming Committee

AAU Diving Committee   AAU Track & Field Committee
USOC Diving Committee   USOC Track & Field Committee

AAU Synchronized   US Gymnastics Federation
   Swimming   US Basketball Federation
AAU Gymnastic Committee   US Track and Field Federation

US Volleyball Association
USOC Volleyball Committee
Joint Committee
   AAHPER-USVBA

Council for National Cooperation in Aquatics
   (AAHPER representative)

*A directory of United States sports' governing organizations and other major athletic groups, including, when available, sites and dates of national and world championships, from the United States Olympic Committee Newsletter, was reproduced in the *Journal of the American Association for Health, Physical Education and Recreation,* April 1972, pp. 52-53.

Women's National Aquatic Forum (unofficial)

National Federation of State High School Associations

National Association for Physical Education of College Women

United States Lawn Tennis Association Women's Collegiate
    Advisory Committee

In 1967 the Commission on Intercollegiate Athletics for Women
(CIAW) was organized in order to encourage organizations to
govern competition for women at the local, state, or regional level,
to hold DGWS national championships as the need for them became
apparent, and to sanction closed intercollegiate events in which
five or more colleges or universities participated. The work of
CIAW accomplished the creation of many sports' governing groups
across the nation and in the conduct of DGWS national championships in several sports.

In 1971 the Association for Intercollegiate Athletics for Women
(AIAW), organized by AAHPER to replace CIAW, was designed
to provide a governing body and continuing leadership for women's
intercollegiate athletic programs. The DGWS, which created, developed, and financially supported the CIAW, also initiated the
formation of the AIAW and continues to provide the new organization with consultant services, program assistance, rules, publications, and officials.

The AIAW, which, in a sense, has become the female counterpart of the men's NCAA, had 275 charter members. The basic
philosophy of AIAW, under the umbrella of DGWS/AAHPER/
NEA, is that as a worthwhile educational experience the program of
intercollegiate athletics for women should be funded by the institutions and not be dependent upon variable sources such as gate receipts, and that women physical educators are best prepared to
determine the directions of intercollegiate sports programs for
women. The broad purposes* of AIAW are to:

1. Foster broad programs of women's intercollegiate athletics
    which are consistent with the educational aims and objec-
    tives of the member schools and in accordance with the
    philosophy and standards of the Division for Girls and
    Women's Sports (DGWS).

2. Assist member schools to extend and enrich their programs
    of intercollegiate athletics for women.

---

* Proposed Operating Code of the Association for Intercollegiate Athletics
for Women, Division for Girls and Women's Sports, American Association for
Health, Physical Education and Recreation, September 15, 1971, pp. 1-7.

3. Stimulate the development of quality leadership for women's intercollegiate athletic programs.

4. Encourage excellence in performance of participants in women's intercollegiate athletics.

The AIAW distributes materials concerning (1) policies and procedures for National Intercollegiate Championships, (2) procedures for submitting a bid to hold a National Intercollegiate Championship, (3) procedures for the Meet Director, and developed the (4) *AIAW Handbook* of Procedures for Women's Intercollegiate Athletic Events.[1]

The Officiating Services Area (OSA) is designated as one of the seven areas of the Division of Girls and Women's Sports.[9] Formerly known as the Women's National Officials Rating Committee (WNORC), which originated in 1922 when the need for basketball officials was acute, the present OSA has over 180 local boards. The purpose of the OSA, that of promoting quality officiating, is undertaken through such services as developing techniques of officiating, establishing standards of conduct for officials, producing educational materials, studying the role of officiating in sports, and examining the needs and problems in officiating. An Executive Board meets annually in order to conduct the business of OSA. In addition to the officers, the Executive Board includes District Officiating Coordinators (DOC), one each from the six AAHPER districts, and chairmen of three committees: Principles and Techniques of Officiating (P & T of O), Examinations and Ratings (E & R), Editorial and Publications.

Official ratings are awarded in badminton, basketball, competitive swimming, softball, tennis, track and field, and volleyball by means of written and practical tests. A rating in fencing, being developed, will constitute the tenth rating. The gymnastics rating is a joint rating with the United States Gymnastics Federation (USGF). In 1968 the Joint Committee of DGWS-USGF also established the Women's Gymnastics Certification Committee and those persons who pass the examination receive a rating card certifying them as judges.

OSA publications include the *Policies and Practices Handbook, Handbook for Teaching Basketball Officiating, The Training of Judges for Gymnastics,* a guide for rating boards, an OSA section in the various DGWS Sports Guides, and it has produced a training film.

In 1972 the OSA revamped the rating system for all sports except gymnastics and synchronized swimming in order to encourage more women to become rated officials, to encourage local boards to try new methods of rating officials, to examine the success of various criteria for ratings, and to identify more accurately the national officials.[12] The Honorary Rating and the Junior National Rating were eliminated; an Apprentice Rating and State Rating were instigated. For additional information the reader should consult the District Officiating Coordinator or the revised edition of the *Policies and Procedures Handbook*.

Numerous other organizations are in liaison with coaching associations and cooperate with the various groups described previously in efforts to make scientific knowledge available and to develop resource material related to the coaching process and, in some instances, to create structures of ethics, standards, systems of certification, and related professional concerns. Although these organizations are too numerous to chronicle in detail here, some with which the enlightened coach may be most familiar include the North American Society for the Psychology of Sport and Physical Activity, the International Council for Sport and Physical Education, and the International Society for Sport Psychology. A relative newcomer to the scholarly study of sports from a philosophic perspective is the Philosophic Society for the Study of Sport, founded in 1972. The interest manifested in sports by these and various other organizations of the world well merits the attention of coaches. Their members are expert in various branches of society —doctors, psychologists, educators, government employees, members of governing bodies of sports, private citizens. In most instances membership is open to coaches in all sports, at all levels of competition, and, at the present time, few women's names appear on the membership lists. Accordingly, it appears logical to suggest that women become more involved in these organizations if they are to create an awareness of the advantages of effective liaison efforts with women's sports organizations and the necessity for women to determine the destiny of women's programs.

In 1973 a DGWS Reorganization Committee inaugurated plans for a new structure designed to serve all those who give leadership to sports programs for girls and women. The title is National Association for Girls and Women in Sports (NAGWS). Although some details are still being worked out and the bylaws are being written at the present time, the various autonomous groups represented in the coordinating structure are outlined in the following chart. In general, it is anticipated that the groups will inform the Board of Directors of the services they need to carry on their work, and the Board, in turn, will coordinate requests for services from the sub-groups and assign specific projects to the appropriate standing committees. The kinds of services

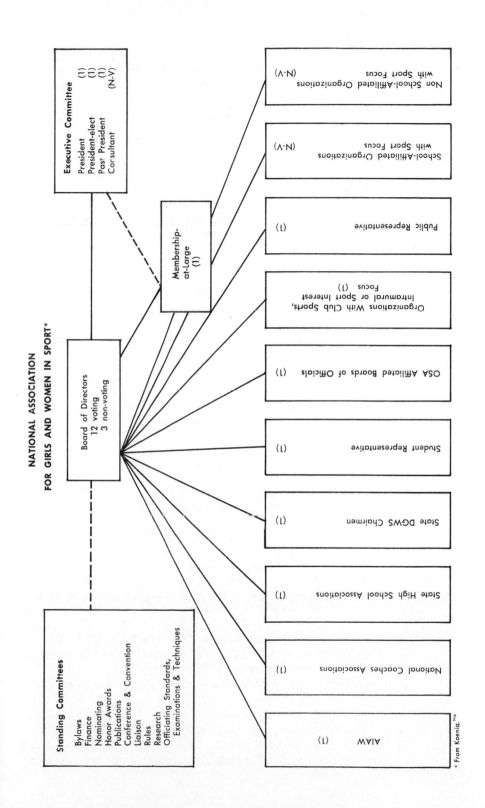

NATIONAL ASSOCIATION
FOR GIRLS AND WOMEN IN SPORT*

Executive Committee

President (1)
President-elect (1)
Past President (1)
Consultant (N-V)

Board of Directors
12 voting
3 non-voting

Membership-at-Large (1)

Standing Committees

Bylaws
Finance
Nominating
Honor Awards
Publications
Conference & Convention
Liaison
Rules
Research
Officiating Standards,
Examinations & Techniques

Non School-Affiliated Organizations with Sport Focus (N-V)

School-Affiliated Organizations with Sport Focus (N-V)

Public Representative (1)

Organizations With Club Sports, Intramural or Sport Interest Focus (1)

OSA Affiliated Boards of Officials (1)

Student Representative (1)

State DGWS Chairmen (1)

State High School Associations (1)

National Coaches Associations (1)

AIAW (1)

NAGWS will be able to provide (as is the case with any association under the new American Alliance for Health, Physical Education and Recreation beginning in June 1974) will depend on the number of Alliance members who join the particular Association, and on the publication profits that the Association brings into the Alliance.[10a]

REFERENCES

1. *AIAW Handbook.* 1201 16th St., N.W., Washington, D.C.: Division for Girls and Women's Sports of the American Association for Health, Physical Education and Recreation.

2. Appenzeller, H. *From the Gym to the Jury.* Charlottesville, Va.: Michie, Educational Division, 1972.

3. Atwood, J. Girls and women's sports philosophy and standards area. *Journal of Health, Physical Education and Recreation,* October 1971, pp. 45-46.

4. Baker, B. E. Physical education and the law. *The Physical Educator, 29,* 1972, pp. 63-65.

5. Crawford, E. DGWS cooperates with national sports organizations. *Journal of Health, Physical Education and Recreation,* January 1965, pp. 25, 86.

6. *Crowd Control.* Sixth National Conference of City and County Directors. Washington, D.C.: American Association for Health, Physical Education and Recreation, 1968, pp. 17-22.

7. *Crowd Control for High School Athletics.* National Council of Secondary School Athletic Directors. Washington, D.C.: American Association for Health, Physical Education and Recreation, 1970.

8. Flinchum, B. Girls and women's sports, DGWS involvement in student sports organizations. *Journal of Health, Physical Education and Recreation,* September 1971, pp. 79-80.

9. Ford, M. W. Officiating services area. *Journal of Health, Physical Education and Recreation,* May 1971, pp. 63-64.

10. Koehler, R. W. Prudence, brother, prudence. *The Physical Educator, 29,* 1972, pp. 29-31.

10a. Koenig, Fran. The now and soon with DGWS. Paper presented at the DGWS National Coaches Conference, Denver, Colorado, October 12-14, 1973.

11. Neal, P. *Sport and Identity.* Philadelphia: Dorrance & Co., 1972.

12. Restructuring of officiating services area. *Journal of Health, Physical Education and Recreation,* September 1972, p. 71.

13. Veller, D. Survey '71. *The Athletic Journal, 52* (2), 1971, pp. 58-60, 74.

Appendix

WEIGHT TRAINING EXERCISES

Weight training exercises are used for several purposes: to strengthen specific muscle groups and lessen the possibility of injury; to improve general body conditioning and contouring; to firm up portions of the body; to change weight status; to recondition muscles following injury.

Although leverage, as well as strength and condition of the athlete, is a factor in computing the amount of resistance to be used, usually a selection of lightweight barbell plates, dumbbells, and iron boots or ankle weights is sufficient to conduct a weight training program for the female athlete.

The *barbell* is a steel bar, usually about 25 pounds in weight, 4 to 8 feet long, with metal collars that encircle the bar and hold the plates or discs in place on the bar. Weight is adjusted by changing the plate (2½, 5, 10 pounds). The *dumbbell* is a short barbell, 8 to 18 inches long, usually of a fixed weight (5, 10 pounds). An *iron boot*, which is attached to the feet by straps, has a hole through which a metal bar is inserted and on which plates are attached to increase weight. An *ankle weight*, although it is of a fixed poundage, is used in the same manner as the iron boot.

There are many theories about and methods of organizing a weight training program. The following suggestions are those stemming from a weight training program for women at the University of Arizona.

Acknowledgment is made to Mary Visker, graduate student in the athletic training program, for her assistance with the preparation of this material and to Lynne Dailey, physical education teacher at Sunnyside High School, for preparation of the exercise illustrations.

1. The needs of the participant and the desired outcomes should be determined. The program should be designed for the individual rather than the individual "squeezed" into a set program. Although many lifts are outlined in detail in weight training books, the coach and performer should know which muscles are being

worked by any standard lift and be able to adapt or to replace a movement if the individual's needs are not being met.

2. A program that will maintain muscle balance in opposing muscle groups should be designed. Although the degree of strength gain in opposing muscle groups will not be the same, gains should be kept in proportion. For example, if knee extensors are strengthened, knee flexors should be strengthened also, even though the flexors are smaller and will be able to gain only about two-thirds the strength of the extensors.

3. Once the muscle (or muscle groups) needing attention is identified, the necessary overload should be determined. The muscle must be made to work 60 per cent and upward of its maximum capacity. For example, if a muscle has the initial strength to lift only 9 pounds maximum, the weight lifted in the exercise would need to be 6 pounds or more. As the muscle gains in strength, the overload must be constantly evaluated and progressive resistance applied. An easy guide to determine whether or not there is sufficient overload is to use enough weight so that the performer is barely able to complete one set of 10 repetitions, then she may be able to complete eight or nine repetitions in the second or third set. However, strain should be avoided by using a weight that can be handled for several repetitions with less-than-maximum effort.

4. A workout is scheduled three times a week with a day of rest between workouts in order to allow the exercised muscles time for recuperation. The workout composed of exercises for specific muscles or muscle groups should be performed the same way each session. Each lift is performed for three sets of 10 repetitions, with a brief rest between each set. The athlete should not cheat (do the exercise incorrectly) or the specific muscles for which the exercise was designed will not benefit.

5. There should be a constant evaluation of the overload for each exercise because not all muscles will gain in strength at the same rate. Little-used or weak muscles show a much more rapid strength gain, initially, than do well-developed muscles. As heavier weights are added, lifting should be done with a partner in order to avoid accidents.

6. Once the desired strength has been obtained, it should be maintained. Maintaining strength does not require as much effort as does acquiring strength. Usually a workout once or twice a week is sufficient to maintain strength.

Some of the commonly used weight exercises in a simplified training program are described in the following section. A brief or condensed program might include *squat, clean,* and *bench press.*

An extended program might include *trunk curl* (abdominal area), *squat* (knee and buttocks), *leg extension* (quadriceps), *leg curl* (hamstrings), *heel raise* (gastrocnemius), *bench press* (shoulders), *clean* (back), *seated press* (shoulders), *arm curl* (biceps), *French curl* (triceps), *bent-over rowing* (arms and back muscles—rhomboids, latissimus).

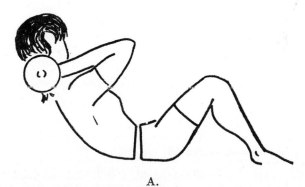

A.

TRUNK CURL (abdominal strength)
Equipment: Dumbbell
Description: Lie on back with knees bent, dumbbell held on chest or behind neck. A partner holds feet on floor. Curl upper trunk as far forward as possible. Return slowly to starting position.

B.

SQUAT (leg and trunk strength)
Equipment: Barbell
Description: Feet in a small side-stride stand, heels elevated 2 inches, barbell resting on back of neck and shoulders. Slowly bend knees to squat position. (If back is rounded, weight is too heavy.) Hold. Return to starting position.

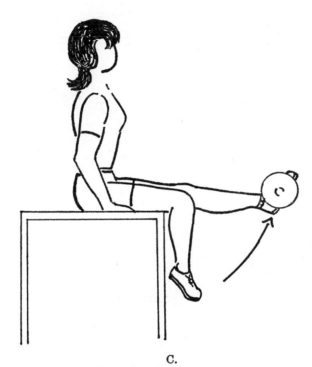

C.

LEG EXTENSION (leg strength—quadriceps)
Equipment: Weighted boot or ankle weight
Description: Sit on edge of table with boot attached to foot. Leg should be hanging free and weights should clear floor. Lift leg to full extension and slowly lower to starting position. Be certain that the last 15 degrees of full extension are achieved. Repeat. Complete entire exercise with both legs.

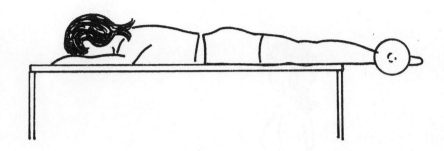

D.

LEG CURL (leg strength—hamstrings)
Equipment: Weighted boot or ankle weight
Description: Lie on abdomen (prone) with feet extended over edge of table, weight attached to one foot. Using weighted foot, completely flex knee and with control slowly return to starting position. Repeat. Complete entire exercise with both legs.

E.

HEEL RAISE (lower leg strength—gastrocnemius)
Equipment: Barbell
Description: Feet in a small side-stride stand, balls of the feet on a 2-inch riser, barbell resting on the back of neck and shoulders. Slowly rise on toes. Hold. Return to starting position. Variations may be performed by having feet either toed out or toed in.

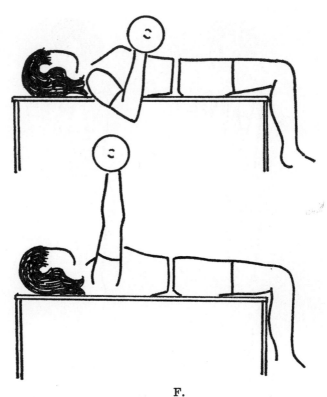

F.

BENCH PRESS (shoulder strength)
Equipment: Barbell, bench press rack, or a partner may give the performer
the weight when she is in the supine starting position
Description: Lie on back (supine), on bench (20 inches wide), knees bent
at right angles, feet flat on floor, barbell held at chest. Slowly extend arms
upward. Hold. Return to starting position.

G.

CLEAN (back and trunk strength)
Equipment: Barbell
Description: Stand erect, bar on floor, toes under bar, feet on a line and a comfortable distance apart. With back held straight, head up, and legs bent, pull barbell to chest. Hold. Return to starting position.

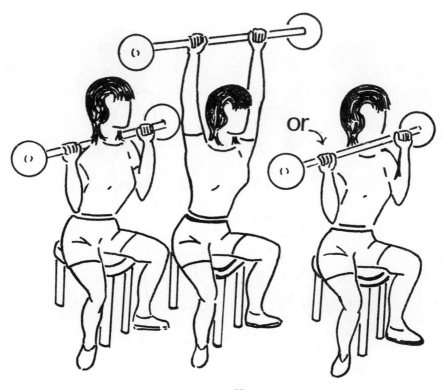

H.

SEATED PRESS (shoulder strength)
Equipment: Barbell
Description: Sit straddle on bench, barbell resting on back of neck and shoulders. Press barbell to arm's length overhead. Hold. Slowly return to starting position. Head must be kept slightly forward in order to avoid being hit by bar as it moves up and down. Since this is a somewhat difficult exercise, a simple *two-hand press,* in which the bar remains in front of head, may be substituted.

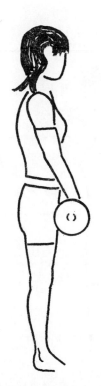 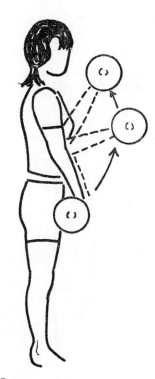

I.

ARM CURL (arm strength—biceps)
Equipment: Barbell
Description: Feet in a side-stride stand, arms extended downward, reverse
or under grip and regular or upper grip. Slowly flex elbows, bringing
barbell to bent-arm position in front of chest. Slowly return to starting
position. Keep eblows near sides of body. Alternate grasp on each set.

J.

FRENCH CURL   (arm   strength—triceps)
Equipment: Barbell
Description: Stand or sit with barbell overhead at arm's length, arms close to ears. Upper arms are kept in position while elbows are flexed, bringing bar down behind head. Elbows must be kept perpendicular while bar is being raised. Variation: lie supine on bench.

K.

BENT-OVER ROWING (arm and back muscle strength)
Equipment: Barbell
Description: Bend forward from waist, with knees slightly bent and back flat, maintaining bent-over position throughout exercise. Using an overhand shoulder-width grip (palms turned inward), lift barbell from floor to abdomen, keeping elbows close to sides (for maximum contraction of latissimus muscles); or lift bar to chest letting elbows go out so that they are in line with shoulders (to involve certain upper back muscles such as rhomboids). Barbell is returned to floor in each repetition. An overall body rowing motion is used rather than jerking bar from floor.

Specific exercises to be used in an individualized training or reconditioning program, depending upon the muscles (or injury) involved, may be selected by the coach or athletic trainer from the following groups of exercises listed according to progressive difficulty and intensity. These exercises have been adapted by Gary Delforge, certified athletic trainer at the University of Arizona, from those recommended and illustrated in Carl E. Klafs and Daniel D. Arnheim, *Modern Principles of Athletic Training* (2nd ed.). C. V. Mosby Company, 1969, Appendix A, pp. 408-416.

A. Foot, Ankle, and Lower Leg Exercises

1. Plantar and dorsal flexion
2. Ankle range of motion (circumduction, plantar and dorsal flexion, inversion, eversion, etc.)
3. Foot arching
4. Achilles tendon stretch
5. Toe raises (three positions)
6. Toe abduction and adduction
7. Marble pick-up
8. Towel gather
9. Bicycle riding

    10. Plantar and dorsal flexion towel exercise
    11. Plantar and dorsal flexion with weighted boot
    12. Inversion and eversion with weighted boot
    13. Toe raises with barbell (three positions)
    14. Jogging, running, and sprinting
    15. Running stadium steps, hills, in sand, and the like

B.   Knee and Thigh Exercises

    1. Quadriceps "setting"
    2. Straight leg raises
    3. Abduction exercise
    4. Straight leg raise against manual resistance
    5. Abduction and adduction against manual resistance
    6. Quadriceps stretching
    7. Hamstring stretching
    8. Hamstring and low back stretching
    9. Knee extension
    10. Knee extension against manual resistance
    11. Knee flexion against manual resistance
    12. Stationary jogging and running
    13. Stationary bicycle
    14. Knee extension with weighted boot or bench
    15. Knee flexion with weighted boot or bench
    16. Abduction and adduction with weighted boot or bench
    17. Toe raises with barbell
    18. Walking, jogging, running, sprinting
    19. Running stadium steps, hills, in sand, and the like

C.   Hip Exercises

    1. Hip range of motion (flexion, extension, abduction, circumduction, and so forth)
    2. Bicycle riding
    3. Leg cross overs
    4. Inverted bicycle exercise
    5. Swimming
    6. Abduction and adduction against manual resistance
    7. Flexion and circumduction with weighted boot (standing)
    8. Flexion with weighted boot (supine)
    9. Abduction with weighted boot (on side)
    10. Extension with weighted boot (prone over end of table)
    11. Walking, jogging, running, sprinting

D. Abdomen and Back Exercises

1. Trunk rotation
2. Trunk circumduction
3. Relaxed hang
4. Chair stretch
5. Leg cross overs
6. Low back flattening against table (supine)
7. Knee to chest stretch
8. Bench bobbing
9. Abdominal curls
10. Sit-ups
11. Twisting sit-ups
12. Lateral raises (on side)
13. Full bridges
14. Back arches
15. Sit-ups with weighted plate
16. Back extension
17. Back extension with weighted plate or barbell

E. Neck Exercises

1. Traction sling
2. Neck range of motion (circumduction, flexion, extension, lateral flexion, rotation, and so forth)
3. Head lift (supine)
4. Head lift (prone)
5. Lateral lift (on side)
6. Extension against manual resistance or towel
7. Lateral lift against manual resistance
8. Flexion against manual resistance
9. Flexion, extension, and lateral raise with weighted helmet
10. Wrestlers bridge

F. Shoulder Exercises

1. Pendulum swing
2. Pendulum swing with weighted dumbbell
3. Shoulder range of motion (circumduction, flexion, extension, abduction, adduction, rotation, and the like)
4. Shoulder shrug
5. Towel stretch
6. Shoulder wheel exercise
7. Swimming
8. Flexion and pectoral adduction with dumbbell (supine)
9. Lateral raise with dumbbell (standing)

10. Rhomboid lift with dumbbell (prone)
11. Flexion and extension with dumbbell (standing)
12. Push-ups
13. Shoulder shrug with dumbbell (standing)
14. Shoulder shrug with barbell (standing)
15. Pull to chest with barbell (standing)
16. Bent over rowing with barbell (standing)
17. Biceps curl with barbell (standing)
18. Bench press with barbell (supine)
19. Parallel bar dips

G. Elbow, Wrist, and Hand Exercises

1. Wrist range of motion (circumduction, flexion, extension, and so forth)
2. Elbow flexion and extension
3. Ball squeezing
4. Towel twisting
5. Flexion and extension with dumbbell or barbell
6. Pronation and supination with dumbbell
7. Wrist roller
8. Biceps curls with dumbbell or barbell
9. Push-ups
10. Parallel bar dips
11. Pull-ups
12. Bench press

Index